WHEN COMEDY GOES WRONG

COMEDY & CULTURE

Nick Marx and Matt Sienkiewicz, series editors

WHEN COMEDY GOES WRONG

CHRISTOPHER J. GILBERT

INDIANA UNIVERSITY PRESS

This book is a publication of

Indiana University Press
Office of Scholarly Publishing
Herman B Wells Library 350
1320 East 10th Street
Bloomington, Indiana 47405 USA

iupress.org

© 2025 by Christopher J. Gilbert

All rights reserved
No part of this book may be reproduced or utilized in any form or by any
means, electronic or mechanical, including photocopying and recording, or
by any information storage and retrieval system, without permission in
writing from the publisher.

First Printing 2025

Cataloging information is available from the Library of Congress.
ISBN 978-0-253-07252-8 (hdbk.)
ISBN 978-0-253-07251-1 (pbk.)
ISBN 978-0-253-07253-5 (web PDF)
ISBN 978-0-253-07254-2 (ebook)

Comedy is everything when we can laugh in communion with others who are as able and willing to laugh at themselves, like the wind and the trees.

Mother Nature, *epilogue*

CONTENTS

Acknowledgments   *ix*

Introduction: High Times for a Comic Dispirit   *1*

1. Comedy at Cross-Purposes: Paul Shanklin and the Show of Conservative Force   *24*

2. Poe's Law and the Moot Points of Million Dollar Extreme   *48*

3. Killing It: *Joker* and Comedy beyond Recognition   *78*

4. Fools on the Hill: Trumpsters and the Capitol Insurrection   *104*

5. Comedy Is Dead, and Living as Rage in the Comic Language of the Alt-Right Machine   *135*

Conclusion: Comedy on the Low Road   *164*

Epilogue: There Is No Denying the Comedy of Earthly Survival   *180*

Bibliography   *193*

Index   *221*

ACKNOWLEDGMENTS

THIS BOOK GREW OUT OF a sense I expressed to numerous colleagues for a number of years at conferences, over Zoom chats in the age of COVID-19, and during conversations when we could once again belly up to a bar. That sense is this: a specter is haunting comedy—the specter of a comic spirit in the United States that began as tragedy and seems to have reappeared as farce. This book is the materialization of that sense brought to fruition. This book is also an outgrowth of early encouragement and support from the editors of this series and the institutional backing that afforded me an opportunity to take some time to simply sit down and write.

Beyond that, suffice it to say that I have had the good fortune of good fellowship among many wonderful individuals in the fields in which I do my work, many of whom are affiliated with the National Communication Association, the Rhetoric Society of America, the American Humor Studies Association, and the Critical Humor Studies Collective. Yet it has never been a forte of mine to name names, save for one. My life partner, Erin, who has proven time and again that love is a place. To borrow some more of E. E. Cummings's words, love is the thing that, in the end, motivates my mind and flesh to make (and make meanings of) worlds and lend voice to reasons for breathing and laughing, in times of daffodils and lilacs and roses and whatever other mysteries come with remembering and forgetting, dreaming and being awake. Love is a space of mutual accommodation and a whereabouts where, in this case, writing can, well, *take place*. It is in this spirit alone that I can say that this book is a labor of love.

To all of my other family members and friends—especially my steadfast and loving parents; my caring brother, Sean; my imaginative, impassioned, and headstrong kiddos, Quincy and Lexi—thank you. I am who I am and do what I do because of how much you let me be me.

WHEN COMEDY
GOES WRONG

INTRODUCTION

High Times for a Comic Dispirit

COMEDY IS FOR NOTHING IF not suffering fools—and making a fuss of human folly.

Let me put it another way.

Joe Rogan is a moron. He says dumb shit. These are not my sentiments exactly. They represent what Rogan says about himself. Consider his engagement with antivaccine postures amid the COVID-19 pandemic. In April 2021, during a conversation with comedian Dave Smith on his podcast, *The Joe Rogan Experience*, Rogan ranted about how healthy people who exercise and eat well should not get vaccinated against the novel coronavirus. He said parents who vaccinate their kids are merely virtue signaling. Smith went further to suggest that vaccine mandates wrongfully put the public weal above personal liberties and that vaccine passports—if they ever came to be—would lead to totalitarianism in the United States. "There are these people in our government," said Smith, "who would go Chinese fascist on us." "If they could," added Rogan, as if to finish Smith's sentence. Smith reiterated, "If they could."[1] The two of them were almost laughing at their own joke.

Following pushback from medical professionals as well as the general public about misinformation and sitting across the table from another comedian a week later, Rogan affirmed his belief in the safety of COVID-19 vaccines and cautioned his listeners to avoid doing "anything stupid" because of his less-than-genuine advice.[2] At the same time, Rogan doubled down on his role as a clown who tells the truth by lending voice to rash, ridiculous thoughts. Rogan is not a doctor. He is what investigative journalist Matthew Remski dubs a "bro scientist" who mixes "humor, irony, grandiosity, [and] muscle mass" to promote well-being as "the outcome of personal choices" and who believes that the best communities are "self-contained" and "self-responsible."[3] Rogan is also a freethinker who is unwilling to think before he speaks, not to mention a self-proclaimed "jackass" who humors pseudoscience for the fun of it, takes testosterone supplements in addition to "every vitamin known to man," unabashedly trumpets rugged individualism, and relishes his role as a renegade intellectual of the dark web and celebutante of popular culture.[4] He is like Panurge in François Rabelais's story of the life and times of Gargantua and Pantagruel—irreverent, witty, and profane, although exceedingly self-indulgent in his worldly criticism.

Even more fascinating than the false trails in Rogan's reasoning and his patently foolish pride is the extent to which he moves seamlessly from the podcast studio to the stand-up stage. A few months after the vaccine debacle, Rogan performed a comedy set in Milwaukee and repeated his "comic" talking point. "I say dumb shit," he proclaimed before warning his audience not to follow his lead.[5] Then it was back to the punch lines. This tendency to disclaim "jokes" about anything from gay people to women to antivaxxers goes back to 2010 when Rogan's podcast began and he was doing bits on stupid people outbreeding smart people. Even so, he has long made it known that *he* is *with* stupid.[6] It is a classic comedic move, and one that he continued making through a later special, *Burn the Boats* (2024), persisting to absolve himself of any responsibility for his not-so-wise folly.[7] In today's vernacular, Rogan represents an archetype of those who are "smarter-than-thou," and therefore one "of those that *gets it*," not one of "those sheeple too lazy or stupid to figure it out."[8] He is, as it were, a clownish snake oil salesman playing a clown prince.

Tellingly, at the end of August 2021, Rogan contracted COVID-19 while on the road for his stand-up show, *The Sacred Clown Tour*. In an Instagram video, Rogan shared the news before admitting that he and his doctors "threw the kitchen sink at it."[9] Monoclonal antibodies. Z-Pak. Prednisone. Ivermectin (the veterinary drug used for deworming in nonhuman animals and strongly discouraged by health professionals). At the end of the short video, Rogan expressed his gratitude for top-notch medical care and lauded the same fruits from the same labors of modern medicine that produced the vaccines. There is irony here. Maybe Rogan is an embodiment of comic idiocy. Maybe none of this is comical at all. If, however, this was a moment when Rogan had to eat his words, then another controversy might provide better food for thought.

In February 2022, a YouTube video circulated online. The video captures times when Rogan used the N-word on his podcast. It concludes with a clip of Rogan making a joke involving Black people and the 2001 remake of *Planet*

INTRODUCTION 3

of the Apes. Pressure was swift from various corners of US popular culture for Spotify to drop *The Joe Rogan Experience*. Rogan once again took to Instagram, this time to apologize for his unchecked use of a racial slur and the casual racism in some of his jokes. Then, at a small stand-up gig in Austin within days of the uproar, Rogan mocked the very notion that anything he says is truly controversial. "I talk shit for a living," he said before likening anyone who takes his advice to those people who are made to eat animal penises on television.[10] By the end of February 2022, Rogan was back on his podcast with philosopher and Jacobin columnist Ben Burgis, proclaiming that comedians are like novelists. Not everything they say indicates their true feelings or beliefs. They create characters. They say what they think is funny or what others will think is funny, which is not always what they really mean. It is wrong, says Rogan, to expect too much of comedy. We expect it to assume a moral superiority. We expect it to occupy a higher ground no matter how low it goes. This from the guy who opened his own comedy club in the spring of 2023, the Comedy Mothership, in the historical site of the Ritz and the One World Theater on Sixth Street in Austin, Texas. According to Rogan, the theater was "built by a cult," called the Buddhafield, for the gay male porn star who was its leader to dance in front of his disciples.[11] The theater eventually provided a venue for talkies, live music, and even pornography. Now, according to Rogan, it is a safe space for "third rail" comedy and anyone hostile to the "fucking cult" of cancel culture.[12]

It is not that Rogan represents some mishandling of the comic license. Rather, it is that his "comic" exploits epitomize comic *licentiousness*. Moreover, it reveals the good reasons to examine these expectations we have of comedic figures who operate *with* a platform, never mind *on* a platform. We tend to think that comedy is used as a truth-telling tool, or a coping mechanism, or as a means of laughing at (or off) something foolish. Comedy, as such, is a way to categorize rights and wrongs in the world. Twenty-first-century comedy is different. Now, comedy is *the* standard of judgment for establishing and expressing normative commitments. Comedy is a way of being, whether "good" or "bad." It is *the* measure of ethical claims and moralistic appeals that get to the truth of a matter even as it is a rhetorical resource for suspending morality, messing up ethics, and mocking the "normal" ways of doing things. Comedy like this is not for figuring out who or what offends or crosses the line. It is for separating in-groups and out-groups and casting judgments like aspersions. It is for measuring what counts as consequential. It is *the* measure. These days, comedy is so much the measure, so much the truth and consequence, it isn't even funny.

THE FUNNY THINGS IS. . . .

One can only take so many declarations that a joke is *just* a joke or that comedy should not be taken so seriously before the declarations themselves become grains of salt. The same goes for scholars and other critics and commentators who declare that we underestimate comedy. Writer and podcaster Jesse David Fox's treatise *Comedy Book: How Comedy Conquered Culture—And the Magic That Makes It Work* (2023) is a paradigm case for giving the comic idea its due by celebrating when it is done right. Comedy is art, says Fox. It is about timing and timeliness. It is a time-tested outlet for comic artists and their audiences to establish relationships based on playful wrangles, and sometimes on shared political ideologies, and very often on what makes people laugh. The book reads a little like a revelation of the greatest hits from years and years of scholarship on comedy and humor. I share in his spirit that comedy matters most when serious matters are made comic. "Comedy," Fox contends, "is the art of manipulating funny."[13] Not jokes. Not laughter. Funny. I agree. Where we differ, of course, is in the tension between his sense that comedy these days is and has long been in its rightful place, and my sense that comedy has, in many ways, gone wrong.

A funny thing about funniness is that it means many things. Something (or someone) funny provokes laughter, or at least some measure of amusement. Funniness also involves what is strange, usually as it pertains to what is familiar. Antiwar activist and philosopher David Thoreau Wieck once posited that "funny things" come from the art of creating an "aesthetic experience of the comical."[14] Insofar as funny things relate to certain qualities of people, situations, and—generally—laughable objects, they rely on "judgments of 'ought to be—ought not to be,'" meaning that the "ego structure" grounding any comic appeal must coalesce with the "group structure" needed for there to be *agreement* that anything is or is not funny.[15] So it goes that funny things for some can be unfunny to others and still be comedy. What is comical causes laughter or amusement just as what is comical inspires shock or unease. Many a funny thing can happen on the way to (and from) the comic form. There is much ado about funny business. "Nothing's funny," it may be said then, "unless it smacks of delight."[16] We can all take delight in such a sentiment.

We must, however, concede that human folly is the fountainhead of *comic* delight. Following Henri Bergson, comic delight springs from anything that preys on foolishness and fools like a hawk preying on a heron or a hound giving chase to a fox.[17] Delight deals with the fun that comes with what is deemed comical. What is comic enables us to indulge in some desire or wish, to enjoy something funny. And it does not take a conscious commitment to schadenfreude for funniness to smack of humor that irritates, abuses, or offends. The pleasure derived from comedy, whether manifest as laughter or unease, is never purely aesthetic, unadulterated, or without its biases; it always retains "an unavowed intention to humiliate, and consequently to correct our neighbour, if not in his will, at least in his deed."[18] The manipulation of funny things entails a singular delight in the use (and misuse) of the comic spirit.

My concern is that comedy gone wrong thrives on degradation without any concessions, and laughter without responsibility for world making and (by the same token) world *breaking* activities. Rogan is a mischief-maker. He agitates people. He antagonizes. With his podcast as well as his comic performances, Rogan has exercised "his willingness to air any perspective, however provocative, especially those shunned or overlooked by mainstream media."[19] He is a deserved firebrand. And the brutish and blunt stand-up comedian, television personality, mixed martial artist, zealous celebrant of vitamin supplements, color commentator for the Ultimate Fighting Championship, and notorious podcast host is also wildly popular. Sometimes Rogan says ridiculous things with impunity. Sometimes he "waxes idiotic" with culture warriors and conspiracy theorists.[20] Sometimes Rogan does racism under the cover of comedy. Sometimes, a comic frame is the principle for his chauvinistic or bigoted or, to be sure, politically reckless content. Sometimes he poses as an ally for (or against) whatever *he* sees as silly or stupid. Sometimes he just says things are comical for the sake of saying they are comical. So, sometimes he is funny, and sometimes he is not. This is comedy built on a mock carnivalesque aesthetic. It is the stock-in-trade for his self-presentation and his persona—truly, for the comic structure of his ego. Comedy like this engenders a fool's paradise wherein saying one thing and doing another is not only the price of admission but also part and parcel of the stakes in being comical *at the expense* of comedy.

Given that Rogan is but one of many in a newfangled comic culture, it is unsurprising that people now speak in terms of a grand American Carnival. We speak of outrage machines and moral decline. We hear of antiwoke humor. We read of self-important influencers and pompous narcissists. The Capitol Insurrection on January 6, 2021, is part low point and part high-water mark in this milieu. The fanaticism. The fury. The vanity. The *festivity*. A crowd of people, self-righteous and spoiling for a fight. So many egos blended into a Big Ego. An alleged March to Save America that was the culmination of a "fantasy-industrial complex" meant to keep divisive cultural politics at a fever pitch.[21] These are the conditions for object lessons in fringe conservative groups like Super Happy Fun America, whose members took to the Capitol in the name of "straight pride" and Western society and traditional values. There are roots in the carnival barking of Rush Limbaugh. There are resonances in the clownery of Stephen Colbert's caricature of a right-wing blowhard on *The Colbert Report*. There are undertones in the fake news reporting of satirical outlet *The Onion*. There are even correlations to things like sports fandom and mascot controversies and absurd memes and a more generalized devil-may-care esprit de corps. Freewheeling humor is a collaborative coping mechanism that doubles as everyday escapism. From the beginnings of the New Right to the bigliness of Trumpism to the machinations of online trolls, one can find a comic spirit embodied by countless farceurs looking for freedom to make fun.

Once again, then, Rogan embodies a comic *dis*pirit by laying turf for its terrain. He is a by-product of comedy that does not so much ascribe an ethics for humor as it encompasses an ethical standard unto itself. This is not comedy in the name of just joking. It is not comedy that conquers all things. It is comedy that gives license to the joke or the jest, to festivity and flippancy, each one a motivating factor for doing comedy by doing wrong by it. This comedy exposes comic forms that we have not fully accounted for. That accounting is the task of this book.

THE COMIC EGO TRIP

Let's begin this accounting with rear ends. There is a moment in *Rabelais and His World* when Mikhail Bakhtin aligns the image of excrement with carnival activities. Excrement, says Bakhtin, is "the most suitable substance for the degrading of all that is exalted."[22] It is not made up of gross material. It is made of "gay matter," relating earth and body, self and other, individual ego and collective identity in a grotesque relation of "regeneration and renewal."[23] Everybody poops. In this fact is a comic reminder that "the egotistic form" is the *ur-form* of comedy, but only insofar as the ego gives way to "one whole laughing aspect of the world."[24] Hence that old comic proverb: *inter faeces et urinam nascimur*. Between piss and shit we are born. How disgusting. Right? No. How utterly *delightful*. How funny! What repulses can be comic in the best of possible senses. But therein lies the risk, for a carnival of comic flaunts can foster a sort of anticomedy that encourages people to toss feces toward walls just to see how it sticks.

According to numerous reports, rioters at the Capitol Insurrection urinated on the steps, smeared fecal matter on the walls, and tracked it through the hallways. Many of them boasted about it on social media. Many others lumped it in with the other activities of a riotous crowd bent on exploiting a "carnival atmosphere."[25] Rioters reveled as they smashed windows, lashed out at police officers, clambered into the Capitol building, and cried foul on democratic

INTRODUCTION

institutions. Outside the building, people flaunted "combat gear, MAGA [Make America Great Again] hats, star-spangled hoodies, coonskin hats, superhero costumes, ghillie suits, [and] flag capes." They brandished the iconography of "Uncle Sam, QAnon signs and slogans ('Q' and 'Trust the Plan'), Confederate flags, the Gadsden flag, and nooses."[26] A group of rioters smiled while setting up a makeshift gallows to hang Vice President Mike Pence. Inside, other "carnivalgoers" exuded a similar comic aesthetic of despoilment. Richard "Bigo" Barnett smirked as he posed with his feet up on House Speaker Nancy Pelosi's desk. Elsewhere, his compatriot Adam Christian Johnson appeared gleeful in a photograph that captured him grinning and waving while stealing away with Speaker Pelosi's lectern. Then there were the raucous antics of the "QAnon Shaman," Jacob Chansley, a Far Right activist who dressed up in a fur headdress with horns, wore face paint betokening the American flag, laid bare all manner of white supremacist iconography in the Norse tattoos covering his torso, and chanted and sang as he marched through the Capitol. The convictions of rioters were deadly serious. As revelers, though, they seemed ready and willing to "die *laughing* at the Capitol."[27]

Hence why some critics saw Bakhtin reborn in this moment, but not in a carnivalesque mood. With overtones of jingoism and racism and specters of fascistic imaginations, rioters exhibited bad faith in festivity as an outlet for seriousness and piety and fervid cults of personality and conspiracy theories, all mixed up with foolish amusement. The Capitol Insurrection was driven by a kind of perilous rage that comes with deep-seated, bilious anger tied up with nostalgia for an old-world order. There was fellow feeling, no doubt. But it was a comic foil for "avarice, jealousy, hypocrisy, bigotry, sterile senility, false heroism, and abstract idealism."[28] The carnivalesque escalated into a grotesque right of trespass with brazen mergers of joy and hate, praise and abuse, rightness and wrongness.

Why dwell on provocateurs like Rogan and on rabble-rousers who took their cues to incite a violent insurrection from an Agitator-in-Chief? One reason is that both examples point to a larger brand of comedy built on berating whatever object of ridicule is put on the comic chopping block. Late-night comedians from Colbert through Seth Meyers and Samantha Bee to Trevor Noah basically systemized such comedy in their dogged raillery against President Trump. Something else stands out too. What seems to pass as carnivalesque is actually more carnival*ish*. It resembles the Bakhtinian carnival. However, it lacks any desire for rejuvenation. Such carnivalish comedy thrives on free expression, laughter in the face of power structures, and celebrations of the now sacred profane. Freedom, laughter, and celebration have deep roots in US

American culture. Brashness, though, is now prevalent in comedy. Violence is festive. Darkness prevails, particularly in comedy online. Comic irreverence translates into real ire.

Then again, what someone else eats will not make you poop. This saying just about sums up the comic zeitgeist. Consumption and excretion are central to the carnival spirit, and they reinforce the positive liberty that comes with a comic license to say what thou will because people can choose what content they want to consume and to whom they pay attention. Feasts of fools, of asses, of time—they are feasts "of becoming, change, and renewal."[29] In the United States, they are feasts of the very victuals of the carnivalesque. A carnival*ish* spirit is shot through with arrogance, not ambivalence. In its comedy are the rhetorical means of disembowelment, dismemberment, and division. Rage mixes with laughter in a manner that readies audience members and participants to "pitch their camps" and "circle and squat."[30] Whether carnivalesque or not, comedy can turn fears, frustrations, and sufferance inside out so that they can be shared by a diverse community. When comedy goes wrong, it leaves what George Meredith once dubbed a "stench of the trail of Ego."[31] Egoistic comedy is comedy gone wrong. It inflates a preoccupation with certain selves over certain others. Comedy is foolish. Errors are the mark of humanity. Egoistic comedy, driven by dispiritedness, is the mark of comic failure. It is the mark of comedy that fails us when its warped rule is used as the very measure for perverting standards of comic judgment.

Ego Sum Qui Comicus

We are comic beings. Or we are who we are comic *with*. The folly of selfhood grounds our human comedy. As Conrad Hyers says, a "comedy of ego" makes fools and carnivals possible.[32] After all, a self that is less serious about its own solemnity, and is thereby more flexible with others, is all the more human. Jesters remind us that kings are courtly fools. Egos are meant to be corrected, not corralled. Make fun of egoism and we make space for "an emancipation, however momentary, from the fanaticisms of the ego and the tyranny of the situation."[33] Egoistic comedy is self-indulgent. In Simon Critchley's words, "ego bloated" comedy provokes "laughter that rails in the face of the firing squad."[34] It is overfed by obsessions with otherness, vanity, and die-hard conceit.

All the same, egoism can help us understand what is comical about the human condition. There is a long line of laughable alter egos that double as embodiments for defects of character in US public culture. Yankee Doodle. Petroleum V. Nasby. Groucho Marx. Charlie Chaplin. Mudbone, aka Richard Pryor. The Colbert of *The Colbert Report*. Miranda Sings. Lauren Caspian. The

INTRODUCTION

list goes on and on, traversing media and comic genres. The point is that the ego is a comic creation. It is a fundamental comic *object*—the butt of a joke. To compare egos, comically, is to locate the substance of superiority (and, to be sure, inferiority) complexes. It is likewise to rebel against those repressive norms and institutions that might suppress fits of self-indulgent revelry. The ego is something to exalt in comedy, says Sigmund Freud. It lets us humor our repressed impulses, intensify our inclinations toward liberation, and find pleasure in the face of pain.[35] Any felt "wrongness" of comedy can therefore be a "rightness of another sort."[36] The upendings of conventions and decrownings of kings in the carnivalesque can help us recollect "the rightness of a world up-righted."[37] To explore comic weightings of the ego is to engage with the limits of a comic spirit.

OK. But what about when a comic spirit is, as one saying goes, as "vacuous as the mask without the face behind it"?[38] Egoism tests the limits of comedy. Why? Because of the tension between the carnivalesque and the carnivalish. The carnivalesque represents comic superiority without condescension. Ideally, it fosters a festive form of comedy that is not just communal or humane but also ecological, relating to bigger conditions of being that account for habits, habitations, and entire groups of inhabitants over and above remarkable individuals or isolable groups. The carnivalish comedy that has pervaded US public culture from the late twentieth into the early twenty-first centuries represents what Terry Eagleton has described as "a riotously deconstructive force."[39] In addition to a widespread sense of imperious humor, this comedy casts others as scornful, condemnatory, and defective in ways that excuse self-congratulations on the part of those who make virtues of malice and ridicule. The senses of humor for *this* kind of comedy are *something else*. Some historical context, then.

In 2005, famed essayist, novelist, and prophet of comic problems David Foster Wallace published "Host." The essay takes stock of talk radio. More specifically, it tackles the conservative egoism in talk radio and how it establishes a "totalizing gaze that fixes everything in relation [to the self]" relative "to the discourse of the other."[40] Wallace profiles John Ziegler. He equates Ziegler's exploits on air with an alter ego that is distinct and yet indistinguishable from his off-air personality. The mix of mordancy and wit that Ziegler harnesses is about neither argumentative nuance nor defensible opinion making. On the contrary, Ziegler exemplifies a familiar comic predilection "to be stimulating" by reducing things to vulgar prurience.[41] Conservative talk radio took hold in the 1980s following the repeal of the fairness doctrine and the rise of commercial media meant to attract attention with provocative content. Limbaugh surpassed Ziegler by turning targets for comic reproach—the "abuse of logic" and "absurd pomposity," "relentless self-promotion," and "a ridiculous ego"—into praiseworthy attributes.[42] Radio personalities created a road map for mocking liberal biases and lambasting icons of progressive cultural politics. They were comic personages, and they constituted a "very popular type of news industry, one that takes advantage of journalistic authority without the stodgy constraints of fairness, objectivity, and responsibility."[43] These personages, according to Wallace, became ironic in the worst of possible ways. Their comedy illustrated both the sorry logic of corporate America and a logical response to cultural production reduced to feel-good transactions. The anger and resentment that came from news outlets was often not funny, but it was driven by a perverse comic spirit to rage against libtards and sheeple and snowflakes. It was horrifying, but it was humorous.

Not long after there arose another industry of satirical "fake news." *The Onion* began in 1988 and grew from a small print outlet to an online Gargantua of comic content. Then it was *Politically Incorrect* (later re-created as *Real Time with Bill Maher*), *The Daily Show with Jon Stewart*, *The Colbert Report*, and an ensuing "Stewart/Colbert Effect" that normalized comedic commentary on public affairs, the toils of political officials, and the travails of presidents.[44] These are touchstones in a historic moment that sparked "an explosion of comic materials of all types."[45] The coinage "infotainment" is now unexceptional. It is a label for informational, usually comedic, entertainment. The early 1980s was a turning point for comedy in the cultural politics of offense. With some hindsight, we can see how comic truths are only as good as the "honest and ethical jesters" that tell them.[46] Retrospection like this has led Paul Lewis and others to trace the rise and fall of comedic commentary much as we might trace the march of historical facts from comedy to tragedy and in the end to farce. There is a specter lurking in this structure of comic feeling, and it is not about the ideologies and cultural struggles that get held up as hills to die on. It is about what Meredith might call a "temple of arrogance" that has grown out of pervasive, unabashed contempt for enemies and opposing sides.[47] An old truism has it that comic laughter is the very thing that ensures our survival—that keeps us from dying. What, though, if Wallace is right? What if we are "dying to give ourselves away to something. To run, to escape, somehow?"[48] What if this is the comic impulse? What if comedy is the foil? What if . . .?

IF THE COMIC DISPIRIT MOVES

An answer to these questions begins with the notion that laughter is a comic effect. So is the simple fact of getting the humor of some jest or laughable

INTRODUCTION 11

situation. A comic effect can be an impact of something comedic too. Its impact on the world. A transposition from an expression about something "into another key or another environment,"[49] like a movement from "insipid buffoonery" to loftiness.[50] In any case, comic judgment deals with what is even worth making fun of or joking about.

Egoistic comedy has made many modern comedians and comic personages into judges of their own cause. Stewart is widely regarded as a satirical reporter on public affairs who transformed what it means to consume news and grasp political culture. In 2008, an article in *The New York Times* dubbed him "the Most Trusted Man in America." *National Public Radio* suggested something similar in 2010. The year Stewart left his post, in 2015, *TIME* hailed him as "the Fake Newsman Who Made a Real Difference." A year before, he topped the PEW Research Center's list of most trusted newsmen. In 2010, Stewart collaborated with Colbert to hold the Rally to Restore Sanity and/or Fear at the National Mall in Washington, DC. A month later, he sat down with Rachel Maddow of MSNBC. Maddow pushed Stewart to acknowledge that he had an actual impact on the politics of the day, that his "fake" news show mattered for more than laughs, that it represented comedy done right. Stewart dismissed the idea. Comedy, he proclaimed, is and always has been about indulgence in folly without any expectation of or responsibility for consequences. It might make people feel good. In the end, though, comedy is haughty, feckless, and impotent. The comedian is a monkey tossing dookie at the players on the field from the sidelines.

Diminishment is common in comedy. We laugh at our foolishness. We revel in pratfalls. Comedians often self-deprecate. Stewart and Colbert regularly discounted their impact even as they built their empires and as the "other side" luxuriated—or, we might say, wallowed—in the House that Limbaugh built.[51] There is a crooked yet discernible line from Stewart's eagerness to poke the beast through Colbert's purveyance of truthiness to Trumpism to memes as outlets for hoaxers to who-gets-the-last-laugh interlocutors and finally to comedy writ large as a crucible for so-called cancel culture. In that lineage, comedy is a "possession without obligation,"[52] like land that is owned without any need to care all that much either for the soil or the tax collector. Comedy in this land is about cults of "comic persona."[53] These cultish constituencies collude with their personages to degrade what is laughed at with no sense that anything needs to be regenerated. Their comedy is carnival*ish*. Stewart's abnegations hint at a comic license granted by audiences who are of a kind in their comic dispiritedness, who share in "the joy, the pride, the intoxication of possessions," and who uphold this or that showman with a sense of humor that aligns with comedy to lumber forth like a "doomed colossus."[54] That might be why Stewart returned to the fold by dabbling in *anti*comedy.[55] In the late modern cultural setup, anticomedy might have a greater comic effect.

So, back to Rogan. Much like Stewart, Rogan is a "pop intellectual" whose comedy is a frame-up for "faux intellectualism."[56] He is also seen as an alternative source of information for making sense of the world. We could harken back to Rogan playing the handyman on the television sitcom *NewsRadio* pretending to fix things at an AM station or to his role in hosting *Fear Factor*, which trafficked in the crude pleasure that comes from subjecting others to coordinated distress. But the point is not to align the comic personas of figures like Rogan and Stewart, let alone figures like Limbaugh and Trump. The point is to mark the turn toward comedy as a means of self-promotion. Rogan betrays a bullish wit. Notwithstanding his obsession with vitamins and supplements, his infatuation with conspiracy theories and culture war apologetics, and his tolerance of bad faith and bad actors, Rogan's real commitment is to himself as a content producer and a consumable brand. Rogan uses comedy to reinforce his rabble-rousing and commentary on whatever he wants to stir up when he "brings on social outliers like comedians, CEOs, scientists, athletes, and dissidents of various flavors to (sometimes) drink and smoke on air with him to talk about stuff like artificial intelligence, steroids, politics, sports, war, transgender people—whatever you could talk about if you spent three hours talking, which is anything."[57] It should not go without saying that Limbaugh's talk radio program ran for three hours a day. Anyway, during a conversation with fellow comedian Joe List in May 2021, Rogan mourned the death of "good" comedy by asserting that "wokeness" had gotten so bad that soon straight white men would not be "allowed to go outside." List laughed. "I'm not joking," Rogan replied in earnest.[58] *That's* the point. He was not joking. Or was he?

This point came to a head in October 2021 when Rogan defended Dave Chappelle after backlash over what has been regarded as brazen gender hatred in his Netflix special *The Closer*.[59] The entire special dealt with the years of criticism Chappelle has received for making fun of "the gays" and "the transgenders" and others who identify according to alternative sexualities. Chappelle has earned acclaim for his social and political commentary, particularly around issues of race. He is a first-rate comedian. Kevin Hart went so far as to name Chappelle "the GOAT," the greatest comedian of all time (an honorific Chappelle also applies to himself), even better than Richard Pryor.[60] Unlike Stewart and others, Chappelle owns his influence and embraces this label. It is part of his self-ascription. Yet like Rogan (and Stewart), he refuses to apologize for how people take his comedy and declares that he is not responsible for how it might be manifested in the real world. "I said what I said" was his response when he was lambasted by members of the LGBTQIA+ community for his litany of transphobic jokes. The jokes echoed those in previous specials, including *Deep in the Heart of Texas* (2017), *Equanimity* (2017), and *Sticks & Stones* (2019). They were also unsympathetic to the fact that LGBTQIA+ communities are regularly done harm. That is of little concern to either Chappelle or Rogan. "His jokes are just that," Rogan said on his podcast. "Jokes." To ascribe hate to humor that is meant to make fun of something or someone is to make enemies of allies, Rogan pronounced. If anyone should be part of a "protected class," it is a comedian.[61]

Comedy is the standard of judgment. It is a crucible for matters of concern. The talk radio host who exploits vulgarity as a virtue of the oppressed. The reckless meme maker who trolls and plays tricks online. The president who made a joke of his campaign only to win and eventually stoke the rage of a riotous mob to a violent insurrection after he lost his reelection bid and then converted ninety-one felony counts across four criminal cases into a comeback tour of sorts. All justify a comic license. When Chappelle "jokes" that the LGBTQIA+ community has not been fighting for equity as long as "the Blacks" and therefore does not deserve greater advances in rights or cultural privileges, he establishes a hierarchy of sufferance. When he makes this hierarchy into a mechanism for using the "anger, hurt, or pain" people feel as comic material, Chappelle re-creates categories of victims and bullies.[62] When he casts himself as a victim of those who take his jokes the "wrong" way, he misrecognizes the comic spirit for a requirement that people "always be able to take a joke."[63] When he laughs off misogyny, Chappelle performs his own "betrayal of the Black comic tradition" that is resident in figures like Pryor, Moms Mabley, and more.[64] When he pretends to be a comic empath who nevertheless feeds into outrage machines and makes fun of fragile audience members and social justice warriors, Chappelle peddles in the apologetics of an embarrassed, raving haranguer. Both Rogan and Chappelle are resentful. They do not want equanimity for everyone. They want impunity for themselves. What is the use of a comic license that provokes oppressive attitudes or that does not upset systems of oppression? Comedy should revel in a common appreciation for "the frailties and follies in the human condition."[65] What is the use of comedy that plays out the antagonisms of society with little to no regard for the caution that Bakhtin aligns with carnivalesque antics? Egoism is a sign of comedy gone wrong. Easy humor (however provocative) that satisfies prejudices is a sign of the wrongful demands we make of comedic takes on the world.

None of this is to say that comedy done right is comedy that follows Bakhtin to the carnival. It is to say, however, that the trick of comedy is to find joy in the folly of our *shared* human condition without singling out "foolish" human beings or playing the victim. What Lauren Berlant and Sianne Ngai brand "comic failure" has been running rampant since at least the turn of the twenty-first century, with "humorless" comedy, selfish comic pleasure, and "comedic aggression" elevating chagrin over and above a grin of the Cheshire Cat.[66] So many comics who profess to be doing the right thing are by and large preaching to the choir. Even the most fervent among them and those putting out the most ardent comic appeals are the first to discount or disclaim the impact of their comedy. The result is part futility and part denialism.

Do not mistake: purity tests and the politics of being offended encourage comedy that gets used either as "a scourge" or as "a broom."[67] In various senses, this sort of comedy gets right to the heart of dispiritedness. It animates an urge to discard, to do the opposite of, to tear apart or move away. It orients its audiences in the direction of ridicule and controversy to belie selfless laughter and humble malice. Comedy for the *couillon*—the sad sack, the coward, the simpleton.[68] Comedy for ambivalence between intellect and idiocy, wisdom and folly, the Last Judgment and the Last Laugh. Comedy lost to a larger moment shaped by "severe intolerance, cruel persecution, official condemnation, and vindictive upheavals."[69] When barkers and hawkers own popular festivity and fold it into a marketplace of laughter that is neither gay nor humorous, there is little room for buffoonery in structures of comic feeling. They participate in cults of laughter that combine the dogmatism, didacticism, narcissism, and sentimentalism of Bakhtin's anticomedic world with the grand pretensions and self-deceptions that animate Meredith's realm of tragic comedians. The conflation of comic cruelty and comedic pleasure turns the comedy edifice into a house of cards. What Meredith once called the "carnival of egoism" predominates like a spade in this house.

No wonder comedy is now an industry of the egoistic and the carnivalish. The trope of "just joking" is weaponized online and across media outlets. Those who brandish it range from scandalmongers who are occupied with staying "woke" to newfangled, aggrieved Birchites who counteract wokeness with anger and resentment—and jokes! Rogan dwells in these spaces. So does Chappelle. So do figures like Sam Hyde, Shane Gillis, Gavin McInnes, Christopher Cantwell, Nick Fuentes, Anthony Cumia, Matt Rife, and more. Others such as Limbaugh and Ziegler and Jones make up something of an old guard, along with figures like Ann Coulter and, yes, Trump. But Stewart, Colbert, Meyers, Noah, and Bee are also still caught up in the mess. So are shows like *Legion of Skanks*

INTRODUCTION

and memes like "Pepe the Frog," aside from oldies like *Opie & Anthony*, which use the comic license like a blank check for procuring "permission to revel in racism and sexism, in homophobia and transphobia."[70] Late-night comedy has safeguarded nostalgic revelry by keeping up an antiquated shtick of being politically glib, culturally smug, and performatively frustrated. Carnivalesque temperaments crop up in the militant politicking of the boogaloo movement. Troll circles and online outlets for "lulz" and irony and the supposed humor of "real America" like image-board websites 4chan and 8chan have emerged as platforms for a comedy of "plausible deniability."[71] The conspiracy theories of QAnon and the odd jeremiads of hate groups, whether in anonymity or in the open air, might come off as humorless and absurd to the uninitiated or as symptoms of polluted conservative wellsprings. Still, comedy is a storehouse for egoistic struggles over the projection, protection, and promotion of certain selves over certain others.

This land is our land. We are reaping what we have sown. It is a land of "comic" personages and other witlings who are wrongheaded in their comedy insofar as that comedy is largely unfree from what Bakhtin saw as the tribalism and territorialism and exploits of wannabe conquering heroes. Rogan proclaims himself a "stranger in a strange land." Chappelle longs to be uninterrupted, unheckled, free to be himself—free to have a family, and acreage, and his estate in Yellow Springs—and time to recover when he has had enough. Both of them embody a gleeful conceit that reverberates through discourses about being woke versus being weak, commentaries that rail against cancel culture and snowflakes and conspiracy theorists, politics of those who want to "own the libs," and comic takes that either deal *with* or deal *in* humor that is "angry and aggrieved, hateful and bigoted."[72] This is a land of comedy in the raw, that hits nerves, and that we can no longer simply laugh at in the name of reaping and sowing. In an observation that reeks of Bakhtin, Meredith once depicted our human comedy as "profusely mixed of good and evil, of generous ire and mutinous desire, of passion for the future of mankind and vanity of person, magnanimity and sensualism, high judgment, reckless indiscipline, chivalry, savagery, solidity, fragmentariness."[73] What to do when the fertile grounds for comedy that could come from this terrain turn to dust? Laugh, perhaps, but with careful attention to a comic dispirit.

WHAT IS AT STAKE AND WHAT IS TO COME

"It's easy to become disillusioned," said comedian Jeremy Levick, "and that's how it works." "I mean, you think about all the pathways that this thing could go," replied his comic partner, Rajat Suresh. "What do the fuckers who pull the levers know that we don't know?" That was Tim Heidecker, serving as host of *Office Hours Live*, a weekly call-in comedy podcast. The thing is that this exchange was featured in a spoof of *The Joe Rogan Experience*. The spoof aired in November 2021.[74] It ran nearly twelve hours, although the actual content took up just over an hour. That content was looped. Its blissful incessancy beckons Meredith's views about "our picked men ruling" with permission to carry on with their "insufferable flights of fancy."[75] How despotic these flights of fancy can be, to say nothing of the comic freedom that comes with them.

The spoof mocks a comedy of inundation. In their roving conversation, Levick, Suresh, and Heidecker capture a sort of know-it-all arrogance that characterizes so many public figures who make a killing by playing fools. From notions of disillusionment and uncertain pathways and lever pullers, Heidecker qua Rogan guides his guests through meandering, nonsensical riffs about corporate interests, government connivery, grassroots politicking, and the various power structures that put people in their place. Suresh banters a bit about the "smart terms" that could be applied to the present circumstance, but invokes the discourse of the everyman, prompting Heidecker to affirm the important "countercurrents" that work against "Old World shit." Levick opines on cultural sea changes. Suresh quips about political currencies. All three laugh about the literal marketplace for comic feelings. Heidecker ultimately punctuates this collective stream of consciousness with a ridiculous sidebar about the health benefits of crab salts before they all share in a faux lament about the black mark of laughter that gets attached to anyone who does wrong by comedy. Suresh, for example, cannot get away with a joke about transgender urinals—a joke that Heidecker proclaims to be both funny and true! There are no details beyond the setup or punch line for the joke, but Heidecker makes clear that there is no real clue as to where we are going with comedy or anything else except that people like him are the trailblazers in an uncharted territory for which they pretend to already have the map. That, and comedy itself is the map to the territory.

This book maps some of the deep, generative principles that lie beneath so many surface grotesqueries in the use and abuse of carnival permissions. Each chapter aims not to root out some bad source of comedy but rather to approach comedy gone wrong in terms of what it might be trying to restore, to reconnect with, or to recover, whether that be something like a lost cause or something like a good old day when people could take jokes *as* jokes. This book reckons with a messy and sometimes mismanaged comedic landscape that bears the fruitage of our late modern follies. There is no rejuvenation of lower bodily strata in these pages, although that might feel appropriate given

INTRODUCTION

the existentialism of the Anthropocene. There is likewise no attempt to regain some humanity that has been lost to a newfangled misanthropy or melancholic nostalgia. Doom and gloom are endemic to our human condition. There is no human comedy without sufferance. Hence the persistence of comic ego trips and attendant trips to the toolshed. My interest is in comedy that blights the landscape.

The book begins with the origins of talk radio and its early injection of comedy into the cultural platforms of the Grand Old Party. Conservative comedian and longtime voice actor on *The Rush Limbaugh Show*, Paul Shanklin, had a foundational role in establishing dittoheads as essential to the cultural production of wrongheaded right-wing movements. The second chapter accounts for the outgrowth, or fallout, of comedy that celebrates a triumph of the worst self (i.e., in the embrace of bigotry, browbeating, and chauvinism) with a look at the exploits of Sam Hyde, a Far Right comedian who made mass shootings into the stuff of mockery in meme culture. In particular, this chapter takes seriously the catchphrase "Sam Hyde is the shooter" as a maxim of comedy that functions as a call to political and cultural and even *literal* arms. Chapter 3 is something of a critical interlude. It dwells on the concept of anticomic, dispirited comedy as it plays out in Todd Phillips's 2019 film, *Joker*, and as it relates to the identitarian bases of precarity, oppression, and violence. This chapter is a hinge for the book. It is a conceptual linchpin for thinking through how we develop and deploy standards of comic judgment and how conventional approaches to comedy lack a certain appeal. Similarly, this chapter grapples with the cultural politics of comedy that prefigure in- and out-group associations in accordance with being in on some joke (or not).

The revelry so apparent in the Capitol Insurrection that took place on January 6, 2021, is the focus of chapter 4, as are the repercussions it has revealed in the follies of promoting a self-centered tyranny of the people. One contributing factor that doubles as a repercussion is alt-right comedy, which animates the fifth and final chapter. Such comedy reinforces a comic dispirit in the mainstream of egoistic political culture and in the cultural politics of narcissistic rage. The book wraps up with a reflection on a comic spirit that fortifies egoism and thereby sets comedy on the low road toward laying "good" humor to waste—hence my concluding gesture to the humanity of comedy and to the problem with last laughs in comedies of survival.

A comedy of brash arrogance, Joe Blow intellectualism, ragtags and bobtails, phony open-mindedness—it radiates from Heidecker's spot-on parody of Rogan. It also bespeaks a comic spirit in high dudgeon. There is no denying a dispiritedness that figures into the folly of comedy that casts a comic gaze at pigeonhole windows and not mirrors, that pits my identity against yours, that thrives on nostalgia for something lost by promoting the destructive forces of rage over the constructive goads of grief, that foments violence, that drifts into what Bakhtin might classify as the "static grotesque," that emphasizes characters who peddle degeneracy and "petty realism."[76] Or that mistakes a death drive for a survival skill. There is also no question that we need to consider where comedy goes when the farces themselves appear so burly and yet so foolhardy. We need to survey the damage, walk around and reacquaint ourselves with a landscape torn apart by warring factions, and contemplate a distorted world that make us misrecognize ourselves as we make our way. At best, when comedy goes wrong, we are left with little more than in-group and out-group modes of *comic* association. At worst, we are left with revelry without joy or comedy for its own sake in the la-la land of infinite jest.

NOTES

1. PowerfulJRE, "Dave Smith Passionately Opposes Vaccine Passports," YouTube video, 8:13, April 23, 2021, https://www.youtube.com/watch?v=x9c3w _QFfbE.

2. PowerfulJRE, "Joe Rogan Clarifies His Vaccine Comments," YouTube video, 5:51, April 29, 2021, https://www.youtube.com/watch?v=PloZ-GB9tzA.

3. Matthew Remski, "Bro Science Manifesto," *Medium*, July 7, 2021, https:// matthewremski.medium.com/bro-science-manifesto-b6f6ec7d5481. See also Matthew Remski, "Bro Science (w/ Dr. Dan Wilson)," *Conspirituality*, December 11, 2020, https://www.podchaser.com/podcasts/conspirituality-1233098/episodes /29-bro-science-wdr-dan-wilson-80775856.

4. Bari Weiss, "Meet the Renegades of the Intellectual Dark Web," *New York Times*, May 8, 2018, https://www.nytimes.com/2018/05/08/opinion/intellectual -dark-web.html. See also Ashley Carman, "What You Learn after 350 Hours of Joe Rogan," *Verge*, December 7, 2021, https://www.theverge.com/2021/12/7 /22821823/joe-rogan-media-matters-hot-pod-spotify-moderation. Note as well the economic elements at play here. Rogan's podcast was rank No. 1 in 2021 on Spotify. In 2022, reports indicated that the deal Spotify made with Rogan for his comic antics and codlike thought leadership is worth $200 million.

5. Piet Levy, "Joe Rogan Addresses Controversial Vaccine Comments, Rips Cancel Culture, at Unapologetically Tasteless Milwaukee Show," *Milwaukee Journal Sentinel*, August 8, 2021, https://www.jsonline.com/story/entertainment /2021/08/08/joe-rogan-addresses-vaccine-comments-tasteless-milwaukee-show -cancel-culture/5478667001/.

INTRODUCTION   19

6. Gábor Hényel, "Joe Rogan–Devolution of Stupid People (Stand-up)," YouTube video, 10:55, September 24, 2014, https://www.youtube.com/watch?v =6YhKZTdqnco.

7. See Kathryn VanArendonk, "Joe Rogan Plays an Unconvincing Fool," *Vulture*, August 5, 2024, https://www.vulture.com/article/joe-rogan-burn-the -boats-netflix-comedy-special-review.html; and Jason Zinoman, "In His Stand-Up Special, Joe Rogan Plays Dumb," *New York Times*, August 4, 2024, https://www .nytimes.com/2024/08/04/arts/television/joe-rogan-standup-netflix.html.

8. Jacob Oller, "*A Glitch in the Matrix* Documentary Is More 'Oh' Than 'Whoa,'" *Paste*, February 3, 2021, https://www.pastemagazine.com/movies /sundance-2021/a-glitch-in-the-matrix-review/.

9. @joerogan, "I GOT COVID," Instagram video, 1:39, September 1, 2021, https://www.instagram.com/tv/CTSsA8wAR2-/.

10. Natalie Prieb, "Rogan Mocks Controversies in Return to Stand-Up Comedy: 'I Talk S—for a Living," *The Hill*, February 9, 2022, https://thehill .com/blogs/in-the-know/in-the-know/593521-rogan-mocks-controversies-in -return-to-stand-up-comedy-i-talk-s.

11. mark normand, "Joe Rogan Explains the Cult Origins of the Mothership | Protect Our Parks," YouTube, June 9, 2023, https://www.youtube.com/watch?v =SzDqbxV2nHc.

12. Hanna Panreck, "Joe Rogan Fights 'F—ing Cult' at New Comedy Club, Welcomes Canceled Comedians," *New York Post*, May 9, 2023, https://nypost .com/2023/05/09/joe-rogan-fights-fing-cult-at-new-comedy-club-welcomes -canceled-comedians/. See also Matt Miller, "Joe Rogan, Whose Podcast Reaches Millions, Is Afraid Woke Culture Will Silence Straight White Men," *Esquire*, May 18, 2021, https://www.esquire.com/entertainment/a36463910/joe -rogan-woke-culture-silencing-straight-white-men/.

13. Jesse David Fox, *Comedy Book: How Comedy Conquered Culture—And the Magic That Makes It Work* (New York: Farrar, Straus and Giroux, 2023), 183.

14. David Thoreau Wieck, "Funny Things," *Journal of Aesthetics and Art Criticism* 25, no. 4 (1967): 443.

15. Wieck, "Funny Things," 443.

16. Roy Blount Jr., "Southern Humor," in *What's So Funny? Humor in American Culture*, ed. Nancy A. Walker (Wilmington, NC: Scholarly Resources, 1998), 167.

17. Henri Bergson, *Laughter: An Essay on the Meaning of the Comic* (New York: Macmillan, 1914), 56.

18. Bergson, *Laughter*, 136.

19. Matt Flegenheimer, "Joe Rogan Is Too Big to Cancel," *New York Times*, July 1, 2021, https://www.nytimes.com/2021/07/01/business/joe-rogan.html.

20. See Jack Crosbie, "Joe Rogan and Jordan Peterson Wax Idiotic on Climate Change and What It Means to Be Black," *Rolling Stone*, January 26, 2022, https://www.rollingstone.com/culture/culture-news/jordan-peterson-joe-rogan-interview-climate-change-1290696/. See also Brandon Yu, "Joe Rogan Is an Idiot—That's Why He Is So Dangerous," *Mic*, January 31, 2022, https://www.mic.com/culture/joe-rogan-spotify-neil-young-response.

21. Sean Illing, "The Fantasy-Industrial Complex Gave Us the Capitol Hill Insurrection," *Vox*, January 8, 2021, https://www.vox.com/policy-and-politics/22217822/us-capitol-attack-trump-right-wing-media-misinformation. See also Michael Sean Comerford, "A Dark Carnival Comes to Life," *Los Angeles Review of Books*, March 27, 2021, https://lareviewofbooks.org/article/a-dark-carnival-comes-to-life/.

22. Mikhail Bakhtin, *Rabelais and His World*, trans. Hélène Iswolsky (Bloomington: Indiana University Press, 1984), 152.

23. Bakhtin, *Rabelais and His World*, 175.

24. Bakhtin, *Rabelais and His World*, 152.

25. Abigail Higgins, "Men Who Joined in Violently Storming the US Capitol Describe a Carnival Atmosphere Inside," *Insider*, January 7, 2021, https://www.insider.com/men-who-broke-into-the-capitol-describe-a-carnival-atmosphere-2021-1.

26. Liam Kennedy, "American Carnival: The Aesthetic Politics of Trumpist Insurrection," UCD Clinton Institute, January 16, 2021, https://www.ucdclinton.ie/commentary-content/american-carnival-the-aesthetic-politics-of-trumpist-insurrection.

27. Katie McDonough, "Die Laughing at the Capitol," *New Republic*, January 11, 2021, https://newrepublic.com/article/160846/die-laughing-capitol.

28. John Docker, *Postmodernism and Popular Culture: A Cultural History* (New York: Cambridge University Press, 1994), 179.

29. Bakhtin, *Rabelais and His World*, 10.

30. George Meredith, *The Egoist: A Comedy in Narrative* (London: C. Kegan Paul, 1879), 7.

31. George Meredith, *Beauchamp's Career* (New York: Charles Scribner's Sons, 1922), 273.

32. Conrad Hyers, *The Laughing Buddha: Zen and the Comic Spirit* (Eugene: Wipf and Stock, 1989), 111. See also Alenka Zupančič, *Odd One In: On Comedy* (Cambridge: Massachusetts Institute of Technology, 2008).

33. Hyers, *Laughing Buddha*, 119.

34. Simon Critchley, *On Humour* (New York: Routledge, 2002), 105.

35. See Sigmund Freud, "Wit and the Various Forms of the Comic," in *Wit and Its Relation to the Unconscious*, trans. A. A. Brill (New York: Moffat, Yard, 1916), 288–384.

36. Hyers, *Laughing Buddha*, 53.

INTRODUCTION

37. Robert D. Zaretsky, "Return of the Grotesque," *Aeon*, July 3, 2017, https://aeon.co/essays/the-grotesque-is-back-but-this-time-no-one-is-laughing.

38. The original phrase in Latin is *ego limis specto sic per flabellum clanculum*. See George Meredith, *An Essay on Comedy and the Uses of the Comic Spirit* (New York: Charles Scribner's Sons, 1913), 10–11.

39. Terry Eagleton, *Humour* (New Haven, CT: Yale University Press, 2019), 156.

40. Michelle Ballif, *Seduction, Sophistry, and the Woman with the Rhetorical Figure* (Carbondale: Southern Illinois University Press, 2001), 106.

41. David Foster Wallace, "Host," *Atlantic*, April 2005, https://www.theatlantic.com/magazine/archive/2005/04/host/303812/.

42. Molly Ivins, "Lyin' Bully," *Mother Jones*, May/June 1995, https://www.motherjones.com/politics/1995/05/lyin-bully/.

43. Wallace, "Host."

44. See Amarnath Amarasingam, ed., *The Stewart/Colbert Effect: Essays on the Real Impacts of Fake News* (Jefferson, NC: McFarland, 2011). See also Stephen J. Farnsworth, S. Robert Lichter, and Farah Latif, *Late-Night in Washington: Political Humor and the American President* (New York: Routledge, 2024).

45. Henry Jenkins, "'Fifi Was My Mother's Name!': Anarchistic Comedy, the Vaudeville Aesthetic and *Diplomaniacs*," *Velvet Light Trap* 26 (1990): 3–27.

46. Paul Lewis, *Cracking Up: American Humor in a Time of Conflict* (Chicago: University of Chicago Press, 2006), 20.

47. Meredith, *Essay on Comedy*, 90.

48. David Lipsky, *Although Of Course You End Up Becoming Yourself: A Road Trip with David Foster Wallace* (New York: Broadway Books, 2010), 81.

49. Bergson, *Laughter*, 118.

50. Bergson, *Laughter*, 123.

51. Ben Shapiro, "The House That Rush Built," *New York Times*, February 20, 2021, https://www.nytimes.com/2021/02/20/opinion/politics/rush-limbaugh-conservative-media.html.

52. Meredith, *Egoist*, 126.

53. Judith Yaross Lee, *Twain's Brand: Humor in Contemporary American Culture* (Jackson: University Press of Mississippi, 2012), 10.

54. Meredith, *Egoist*, 126.

55. Sophie Gilbert, "The New Anti-comedy of Jon Stewart," *Atlantic*, October 1, 2021, https://www.theatlantic.com/culture/archive/2021/10/problem-jon-stewart-apple-tv-plus/620277/.

56. Devin Gordon, "Why Is Joe Rogan So Popular?," *Atlantic*, August 19, 2019, https://www.theatlantic.com/entertainment/archive/2019/08/my-joe-rogan-experience/594802/. See also Flegenheimer, "Joe Rogan Is Too Big to Cancel."

57. Matt Pearce, "This Is Another Article about Stuff Joe Rogan Has Said about the Coronavirus. With Bonus Timeline!," *Los Angeles Times*, September 3,

2021, https://www.latimes.com/entertainment-arts/story/2021-09-03/joe-rogan-podcast-coronavirus-vaccine-hestitancy-ivermectin.

58. Ian Schwartz, "Joe Rogan: We Will Get to the Point Where 'Straight White Men Aren't Allowed to Talk' Due to Privilege," RealClearPolitics, May 18, 2021, https://www.realclearpolitics.com/video/2021/05/18/joe_rogan_we_will_get_to_the_point_where_straight_white_men_arent_allowed_to_talk_due_to_privilege.html.

59. Daniel Kreps, "Surprising No One, Joe Rogan Defends Chappelle: 'His Jokes Are Just That: Jokes,'" *Rolling Stone*, October 20, 2021, https://www.rollingstone.com/tv/tv-news/joe-rogan-defends-dave-chappelle-the-closer-1244854/.

60. JRE Clips, "Kevin Hart: Dave Chappelle is the GOAT!," YouTube video, 11:53, May 25, 2020, https://www.youtube.com/watch?v=8kJacGNg_9w.

61. Dylan Matthews, "The Joe Rogan Controversy Revealed Something Important about the American Left," *Vox*, January 27, 2020, https://www.vox.com/future-perfect/2020/1/27/21081876/joe-rogan-bernie-sanders-henry-kissinger.

62. Aja Romano, "What Dave Chappelle Gets Wrong about Trans People and Comedy," *Vox*, October 23, 2021, https://www.vox.com/culture/22738500/dave-chappelle-the-closer-daphne-dorman-trans-controversy-comedy.

63. See Romano, "What Dave Chappelle Gets Wrong." See also Helen Lewis, "Dave Chappelle's Rorschach Test," *Atlantic*, October 13, 2021, https://www.theatlantic.com/ideas/archive/2021/10/dave-chappelle-the-closer/620364/.

64. John Blake, "Dave Chappelle Insulted Another Audience No One Mentions," CNN, October 21, 2021, https://www.cnn.com/2021/10/20/entertainment/dave-chappelle-controversy-netflix-black-comic-tradition/index.html.

65. Conrad Hyers, *The Spirituality of Comedy: Comic Heroism in a Tragic World* (New Brunswick, NJ: Transaction, 1996), 113.

66. Lauren Berlant and Sianne Ngai, "Comedy Has Issues," *Critical Inquiry* 43 (2017), https://www.journals.uchicago.edu/doi/full/10.1086/689666.

67. Meredith, *Laughter*, 21.

68. Bakhtin, *Rabelais and His World*, 418–20.

69. Osita Nwanevu, "The 'Cancel Culture' Con," Soapbox, *New Republic*, September 23, 2019, https://newrepublic.com/article/155141/cancel-culture-con-dave-chappelle-shane-gillis.

70. Seth Simons, "The Comedy Industry Has a Big Alt-Right Problem," *New Republic*, February 9, 2021, https://newrepublic.com/article/161200/alt-right-comedy-gavin-mcinnes-problem.

71. Helen Lewis, "The Joke's On Us," *Atlantic*, September 30, 2020, https://www.theatlantic.com/international/archive/2020/09/how-memes-lulz-and-ironic-bigotry-won-internet/616427/.

INTRODUCTION 23

72. Simons, "Comedy Industry."

73. George Meredith, *The Tragic Comedians: A Study in a Well-Known Story* (New York: Ward, Lock, Bowden, 1892), 177.

74. Tim Heidecker, "Jeremy Levick, Rajat Suresh on Office Hours Live (Ep 184 11/25/2021)," YouTube, November 25, 2021, https://www.youtube.com /watch?v=P6Iyg9fznvM.

75. Meredith, *Beauchamp's Career*, 201.

76. Bakhtin, *Rabelais and His World*, 53.

ONE

COMEDY AT CROSS-PURPOSES

Paul Shanklin and the Show of Conservative Force

THE SELF-PROCLAIMED ANCHORMAN OF AMERICA was fond of making fun of the dead. As columnist Erin Gloria Ryan put it in a mock encomium, Rush Limbaugh joked about "people who died of AIDS, of people who died by suicide, of people who were dying of Parkinson's disease, and unarmed Black children who were murdered under racist pretenses."[1] Once, on his radio show, Limbaugh quipped that gay men who turn their backs on you are not doing so as an insult but rather as an invitation. All composite pictures of wanted criminals, said the radio personality in another instance, look like iconic Black political activist and two-time candidate for the Democratic presidential nomination, Jesse Jackson. For Ryan and others who reacted to Limbaugh's own death in February 2021, these and so many more remarks make up a posthumous license to speak ill of a man whose sense of humor underwrote his reputation as "a huge piece of shit."[2] Mock Limbaugh in death, and let the dead bury the dead.

It is old news to me now that Limbaugh died as he lived, reveling in his campaign of political and cultural warfare (so-called Operation Chaos). Still, I was not yet a teenager when Limbaugh was securing his status as a political and cultural icon in the late 1980s and early 1990s. But I do remember when he espoused this sentiment about perhaps my favorite artist of all time: "Kurt Cobain was, ladies and gentleman, I just—he was a worthless shred of human debris."[3] It was April 11, 1994, just days after Cobain was found dead in the greenhouse of his home in Seattle, Washington, having taken his own life. It is hard to imagine a man as braggadocian as Limbaugh even considering pots and kettles while proclaiming such a thing. It is even harder to admit that this element of cruel sentimentality was the reason for Limbaugh's fame as the "Happy Warrior" of conservatism.[4] It was his reason for being a nonpareil of comedy.

COMEDY AT CROSS-PURPOSES   25

For sure, his "merry brand of malice" *was* a brand.[5] Limbaugh was not a pollster or a political adviser or a policymaker. He was an entertainer. He employed a comic license to deride what he regularly dubbed the absurdity of America. According to outlets like Fairness & Accuracy in Reporting (FAIR) and publications like *Extra!* (the newsletter published by FAIR), Limbaugh's lengthy, even ranting commentaries were shot through with "sloppiness, ignorance and/ or fabrication."[6] A profile in *TIME* magazine from October 1992 considered whether Limbaugh was a "Conservative Provocateur" or just a "BIG BLOW-HARD." Either way, he was "a one-man conglomerate," with books, a newsletter, swag for purchase, and a general air of the carnivalesque in his penchant for making people wonder if he is "the tight-wire walker or the Tilt-a-Whirl, the sideshow barker or the geek."[7] For some, Limbaugh was an all-American polemicist. For others, like Mary Strom Larson, he was a "broadcast demagogue."[8] Limbaugh had a big audience, and it was precisely the kowtowing of doting listeners who called in daily to his three-hour talk radio program that reinforced his demagoguery. On air, Limbaugh fanned his own ego and gave his fans what they wanted with "rude," sometimes "stale," and routinely "mean-spirited" raillery that epitomized a politics of grievance.[9] Elsewhere, like in his monthly newsletter, the *Limbaugh Letter*, Limbaugh expanded his reach by baiting would-be critics and amusing his supporters with appeals to conservative superiority in features like "Stupid Quotes," wherein he would add comic insult to apparently injurious comments made by public officials, actors and actresses, journalists, and political leaders. Crucially, the wit and whimsy in these pages were about staying on brand. They were the same ingredients he cooked up in his badinage around this or that source of liberalism. They materialized in the flippancy with which he joked about "feminazis." Limbaugh delighted in being a rabble-rouser right along with his fawning dittoheads. Nevertheless, the delight was terribly serious.

On January 6, 2021, comic politics turned into political violence. The Capitol Insurrection that followed Joe Biden's win over Donald J. Trump in the 2020 presidential election was partly stoked by talk radio hosts like Limbaugh who urged not just a protest but a fight. This urgency took on greater severity given the fact that Trump was shot in the ear during an attempted assassination at a campaign rally in Butler, Pennsylvania, in July 2024. He was pulled to his feet by Secret Service agents just seconds after shots rang out, and he huddled behind his podium. When he rose, blood was smeared on his face. "We gotta move," an agent insisted. Trump told them to wait, turned to the crowd, raised his right fist and repeatedly mouthed a single word: fight. The day after the insurrection, Limbaugh took to the air and likened the insurrectionists to historical figures like Sam Adams, Thomas Paine, tea partiers, and the soldiers at Lexington and Concord. To Limbaugh, the rage machine of Trumpism represented the makings of a Second American Revolution. As much is made apparent in his series of children's books, the Adventures of Rush Revere, which are *New York Times* bestsellers. The sidekick to Limbaugh the History Teacher is Liberty the Horse. One can purchase plush stuffed animals of Liberty along with the complete book set. Crucially, the same spirit of revisionist history that animates these books animates Limbaugh's career-long assertions that *his* Second American Revolution would be a "restoration."[10] An insurrection is a culmination of his life's work. Limbaugh was forecasting such a "revolutionary" moment as early as 1995 in the *Limbaugh Letter*, with a cartoon cover image depicting the radio host as a soldier in military garb. The comic basis for this "culture-war-uber-alles approach" is what remains most disconcerting.[11]

Happy warism in the radio play of culture and politics should not be taken lightly. In William Wordsworth's poem, such a soldierly stance demands comfort in self and cause and a will to fabricate worldviews for the "toward" and "untoward" lots, in kind.[12] These are precepts of Limbaugh's cartoonishness and manifest in his reliance on offensiveness as a means of persuasion. They are also manifest in newsletter articles that fall under titles such as "Are Americans Stupid?" and the cynicism in his own answer, which Limbaugh frames as a lambasting against all those fraudsters who "pursue the prurient interests of entertainment" to the detriment of the "thinking, engaged citizens" who constitute his listenership.[13] À la Cobain, the happy warism of this Mr. Big of the Vast Right-Wing Conspiracy relies on a mystification of who is serving the servants.

My references to Cobain hint at a further theme in this chapter, and that is the glib, jokey nature of Limbaugh's commentary and the role of popular culture—and, more specifically, music—in his comic spirit. Before flaunting what he repeatedly portrayed as talent on loan from God, Limbaugh was a Top 40 disc jockey at KQV in Pittsburgh and then at various stations along his way to national syndication. He went by the alias Jeff Christie or sometimes Rusty Sharpe. As a deejay, Limbaugh played music and delivered traffic reports. He also tried out bits "to make his audience laugh."[14] At the time, "insult comedy" was becoming more and more popular among radio listeners.[15] It provided a space for Limbaugh to hone his craft. As Limbaugh put it, the experience of doing bits on FM music stations made him realize that he was "really, really good at insulting people."[16] This is what ultimately made him a dominant force in conservative politics, a force to be reckoned with—a comic force.

There is something else lurking behind Limbaugh's comic politics. Well, not so much some*thing* as some*one*: Paul Shanklin. If music is part and parcel of a culture industry in the United States, music in the Limbaugh era exploited the power of insults as rhetorical foundations for comedy. Shanklin is a masterful parodist, impersonator, and vocal mime. He was also the writer of comic songs that became the source material for so many of Limbaugh's comedy sketches from the years of the Bush dynasty through the age of Trumpism. Parodies and skits like "I Lied To You," "Ain't Got No Proof," "Amerika," "The Manchurian President," "This Land Was Your Land," "Slick Willie," "Werewolves in Congress," "Conservative Boy," "Osama Obama," "Barack the Magic Negro," and countless others provide the drumbeat of Limbaugh's brand of conservatism. This chapter takes stock of Shanklin's influence on a new way of doing cultural politics and being political in American culture that enabled Limbaugh to make a brand of selfishness out of comic ideas. Even more, it establishes the cross-purposes in this comic way, in this manner of seeing the world as if through a looking glass, comically. These cross-purposes offer evidence for a turning point in the history of comedy not as an activity or genre but as an attitude, a collective mode of conduct, and, in the long run, a chauvinistic form of egoism.

FARCING THE MUSIC

Comedy is central to the political order of things—and this in an age when one of the most recognized "political" comedians, Bill Maher, implores us to stop making everything about politics.[17] In November 2022, he praised famed comedy songwriter, "Weird Al" Yankovic, for modeling what it means to be comical without being political.[18] Yankovic is a renowned parodist, known for avoiding politics in his songs, not to mention living a life that is uncontroversial, safe, and even boring. He made an exception in 2020 with "We're All Doomed" (also known as "Who's It Gonna Be?"), which he cocreated with the Gregory Brothers. The title conjures up *A Perfect Circle*'s ominous track, "The Doomed" (2018). The song is premised on Weird Al being a moderator for a debate between Joe Biden and President Trump, which he acts out in the music video. At first, Weird Al is hysterical, ranting and raving about COVID-19 and TikTok mania. After receiving a plea in his earpiece to be dignified, he bursts into a question-and-answer singsong wherein he warbles a question before clips of the candidates from the actual debate come back as modified, melodic responses. "Any ideas how to stop a worldwide plague?" he asks. The candidates respond with pabulum about wearing masks. The economy? Trump intones about how he brought back football. Weird Al admits in short order that he is out of questions and lets the candidates just freestyle. Trump spouts about the "forest cities" of Europe, the Proud Boys, and China. Biden prates about

Trump's inanity and fearmongering. In the last part, Weird Al delivers his own verse about conspiracy theories, World War III memes, and his relative inability to distinguish between reality and make-believe. The video for "We're All Doomed" ends with the debate space going up in flames.

Even if "We're All Doomed" stands out for its overt engagement with political culture, it retains the playful mockery that defines songs like "My Bologna" (a parody of the Knack's "My Sharona," released in 1983), "Eat It" (a parody of Michael Jackson's "Beat It," released in 1984), "Living with a Hernia" (a parody of James Brown's "Living in America," released in 1986), "Like a Surgeon" (a parody of Madonna's "Like a Virgin," also released in 1986), "Amish Paradise," (a parody of Coolio's "Gangsta's Paradise," released in 1996), and many, many more songs that make fun not *of* but rather *out of* chart-topping music. Their lyrical content reflects something utterly nonsensical or something funny because of its engagement with the mainstream or its connection to the cultural politics of the day. The parodies, though, are far less about ridicule than reverence. For example, when Weird Al parodied Nirvana's hit song "Smells Like Teen Spirit" with "Smells Like Nirvana," he paid homage to Cobain's infamously cryptic lyrics while finding humor in the presumed inability of a listener to comprehend what is being said through the mix of drones and screams. As such, the song also captures persistent media speculation about the meaning of Cobain's lyrics, never mind the odd martyrdom and collective mood that were mapped onto this so-called voice of a voiceless generation. Lyrics in "Smells Like Nirvana" turn lines like "Our little group has always been and always will until the end" into "It's hard to bargle nawdle zouss with all these marbles in my mouth." According to one commentator, the song says something about "weirdness versus normalcy, insider versus outsider," the inner workings of "the American soul."[19] Cobain gave Weird Al his blessing to do the parody. On the word of Weird Al, the Nirvana front man was mostly curious about whether or not the comic version would be about food. When the two interacted in person again after "Smells Like Nirvana" became a hit single on the album *Off the Deep End* (1992), Weird Al thanked Cobain "profusely" and said, "Anything I can do for you, let me know." Kurt put out his hand and said, "Polish my nails."[20] Two wonderfully weird purveyors of the comic arts.

That Weird Al exemplifies parody as reverence rather than scorn is significant. It derives its sense of humor from what Mikhail Bakhtin might call "gay parody" by using songs to constitute (and, yes, to comment on) a "comic world."[21] It therefore exhibits parody, in Linda Hutcheon's terms, as "a form of imitation" that relies on "ironic inversion," but not with any need to make fun "at the expense of the parodied text"—or, for that matter, the parodied

COMEDY AT CROSS-PURPOSES 29

person.[22] So, when President Trump and candidate Biden deliver refrains in "We're All Doomed" that seem to demonstrate how offbeat and out of touch they are with, say, the better angels of America, those refrains resemble the solemn playfulness in lyrics from a grunge rock parody. Parody like this strips comedy of a palpable egoism that otherwise relies on contempt at worst and condescension at best.

Remember *Beavis and Butt-Head*—Mike Judge's popular animated series about two teenage morons who watch MTV and critique popular music and the videos that accompany them? An episode pertinent to this theme aired in May 1993. In it, Beavis and Butt-Head review the same Nirvana hit song that Weird Al parodied. "Yes!" exclaims Beavis when he hears the opening riff of "Smells Like Teen Spirit." "This kicks butt," Butt-Head proclaims. "Nirvana is cool." *Heh, heh. Hem-hem.* Butt-Head laughs. Beavis grunts. The song plays, and the teenagers wax imbecilic about the meaning of "teen spirit" and the symbolism in music videos. The video is set in a high school gymnasium where Nirvana plays a mock pep rally alongside cheerleaders dressed in black uniforms bearing the red circle-A, for anarchy. A middle-aged male janitor dances in tune as the song spirals into a melee and the rallygoers become a mosh pit. The version by Weird Al is quite similar but concludes with a Girl Scout crowd surfing after attempting to sell cookies to students in the mob. Here again the parody is ridiculous, even critical, but not predicated on ridicule.

So what?

Matters of ridicule and the ridiculous help close the loop with Limbaugh and, more precisely, with Shanklin. Accompanying the article "Are Americans Stupid?" is an editorial cartoon by Bob Gorrell. It features Beavis and Butt-Head clad in nationalistic attire emblematic of Uncle Sam. They are visible from the waist up; however, their wing collars hint at tailcoats, and each has on a top hat with the markings of an American flag. Underneath their open coats are T-shirts. Text on Beavis's T-shirt reads "U.S. Values." Butt-Head, in kind, represents "U.S. Culture." This cartoon makes overt reference to not only these animated icons of the 1990s but also their embodiment of comic ways that justify what Limbaugh characterizes as "brilliant societal analysis." What is more, the cartoon, along with Limbaugh's argument for "conservative ideas" in the face of certain types of American stupidity, betokens what has been recognized as "the best part of his show": the broadcast of Shanklin songs that convert hit songs "into parodies with a 1990s conservative message."[23] In short, egoism was the basis for Limbaugh's comic mockery. Comedy was his vehicle for making selfishness into a virtue and ridicule for analyzing political culture and cultural politics. Shanklin, in turn, provided the soundtrack for this comic appeal.

A COMIC RUSH

Limbaugh used to say that he possessed "talent on loan from God." A column in the *Washington Post* from January 1994 characterized this expression as part and parcel of the "egotistical fantasy" that underlined his on-air persona.[24] Limbaugh's self-presentation toed the line between attraction and repulsion. Where Limbaugh and others saw loaned-out talent, though, others saw the ambition of an entertainer who sold his soul.[25] In other words, Limbaugh borrowed an ego, not talent.

It is hardly controversial to suggest that Limbaugh was egotistical, overbearing, and stagy. Notwithstanding his own bigheadedness, he was widely regarded as a celebutante of political commentary and cultural prophesying. *The Rush Limbaugh Show* debuted with national syndication in 1988. From that point all the way up until his death, Limbaugh nurtured his role as "a consummate showman who excited listeners by being zany and fun and obliterating boundaries."[26] He was unabashedly partisan, and his conservative politics were "purely Manichean," not unlike those we now recognize in "conspiracy cranks" like "the John Birchers, the Christian Zionists, the science deniers, the InfoWarriors,"[27] and lately the Proud Boys, Oath Keepers, and adherents of QAnon. But even if he had the message-making appeal of a rabble-rouser for the culture wars, he did not establish himself in a vacuum. The medium matters.

Talk radio is a familiar medium, and commonly seen as a core stomping ground of the right wing. Following Nicole Hemmer, a first generation of talk radio hosts that preceded Limbaugh, Sean Hannity, Glenn Beck, Laura Ingraham, and other "Messengers of the Right" came of age in the 1950s.[28] Even then, the ideological marketplace was conceived as the space for a "battle of ideas" pursuant to a "sense of persecution" among conservatives.[29] Some of that sensibility stemmed from the idea that broadcast regulations were mechanisms of political oppression. News networks were leading forums for getting messages out there. To stifle this or that kind of speech was to stymie a way of being in the world. Presumptions of a liberal bias in the media were not prominent until the 1960s, but broadcasters like reputed godfather of conservative media Clarence E. "Pat" Manion leaned into radio as a means of speaking out against civil rights reforms and left-leaning policies. Indeed, the cultural warfare of the 1960s led to the use of radio as an outlet for conservative speechifying and fomenting a right turn such that "conservatism transformed itself from an obscure fringe movement into one of the most powerful political forces in the country."[30] It was codified in the late 1980s with the repeal of the fairness doctrine. The repeal

COMEDY AT CROSS-PURPOSES   31

deregulated the airwaves and removed requirements for fair or balanced pro-gramming. Consequently, it provided a platform for talk radio hosts to work out "what went 'wrong' in America and what could be done to fix it."[31] This platform, per Ronald Reagan's infamous 1980 presidential campaign slogan, was for making America great again.

The element of entertainment matters most here. There was conservative pushback against liberal orientations toward race, gender, sexuality, religion, militarism, and more, but it was not politics per se that drove the radio right; it was personality. Limbaugh was the conservative radio personality par excellence. He was self-righteous. He was expressly aggrieved about not being heard, about being shut out of the mainstream, about losing some olden idea of US American culture. As importantly, Limbaugh embodied "an id of American conservative thought," lending voice to feelings of alienation and resentment shared by conservative paranoiacs yearning to be judge and jury of "who could or could not participate in the American experiment."[32] Trump is different by degrees. Like Limbaugh before him, he was only ever interested in "selling political *attitude*. The swaggering certitude. The mocking dismissive-ness. The freedom to offend. The right to assert your privilege without guilt or embarrassment."[33] With Limbaugh, talk radio took on the air of "a carnival."[34] Trump "brought the world of talk radio to life" with "carnival-like" rallies and his wildly yawpish campaign trail antics.[35] Limbaugh performed under the auspices of his self-described EIB Network, or Excellence in Broadcasting. It could just as easily have been *Entertainment* in Broadcasting or Excellence in *Bluster*.

The repeal of the fairness doctrine exempted Limbaugh from any respon-sibility to the public interest. As a medium of entertainment, talk radio freed him to attract attention, acquire listeners, and ultimately turn a profit. He was not accountable for actual governance. He had no need for any real concern over policy initiatives. He was beholden to his audience. There is, however, an even more fundamental issue. Limbaugh was not just an entertainer who built a fantasy world "based on a television sitcom memory of the American dream."[36] Neither was he simply a blowhard with a big ego and a penchant for "peddling political outrage and fueling the fires of polarization" while disguising "racist, sexist, and homophobic commentary" as serious "civic engagement."[37] Lim-baugh was a *comic* entertainer.

From the get-go, Limbaugh—with what President Clinton labeled in 1995 as his "loud and angry" voice and then again in 1996 as his "hostile" and "shrill" discourse of "ridicule" and "hatred"—advertised himself as a wise fool do-ing the work of a funnyman, and *The Rush Limbaugh Show* was closer to the

WHEN COMEDY GOES WRONG

genre of comedy than investigative journalism.[38] Disgraced television execu
tive and chair and CEO of Fox News Roger Ailes liked Limbaugh precisely
because he was "a lot of laughs."[39] He was. First of all, Limbaugh was a master
of witty nicknames. He called himself the Doctor of Democracy, America's
Truth Detector, and Professor of the Limbaugh Institute for Advanced Studies.
President Clinton was "Slick Willie." In the midst of the Clinton-Lewinsky sex
scandal, the Oval Office became the Oval *Orifice*. Limbaugh was also a jokester
prone to comic hoaxes. Sometimes he would tell his audience that he had an
epiphany and decided to transform himself from a hard-line conservative into
a "sensitive liberal," for instance, by supporting Clinton for president in 1992.
Some of his pranks were playful, as when he warned his listeners to be on the
lookout for women who "fard" on the highway. To "fard" is to apply makeup.
Limbaugh did not stop there.

In the spring of 2007, he was criticized for playing "Barack, the Magic Negro" (a song by Shanklin, whom Limbaugh referred to endearingly as the "white
comedian," meant to parody the popularity of the first Black president among
white voters). In response, Limbaugh joked about "the idiocy and phoniness
of the Left."[40] The song features civil rights activist and Baptist minister Al
Sharpton singing bitterly about Obama's run for president. At the time, rumors
were circulating about how jealous Sharpton was that Obama was popular not
for being a "real" Black man but rather a "white interloper's dream." The song,
though, is not just about those rumors. It is also about a column by David
Ehrenstein in the *Los Angeles Times* that applied the term "Magic Negro" to
Obama as a way to make the case that his popularity emerged out of the need
for white people to dismiss dark histories of slavery and racism by propping up
a palatable Black man for high political office.

> "Barack, the Magic Negro," sings Shanklin as Sharpton (to the tune of "Puff,
>   the Magic Dragon"), lives in D.C.
> The L.A. Times, they called him that
> 'Cause he's not authentic like me.
> Yeah, the guy from the L.A. paper
> Said he makes guilty whites feel good.

You get the idea.

Many people were offended. Limbaugh was lambasted. Some members of
his audience criticized the ill-chosen content of the song. Limbaugh responded
by doubling down on the song's comic spirit, proclaiming that it represents the
lunacy of those on the Left who perpetuate a racial stereotype that they revile at
the same time as they repurpose it. As he told a caller, the song reinforced "what
we do on this program," which is "illustrate absurdity by being absurd."[41] So,

the Left wants to use the "Magic Negro" trope as a rhetorical trick for calling out the racism of white America? "OK," joked Limbaugh. "Let's . . . just get an auction block and grab as many blacks as you want to put them up there and let's start the sales, *L.A. Times*, and let's see who it is that fetches the highest prices."[42] Leftists are the racists for positioning Black people as commodities of white culture and establishment politics. That's the punch line.

Perhaps the most telling thing in Limbaugh's joke cycle is his own contention that, despite the apparent absurdity, *he* is the one to be "tarred and feathered."[43] His caller agrees. Or as a staff writer for the *Columbus Dispatch* put it, "birds of a feather mock together."[44] It only makes sense that the very next year, after Obama was elected, Limbaugh promoted his longtime Black call screener, James Golden, aka Bo Snerdley, to Official Criticizer of Barack Obama. Why? Because Snerdley was a self-professed "African-American-in-good-standing-and-certified-black-enough-to-criticize-Obama guy." As Ehrenstein wrote in his column, a "magical negro" is one who "is there to help" white people. He is a sidekick. Lest we be on the lookout for pots and kettles.

After he died, some lamented the wide-ranging impact of Limbaugh's "wicked glee."[45] Some saw in it the entertainment value of nationalistic fantasies and cruel prejudices.[46] Long before that, though, judgments of his wit and wisdom ran the gamut. For some, he was "a vicious clown";[47] for others, a "comic genius."[48] Trump earned similar praise and reproach.[49] Like Limbaugh, the candidate and eventual president "was always captivating, even to those who paid attention only to wince and seethe."[50] Limbaugh normalized character attacks, profanity, ribaldry, insults, and grievances as the comic materials for decrying culture and politics. He established trustworthiness among listeners based on emotional investments and catharsis on demand. This only enhanced his ability to move egotism into echo chambers of what became a form of thought leadership.[51] He offered "frivolous entertainment" normally associated with tabloid newspapers that "clearly refuse to take themselves too seriously (witness the plethora of Elvis and alien sightings in their pages)."[52] Limbaugh, however, made it his business to purvey his content comically and get it to be taken seriously—but *not* as comicality and never in terms that could be written off as just jokes.

When we think of Limbaugh, then, we should not think of him in the tradition of conventional talk radio as much as in a comic tradition of blending bigotry with calculated buffoonery. He was not like Jon Stewart, or Stephen Colbert, or Bill Maher, or so many of the comedians who permeate political comedy. Rather, he was more like a cantankerous vaudeville performer with a radio show. He was like a perversion of Jack Benny, a self-caricature whose "de rigueur form of humor" entailed invective and effrontery, and whose persona exemplified the man who refused to suffer through any of the perceived mortifications caused by what Limbaugh called "cock-eyed liberals."[53] The hook is that if Limbaugh was a wayward Jack Benny, then Shanklin—the "Man of Many Voices"—was a travesty of the "Man of a Thousand Voices," Mel Blanc. After earning the endorsement of program announcer Johnny Donovan, Shanklin began working with Limbaugh in 1993, thus securing a career of contributing droll sketches and satirical songs as a caricaturist for hire. Shanklin's shtick was not all that different from comedians like "Weird Al." He impersonated people by composing "wickedly funny riffs on popular tunes."[54] The difference is that he did not strive to pay homage to his subjects of ridicule or be self-reflexive in his mockery. Instead, he used comedy against anyone or anything that enraged his sense of how the world should be. Shanklin mimicked and mocked liberal politicians, progressive cultural politics, and left-leaning ideals. His goal was to capitalize on Limbaugh's brand of intransigence. His riffs were therefore refrains for the Limbaughesque way of life. This musical comedy was not simply an accessory to Limbaugh's own sense of humor. It was a core feature, making Shanklin's comic alter ego an exemplar of what *The Rush Limbaugh Show* did. It made cultural politicking and political commentary into egotistic, comic conceits, with bunco artistry as the basis for festive outrage that was music to the ears of a dittohead.

CONSERVATISM AS MUSICAL COMEDY

In his essay on the meaning of the comic, Henri Bergson made an observation about the relationship of music and comedy. Music deals with the senses. It captures what is real by expressing what might not be expressible in the normal course of speaking and acting. Like comedy, music gets us close to "inmost feelings," perhaps most markedly when it moves us "willy-nilly, to fall in with it" and act out "the depths of our being."[55] Music strikes a chord. It makes us experience a truer "contact with reality," not unlike the laugh that reveals a bona fide sense of humor.[56]

The musical exploits of his "Parody Czar" emerged out of Limbaugh's longtime use of comedy to approximate what he saw as a reality inspired by the four corners of deceit—big government, academia, science, and the mainstream media. On his radio show, Limbaugh would spout off diatribes laced with blather. He would joke with and sometimes even about listeners who called in to the show. He would also offer regular updates. Homeless Updates. Animal Rights Updates. Feminist Updates. Condom Updates. AIDS Updates. Along with each update, Limbaugh would play a song. For updates about the

COMEDY AT CROSS-PURPOSES   35

homeless, it was "Ain't Got No Home," by Clarence "Frogman" Henry. When he would discuss animal rights, Limbaugh would laughingly play Andy Williams's easy-listening classic, "Born Free," which he "mixed with the sounds of animal cries and gunfire."[57] For his AIDS Update, there were various songs, including Steam's hit "Na Na Hey Hey Kiss Him Goodbye" and Johnny Lee's version of "Lookin' for Love," a number-one country tune from the *Urban Cowboy* soundtrack.[58] The comedy was in the lyrics. Lookin' for love *in all the wrong places*. Na na na na, na na na na, hey hey hey, goodbye! Limbaugh made harsh harangues come off as comedy, in many cases by turning tragedy into farce.

Farce is forcemeat stuffing. For Limbaugh, it was the by-product of comedy stuffed into places where it was normally unfit. Contra Bakhtin, his comedy used travesty as a device to profane, and it translated to his television show (1992–96). During Christmastime in the first year that Limbaugh was the talk of the small screen, he ended an episode with a comic sing-along. Limbaugh began his denouement by walking from a room filled with TV sets and meant for working through current affairs to the "audience area" of the studio. He then invited a member of the audience onstage to serve as "conductorette" for a choral rendition of "God Rest Ye Merry, Gentlemen." The lyrics of this rendition, though, were altered to reflect the sentiments of "feminazis" from the Women's Action Coalition who were supposedly protesting by singing emended songs around New York City. Here is a verse from Limbaugh's version, as it was sung by his studio audience.

> Don't rest so merry, gentlemen. There's much to cause dismay.
> For women's lives are limited, by unfair rank and pay.
> Continuing repression whether black, white, straight or gay.
> Oh, tidings of action and change, action and change.
> Oh, tidings of action and change.

Be mad, urged Limbaugh before the audience began to sing. Be angry. Fill yourselves with rage! But the people smiled as they sang the refrain. In the end, they were too gleeful. Limbaugh told them as much. That was the travesty in his not-so-gay parody, because he smiled right along with them. Farce in festivity.

In song after song, Shanklin exploited a similar comic license to organize and orchestrate his tuneful political style. Comedy imbued Limbaugh's political style with egocentrism, mockery, and contempt. In Shanklin's music, this egocentrism and contempt plays out as a singsong way of mocking liberals and anyone or anything they might represent. The Clinton presidency was an apt comic foil, and the president himself was Shanklin's pilgarlic. Aside from wryly endorsing Clinton's bid in 1992 and doing an infamous overnight at the White

House in order to bolster the standing of then president George H. W. Bush, Limbaugh famously made his mark on the Clinton administration by referring to it as the "Raw Deal." The elements of this deal were detailed in songs that Limbaugh played on his radio show. Many of these songs ended up on Shanklin's first album, *Bill Clinton: The Early Years* (1995), which is a sort of greatest hits record of Limbaugh's brickbats. Like numerous comedy albums that would follow, this exemplifies a comic style for making fun of liberal politics and cultural politicking with impersonations that are peddled as amplifications of the absurd in real life. This is hardly novel in comedy that relies on parody and caricature. However, in Shanklin's music, comedy comes off as what George Meredith might call a "love-season" for conservatism in "the carnival of egoism."[59] The scandals and outrages of the Clinton administration are turned into the rationale for a return to the rugged individualism that Limbaugh set against any common weal that could be created by Big Heads in Big Government.

The album begins with "The Beginning." One hears someone walking up to a microphone. That someone is Shanklin pretending to be Paul Tsongas, a Massachusetts senator who ran an iconoclastic campaign in competition with Clinton on a platform of progressive policymaking and what he described in a manifesto as "A Call to Economic Arms." You could have had me as your president, he says as if to laugh at his listeners, but you chose the Panda Bear. "Nyah nyah nyah nyah nyah nyah," he chides and, in so doing, stylizes conservatism as a mood affected by a sense that liberal policies poison the soul. Democrats are bent on social engineering, he says, and self-reliance is the only real virtue in society. Consider the comic stylization of Limbaugh's "Undeniable Truths of Life," like "Freedom is God given," "There is a distinct singular American culture—rugged individualism and self-reliance—which made America great," "Feminism was established to allow unattractive women access to the mainstream of society," and "Condoms only work during the school year." It is comedy done by "the boil-in-the-ass version" of a fool in *King Lear*.[60] A scourge, not a jester.

So it goes in Shanklin's comic redux of Clinton's early years. Variously replicating the tunes of popular songs, like "All My Loving" by the Beatles, and performing mock interviews and bogus infomercials, Shanklin exhorts listeners to find a boon in liberal banes. In "All Your Money," he impersonates Clinton as a scheming politician pushing tax reforms and budget reconciliations. In "I Lied to You," sung to the tune of the Beatles' song, "Do You Want to Know a Secret," Clinton flaunts his own power plays despite the fallout from white lies about not inhaling when he first tried marijuana and cock-and-bull stories about how he dodged the Vietnam War draft. Yet other songs, such as "The Tax and Spend," feature Clinton singing about his economic policy as the confiscation of public monies. At one point, Shanklin pretends to be Al Gore echoing Clinton's appeals and putting forth his own environmentalist and animal rights agendas. In each case, Shanklin parrots Limbaugh in making fun of those who think they can fool the American people. The album is replete with markers for the intellectual roots of the conservative movement in William F. Buckley Jr., the hypocrisies in liberal demands that people pay their fair share, and the sentiment that Clinton's American dream amounted to Reagan's American nightmare. One sketch has Clinton delivering a public service announcement that is really a request for contributions to his legal defense fund. Another song retells the Whitewater scandal as the "Whitewater Blues," a requiem on crooked real estate investments and sexual misconduct. In Shanklin's parodies, the Right is right to be self-righteous given the Left's politics of corruption, cover-ups, and cronyism.

The timing of this album is crucial, and not just because it coincides with the Clinton presidency. Shanklin's album coincides with Limbaugh's early influence and public pushback against talk radio. President Clinton himself took to the airwaves in an effort to scold Limbaugh for his rhetorical violence and jeering expression of political commentary as insult comedy—an early example of which is Limbaugh's insinuation in 1992 and then outright contention in 1993 that Chelsea, the president's teenage daughter, was the White House dog. President Clinton called into St. Louis radio station KMOX in June 1994. He denounced Limbaugh as an embodiment of the constant backbiting that seemed to make opposition politicking into mean-spirited gamesmanship. According to Clinton, the talk radio demigod was the patron saint of cynicism.[61] Some members of the press reacted to President Clinton's call-in by portraying it as a "sad-sack lament" that left the nation "wading in tears—tears of laughter."[62] It would have been hard for Shanklin to render Clinton a more pitiful laughingstock.

With these kinds of reactions, Limbaugh indulged in what he viewed as an onslaught "from every corner of liberalism."[63] A showman. A hatemonger. A slabhead. A jerk. A political dinosaur. A racist. These are among the labels that were used to express just how insufferable Limbaugh could be. For Limbaugh, they are euphemisms for how liberals really felt: afraid. In an essay he penned for *Policy Review* in the fall of 1994, Limbaugh celebrated his stature as a consummate "performer" who represented "a body of beliefs that strikes terror into the heart of even the most well-entrenched liberals."[64] He once again championed rugged individualism and positioned himself as a proud, nay, prideful, *persona grata* for the rejection of liberalism and its core tenets.

Moreover, he highlighted the superiority of his "bumper music" and the comic truths it could lay bare.

These principles motivated Shanklin all along. On September 24, 1994, Shanklin was a featured speaker at a hearing of conservative watchdog organization Accuracy in Media. The hearing was entitled, "Resistance to Politically Incorrect Stories."[65] In his speech, he teased conservatives for their winning ways (the "Republican Revolution" of the midterm elections had not yet occurred). He hailed Jimmy Carter as a homebuilder with Habitat for Humanity and a "fine ex-president." He taunted the populist, billionaire, industrialist, and Independent presidential candidate Ross Perot. To be fair, he teased George H. W. Bush for being what impressionist Dana Carvey once described as a cross between Mister Rogers and John Wayne. This was before Shanklin got to his depictions of President Clinton as a flimflamming, womanizing Commander in Briefs. These are familiar mockeries on Shanklin's comedy albums. Less compelling than his comic iterations of presidents and party politics, then, was Shanklin's claim that he does not write his own material. The material writes itself. He simply amplifies and exaggerates the absurdity.

Interestingly, Shanklin's defense of comedy resonates with what actor Alec Baldwin more recently said in a reflection on his portrayal of President Trump on *Saturday Night Live*. With all of his scandals and scurrilous talk both before and after his election, Trump was "the head writer of his own comedy routine."[66] A key difference is that while Baldwin initially found his impersonation to be "fun, fun, fun," it was ultimately agonizing because of what it was doing to comedy and *not* doing to minimize the damage being done by Trump.[67] To wit, in the Trump era, comedy lost some of its capacity to do good by diminishing the collective will to revel in shared human folly. Shanklin is a precursor. He exemplifies a turning point in the history of comedy in the United States because of the cross-purposes to which he put it, on one hand as a recognizable form of political humor and, on the other, as a bitter form of entertaining resentment.

Shanklin has a robust oeuvre. In *Bill Clinton: The Comeback Kid Tour* (1999), he kept up his disdain for Clinton's "phony baloney." He sang of "Werewolves in Congress," made Clinton speak of his "casual life" in Arkansas as if it was an insurance policy predicated on nondisclosure, and mimicked Vice President Gore's rumination about Nixonian legacies and impeachment. To these typical takes Shanklin added comic characters like the "simpletons" to distinguish between honest, hardworking Americans and members of (or adherents to) the elite. He also fabricated public service announcements that even more overtly situated liberalism as the last political refuge of scoundrels. Conservatism, for Shanklin (like Limbaugh), was the last resort for real Americans. For instance, in "Montana," Shanklin reiterates a sense that the Treasure State is the Last Best Place to live on one's own land in one's own country with one's own court of opinion. He makes of Montana a faux utopia for conservatives looking to escape an America beyond salvation, even as he quips about those of his lot being "nutcase" extremists bent on inbreeding, child abuse, wifebeating, and racism. Do not be fooled. Shanklin uses the classic strategy of a satirist who projects onto *others* what could be considered "the weaknesses and temptations that are really *within himself.*"[68] Revisit the essay about stupid Americans and you will discover that Limbaugh operates in a comparable vein, signing off with appeals to low taxes, small government, traditional values, personal responsibility, and freedom—appeals he makes to his "fellow extremist." The fringe becomes the would-be mainstream.

Cultural warism and conspiracy theorizing were prevalent in Shanklin's comic way. It created a framework for popular conservatism that "grew wilder, more menacing, more elaborate, and more violent" as the "gospel according to Rush" gave way to Trumpism.[69] Limbaugh defended the Capitol Insurrection on January 6, 2021, as a legitimate act carried out by those who were fed up with an America that had been stolen from them. No surprise. Among his undeniable truths is the avowal that peace sometimes requires war in a land of free peoples (never mind the paradox in another "undeniable truth" that opposition to America by Americans "is not always courageous and sacred; it is sometimes dangerous"). There is a twisted line from right-wing radio to the Capitol siege, and it forges a path through tragedy as farce to the use of comic ideas for entertaining, yet all too consequential, political action.

A certain joy comes with comedy that is aligned with drollery as well as danger. Shanklin's songs and skits constitute an almost frolicsome drumbeat behind the rants and raves of "the most Dangerous Man in America." Following the Capitol Insurrection, Trump borrowed the tone of this playlist by "laughing at the trauma" of those who suffered in real time and in the aftermath.[70] The whole goal is honing a sense of humor based on horrible visions of reality. This land was your land, Shanklin lamented at the turn of the twentieth century. Later it was jeremiads about executive privileges and the familiar faces of globalism, who editorial cartoonist Michael Ramirez represented in lockstep with caricatures of Bill Clinton, Saddam Hussein, Jesse Jackson, and Osama Bin Laden. These caricatures were pictured in a cartoon identity parade that was used as cover art for Shanklin's 2002 album, *The Usual Suspects.* In the buildup to Obama's presidency, Shanklin seemed to codify a veritable comic vocabulary for popular conservatism as conceived by Limbaugh with songs and skits like "Blazing Liberal," "I Am Woman," "Bank of Amigo," "U Can't Say That," "The Star-Spanglish Banner," and—suggestively—"We Hate America." To read this list and recognize that there is more to it than a collection of comic ideas is, of course, to acknowledge how much Limbaugh turned the screw on economies of attention. But lest we forget the ultimate undeniable truth of life, according to Limbaugh: "Too many Americans can't laugh at themselves anymore." It is the *can't* here that remains a sticking point.

CONCLUSION: A COMIC TRUDGE

In 1996, comedian Al Franken published a book. It is called *Rush Limbaugh Is a Big Fat Idiot and Other Observations*. As Franken describes it, the book is satirical in tone albeit "entirely serious" in "its intent."[71] Numerous moments in the book are testaments to this sensibility. One involves Franken recounting a public exchange between Limbaugh and a dittohead. The exchange took place in early April 1996 on alt.fan.rush-limbaugh, an online discussion group. It was framed as a response to Franken's book and his attempts to poke the bear. "It would seem," Limbaugh wrote, "that the Liberals have to resort to name-calling instead of common sense. But common sense will prevail, so don't worry you people." To this a dittohead responded with topics for books that Limbaugh could write about Franken, for example, how he "is a desperate, washed-up loser," the "butt uglyman" with a "grotesque froglike appearance," an "Abortion Posterchild," and so on. Limbaugh wrote back with an expression of gratitude that doubled as a gesture of self-promotion. "Thank you," he wrote. "I like my fans praising me and my great wisdom." Limbaugh also liked the book ideas. They were good resources for countering Franken's observations, which Limbaugh characterized as not "very funny, just stupid."[72] Franken took the high road. Sort of. He opted not to "point out the logical inconsistency" in Limbaugh's retort. He refused to be indignant. Instead, Franken wrote, "I think I'll just let Rush's own words speak for themselves."[73]

The comedy is in Franken's aim to satirize Limbaugh by doing precisely what the "big fat idiot" does to deride others. Limbaugh baited people with his braggadocian comic appeal. Franken baited back. To do this, he made the crucial observation that he and Limbaugh were "sort of in the same business" and that business is part entertainment, part ego inflation, and *large* part "comedic process."[74] I want to bring these threads together by returning to the element of farce and the fodder of carnival that propelled what Shanklin reinforced as the core resources for approximating real life in order to showcase particular comic ways of being.

Poet Jay Sizemore wrote a "satirical" elegy on the occurrence of Limbaugh's death in February 2021. Limbaugh was "the Hindenburg disaster" incarnate,

COMEDY AT CROSS-PURPOSES

a zeppelin "filled with flammable gas," and yet a man not unlike the Cheshire Cat who pioneered talk radio as a gateway for propaganda in democratic politicking and on whose corpse there should be pinned a medal for lifelong remorselessness.[75] Sizemore's poem is well suited for a political arena wherein the only choices are to laugh or go mad. One is not wrong to wonder whether Limbaugh was ever and always grinning like the Cat or going mad like the Hatter. For the purposes of this conclusion, it is better not to speculate on whether either possibility is better or worse but rather to imagine how Limbaugh poses a problem for the comic spirit that moves from a parodic mode of doing, say, cultural politics, to an ontology of political identity. Shanklin's comedic tunes did not just inscribe this or that norm of discourse or civic engagement through mockery. Rather, they instituted mockery as a means of, in Sizemore's words, puffing the smoke from a cigar much as the devil did on the day Limbaugh died. Neither the devil nor the dead have remorse. Limbaugh certainly did not.

> "Pin the medals on his corpse.
> Spin the carousel of lights again,
> and wait for the music
> to magically erase
> the history of his sin."

Wait for the music . . .

The music excites. It feeds the beast. In a comic spirit of the carnivalesque, music is "closely combined with slaughter, dismemberment, bowels, excrement, and other images of the material bodily lower stratum."[76] This means that, on the radio, talk inspirited by comicality is meant to break things down to their basest elements. With Limbaugh, we find a comic spirit that is not a source of fertility so much as it is a source of degradation. You do not have to look hard on the internet or listen long in the archives of *The Rush Limbaugh Show* to discover that Ayn Rand, with her Objectivist, egoistical approach to the world, is a major spirit animal. In Rand's work, the egoist is the lowest common denominator and that self-important creature does right by doing away with any idea that anyone other than the self—the king among fools—matters. Limbaugh's persona is shot through with Rand's conception of the egoist. Shanklin's comic character is too. The happy viciousness in their comedy blends into the virtues of their conceit.

The irony is that, as much as Rand inspired Limbaugh and Shanklin, she embodies the very take on egocentric politics that flies in the face of their silly bits and trivial ditties. To laugh at oneself, says Rand, is "monstrous." It is akin to "spitting in your own face."[77] Call others contemptuous and laugh at them. That is virtuous. That is the act of unmasking that counteracts "the camouflage of moral cowardice."[78] In Bergson's terms, that is how music can be used, comically, to revel in "everything that veils reality from us, in order to bring us face to face with reality itself."[79] With an esprit de corps in common with Bergson, poet and novelist George Meredith conceived of egoism as an absurdity unto itself. Comedy is about recasting the absurdity of egoism in the folly of promoting any one person or idea or thing over and above a collective.[80] The comedy in Limbaugh, and then again in Shanklin, dilutes this brand of absurdity by making delusions of self-interest into the fountainhead for the comic spirit. The ego, as Rand would say, is sacred. Comedy is profane.

Herein lie the cross-purposes of comedy that combines "derisive laughter" with what is advertised as "thoughtful laughter."[81] This brand of comedy demonstrates a rigid comic spirit that relies on the "puppet-like movements" of laughers-at.[82] The turning point in comedy so inspired by Limbaugh and Shanklin has everything to do with the idea that what Bergson once dubbed the root of comedy, rigidity, should no longer be eyed with suspicion or ridicule but rather met with praise and high (or we might say *low*) esteem. What Meredith might characterize as a "comic perception" is the prime mover for fools who aim to be kings or kingmakers in US American culture and politics. These trifling fools are the stuff of easy entertainment. Shanklin is a case in point with his use of music and satirical sketches to conjoin "two opposite currents of comic fancy."[83] One is stern foolishness. The other is false morality.

A comedy of degradation is everywhere in and around those who laughed at Limbaugh or laughed him off or found him to be a breeding ground for contempt. Those who were with him, his dittoheads, took the privileges that come with being put under the rubric of comedy and ran with it. That is, they played along with him to spew the very plaudits that made Limbaugh a king among men, making fun as a way of making hay. Some might see this as force multiplication in degraded comedy. In the singsong conservatism of Limbaugh and Shanklin is something more ignominious. In the degradation of comedy is a recourse for counteracting the festivity of our ego system.

The ego trip therefore becomes the ego trudge. The next few chapters bear this out and elaborate on the antics of those who seem to enact the tenets of more contemporary shows like popular right-wing podcast *Louder with Crowder*.[84] At the time of this writing, visitors to host Steven Crowder's website would be invited to either sign up for his newsletter with an affirmation that you are sick of the Left or decline the invitation by clicking on a button labeled "I hate myself." Orientations like this normalize revelry in straight talk as horseplay, in bigotry as buffoonery, and—ultimately—in the peculiar privileges conferred by the label "comedian." They welcome a comic spirit for provoking critics to be fools running errands in circles. Or else, they stir up a way of being seriously comic by being with stupid.

NOTES

1. Erin Gloria Ryan, "Rush Limbaugh Spent His Lifetime Speaking Ill of the Dead," *Daily Beast*, February 17, 2021, https://www.thedailybeast.com/rush-limbaugh-spent-his-lifetime-speaking-ill-of-the-dead.

2. Ryan, "Rush Limbaugh."

3. See "The Way Things Aren't: Rush Limbaugh Debates Reality," Fairness & Accuracy in Reporting, July 1, 1994, https://fair.org/home/the-way-things-arent/.

4. Tony Katz, "Rush Limbaugh Was Conservative Radio's 'Happy Warrior.' That's What Liberals Don't Understand," *THINK*, February 18, 2021, https://www.nbcnews.com/think/opinion/rush-limbaugh-was-conservative-radio-s-happy-warrior-s-what-ncna1258193.

5. Matt Sedensky, "Rush Limbaugh, 'Voice of American Conservatism,' Has Died," *Salt Lake Tribune*, February 17, 2021, https://www.sltrib.com/news/2021/02/17/rush-limbaugh-voice/.

6. "The Way Things Aren't."

7. Richard Corliss, "Conservative Provocateur Or BIG BLOWHARD," *TIME*, October 26, 1992, https://time.com/archive/6721514/conservative-provocateur-or-big-blowhard/.

8. Mary Strom Larson, "Rush Limbaugh—Broadcast Demagogue," *Journal of Radio Studies* 4 (1997): 189–202.

9. Virginia Heffernan, "Trump Dittoes Limbaugh's Bigotry with a Presidential Medal of Freedom," *Los Angeles Times*, February 7, 2020, https://www.latimes.com/opinion/story/2020-02-07/rush-limbaugh-presidential-medal-of-freedom-donald-trump.

10. See "Limbaugh on 'Second American Revolution,'" Media Matters for America, August 2, 2010, https://www.mediamatters.org/rush-limbaugh/limbaugh-second-american-revolution-i-would-not-call-it-revolution-id-call-it.

11. Philip Bump, "Rush Limbaugh Created the Politics That Trump Used to Win the White House," *Philadelphia Inquirer*, February 18, 2021, https://www.inquirer.com/opinion/commentary/rush-limbaugh-obituary-death-trump-20210218.html.

12. William Wordsworth, "Character of the Happy Warrior," Poetry Foundation, accessed January 7, 2023, https://www.poetryfoundation.org/poems/45512/character-of-the-happy-warrior.

13. Rush Limbaugh, "Are Americans Stupid?," *Limbaugh Letter* 3, no. 4 (April 1994): 13. Retrieved from the Internet Archive, https://archive.org/details/the-limbaugh-letter-1994-04/page/n11/mode/2up.

14. Ze'ev Chafets, *Rush Limbaugh: An Army of One* (New York: Sentinel, 2010), 32.

15. Chafets, *Rush Limbaugh*, 37.

16. Rush Limbaugh, *See, I Told You So* (New York: Pocket, 1994), 31.

17. See "New Rule: Just Don't Go There," *Real Time with Bill Maher Blog*, November 17, 2018, https://www.real-time-with-bill-maher-blog.com/index/2018/11/17/new-rule-just-dont-go-there.

18. See Club Random Podcast, "'Weird Al' Yankovic," YouTube, November 13, 2022, https://www.youtube.com/watch?v=oTgoL5aT2cg.

19. Sam Anderson, "The Weirdly Enduring Appeal of Weird Al Yankovic," *New York Times*, April 9, 2020, https://www.nytimes.com/2020/04/09/magazine/weird-al-yankovic.html.

20. Arun Starkey, "How Kurt Cobain Reacted to 'Weird Al' Yankovic's Nirvana Parody," *Far Out*, August 17, 2022, https://faroutmagazine.co.uk/kurt-cobain-reacted-weird-al-yankovic-nirvana-parody/.

21. Mikhail Bakhtin, *Rabelais and His World*, trans. Hélène Iswolsky (Bloomington: Indiana University Press, 1984), 39, 88.

22. Linda Hutcheon, *A Theory of Parody: The Teachings of Twentieth-Century Art Forms* (Urbana: University of Illinois Press, 1985), 87–88.

23. James Fallows, "Talent on Loan from the GOP," *Atlantic*, May 1994, https://www.theatlantic.com/magazine/archive/1994/05/talent-on-loan-from-the-gop/303852/.

24. Gigi B. Sohn and Andrew Schwartzman, "FAIRNESS—NOT SILENCE," *Washington Post*, January 31, 1994, https://www.washingtonpost.com/archive/opinions/1994/01/31/fairness-not-silence/cbe8b618-de11-4da3-8b63-83e04b4dec1c/.

25. Mark Horne, "Rush Limbaugh: An Ego on Loan from God," *Christianity Today*, July 18, 1994, https://www.christianitytoday.com/ct/1994/july18/4t8062.html.

26. Brian Rosenwald, "They Just Wanted to Entertain," *Atlantic*, August 21, 2019, https://www.theatlantic.com/ideas/archive/2019/08/talk-radio-made-todays-republican-party/596380/.

27. Bob Moser, "Rush Limbaugh Did His Best to Ruin America," *Rolling Stone*, February 17, 2021, https://www.rollingstone.com/politics/politics-features/rush-limbaugh-dead-trump-ruined-america-1129222/.

28. Nicole Hemmer, *Messengers of the Right: Conservative Media and the Transformation of American Politics* (Philadelphia: University of Pennsylvania Press, 2018).

COMEDY AT CROSS-PURPOSES

29. Hemmer, *Messengers of the Right*, 27, 124.

30. Matthew Dallek, "The Conservative 1960s," *Atlantic*, December 1995, https://www.theatlantic.com/magazine/archive/1995/12/the-conservative-1960s/376506/.

31. Paul Matzo, *The Radio Right: How a Band of Broadcasters Took on the Federal Government and Built the Modern Conservative Movement* (New York: Oxford University Press, 2020), 12.

32. Grynbaum et al., "How Right-Wing Radio Stoked Anger before the Capitol Siege," *New York Times*, February 12, 2021, https://www.nytimes.com/2021/02/10/business/media/conservative-talk-radio-capitol-riots.html. See also Matzo, *Radio Right*, 9, and Peter Laufer, *Inside Talk Radio: America's Voice or Just Hot Air?* (New York: Birch Lane Press, 1995), 8.

33. Moser, "Rush Limbaugh Did His Best." See also the discussion of Trumpism as a mood in Lawrence Grossberg, *Under the Cover of Chaos: Trump and the Battle for the American Right* (London: Pluto Press, 2018).

34. Laufer, *Inside Talk Radio*, iv.

35. Brian Rosenwald, *Talk Radio's America: How an Industry Took Over a Political Party That Took Over the United States* (Cambridge, MA: Harvard University Press, 2019), 244.

36. Laufer, *Inside Talk Radio*, 58.

37. Jeffrey M. Berry and Sarah Sobieraj, "Understanding the Rise of Talk Radio," *PS: Political Science and Politics* 44 (2011): 762–67. See also Frank Rich, "Can Conservatives Be Funny?," *New York Magazine*, May 15, 2014, https://nymag.com/news/frank-rich/conservative-comedians-2014-5/.

38. See Greg Pollowitz, "Rush Limbaugh vs. Bill Clinton," *National Review*, April 19, 2010, https://www.nationalreview.com/media-blog/rush-limbaugh-vs-bill-clinton-greg-pollowitz/. See also Laufer, *Inside Talk Radio*, iv, 16.

39. Staci D. Kramer, "The Gospel According to Rush," *Chicago Tribune*, November 30, 1992, https://www.chicagotribune.com/news/ct-xpm-1992-11-30-9204190360-story.html.

40. Adam Serwer, "Latching onto L.A. Times Op-Ed, Limbaugh Sings 'Barack, The Magic Negro,'" Media Matters for America, March 20, 2007, https://www.mediamatters.org/rush-limbaugh/latching-la-times-op-ed-limbaugh-sings-barack-magic-negro.

41. "Barack the Magic Negro, Explained," *Rush Limbaugh Show*, March 23, 2007, https://www.rushlimbaugh.com/daily/2007/03/23/barack_the_magic_negro_explained2/.

42. Serwer, "Latching onto L.A. Times Op-Ed."

43. "Barack the Magic Negro, Explained."

44. "Limbaugh Colors Debate on Obama with a Song," *Columbus Dispatch*, May 10, 2007, https://www.dispatch.com/story/opinion/cartoons/2007/05/10/limbaugh-colors-debate-on-obama/23462989007/.

45. Moser, "Rush Limbaugh Did His Best."

46. Justin Peters, "Rush Limbaugh Wasn't Funny," *Slate*, February 18, 2021, https://slate.com/news-and-politics/2021/02/rush-limbaugh-wasnt-funny.html.

47. Penny Laurie, "Laurie Penny on Rush Limbaugh: A Vicious Clown," *New Statesman*, March 9, 2012, https://www.newstatesman.com/world/2012/03/limbaugh-women-sex-real-attack.

48. Steve Young, "Rush Limbaugh, Comic Genius," *Philadelphia Inquirer*, March 7, 2012, https://www.inquirer.com/philly/opinion/inquirer/20120307_Rush_Limbaugh__comic_genius.html.

49. Emily Nussbaum, "How Jokes Won the Election," *New Yorker*, January 15, 2017, https://www.newyorker.com/magazine/2017/01/23/how-jokes-won-the-election.

50. Rosenwald, *Talk Radio's America*, 228.

51. See Kathleen Hall Jamieson and Joseph N. Cappella, *Echo Chamber: Rush Limbaugh and the Conservative Media Establishment* (New York: Oxford University Press, 2008).

52. Laufer, *Inside Talk Radio*.

53. Kathryn Fuller-Seeley, *Jack Benny and the Golden Age of American Radio Comedy* (Berkeley: University of California Press, 2017), 226.

54. Rod Schwartz, "Remembering Rush Limbaugh," Pullman Radio, February 23, 2021, https://pullmanradio.com/remembering-rush/.

55. Henri Bergson, *Laughter: An Essay on the Meaning of the Comic*, trans. Cloudesley Brereton and Fred Rothwell (New York: MacMillan, 1911), 156–57.

56. Bergson, *Laughter*, 157.

57. Schwartz, "Remembering Rush Limbaugh."

58. Dan Evon, "Did Rush Limbaugh's 'AIDS Update' Mock the Deaths of Gay People?," *Snopes*, February 17, 2021, https://www.snopes.com/fact-check/rush-limbaugh-mock-aids-gays/.

59. George Meredith, *The Egoist: A Comedy in Narrative* (New York: Charles Scribner's Songs, 1908), 110.

60. Jackson Baker, "Playing the Fool," *Memphis Flyer*, January 15, 2009, https://www.memphisflyer.com/playing-the-fool.

61. "Presidential Radio Interview," C-SPAN, June 24, 1994, https://www.c-span.org/video/?58239-1/presidental-radio-interview.

62. Howard Rosenberg, "Truthman Slips Up in His Rush to Judgment," *Los Angeles Times*, June 29, 1994, https://www.latimes.com/archives/la-xpm-1994-06-29-ca-9739-story.html.

63. Rush Limbaugh, "Why Liberals Fear Me," Heritage Foundation, February 18, 2021, https://www.heritage.org/conservatism/commentary/why-liberals-fear-me.

64. Limbaugh, "Why Liberals Fear Me."

65. "Resistant to Politically Incorrect Stories," C-SPAN, September 24, 1994, https://www.c-span.org/video/?60430-1/resistance-politically-incorrect-stories.

66. Kelsey Sutton, "Alec Baldwin on Trump: 'He's the Head Writer of His Own Comedy Routine,'" *Politico*, November 8, 2016, https://www.politico.com/blogs/on-media/2016/11/alec-baldwin-on-trump-hes-the-head-writer-of-his-own-comedy-routine-230939.

67. Greg Evans, "Alec Baldwin Still Hates Playing Trump on 'SNL' but Says Parody Helps Fans 'Manage Their Pain,'" *Deadline*, September 6, 2019, https://deadline.com/2019/09/alec-baldwin-snl-saturday-night-live-donald-trump-kevin-nealon-interview-1202713730/.

68. Kenneth Burke, *Attitudes toward History*, 3rd ed. (Berkeley: University of California Press, 1959), 49.

69. Moser, "Rush Limbaugh Did His Best." See also Kramer, "The Gospel According to Rush."

70. Asawin Suebsaeng and Will Sommer, "Trump's Favorite Part of Jan. 6 Is Laughing at the Trauma," *Daily Beast*, January 6, 2022, https://www.thedailybeast.com/trumps-favorite-part-of-january-6-is-laughing-at-the-trauma.

71. Diane Ravitch, "Al Franken on Rush Limbaugh's Squalid Legacy," *Diane Ravitch's Blog*, February 23, 2021, https://dianeravitch.net/2021/02/23/al-franken-on-rush-limbaughs-squalid-legacy/.

72. See "Message to My Fans," Google Groups Conversations, accessed November 11, 2022, https://groups.google.com/g/alt.fan.rush-limbaugh/c/p3FeoDbdvwE/m/FolMfx1-QoAJ.

73. Al Franken, *Rush Limbaugh Is a Big Fat Idiot and Other Observations* (New York: Dell Trade Paperback, 1996), 275.

74. Franken, *Rush Limbaugh Is a Big Fat Idiot*, 14, 295.

75. Jay Sizemore, "The Day Rush Limbaugh Died," *Medium*, February 17, 2021, https://medium.com/parlor-tricks/the-day-rush-limbaugh-died-83cf04472a1f.

76. Bakhtin, *Rabelais and His World*, 224.

77. Ayn Rand, quoted in *The Ayn Rand Lexicon: Objectivism from A to Z*, ed. Harry Binswanger, (New York: Meridian, 1986), 207.

78. Rand, quoted in Binswanger, *Ayn Rand Lexicon*, 207.

79. Bergson, *Laughter*, 157.

80. George Meredith, *An Essay on Comedy and the Uses of the Comic Spirit*, ed. Lane Cooper (New York: Charles Scribner's Sons, 1918), 82–83.

81. Meredith, *Essay on Comedy*, 140, 141.

82. Bergson, *Laughter*, 141.

83. Bergson, *Laughter*, 123.

84. Seth Simons, "Right-Wing Comedians Are Right-Wing Media," *Paste*, March 22, 2021, https://www.pastemagazine.com/comedy/right-wing-media/ring-wing-comedians-are-right-wing-media.

TWO

POE'S LAW AND THE MOOT POINTS OF MILLION DOLLAR EXTREME

TO WATCH THE SKETCHES OF comedy troupe Million Dollar Extreme (MDE) is to watch twenty-first-century re-creations of Aesop's fable of the Frog and the Ox. While grazing in a meadow, an Ox accidentally "set his foot among a parcel of young Frogs." They all escaped danger, except one, who was squashed. The other young Frogs told their mother of "the hugest creature that they ever saw" and of its murderous ways. Mother Frog tried to fathom the true size of the beast. So, she swelled up her body and asked, "Was it so big?" "Oh, bigger," the young Frogs replied. She swelled up even more. "And so big?" "Indeed, mother," said the young Frogs, before informing her that she could blow up big enough to burst and would still never reach the magnitude of that Ox. Mother Frog "strove yet again," though, until she burst.[1]

Here is another way to approach MDE's comedy. Imagine that you are a fly on the wall in a room of individuals saying what they really think and feel, with no filter, and with a shared sense of what is funny. Now imagine that those individuals publicize that comic sensibility. Imagine they say and do things that might otherwise be reserved for private spaces, if not the space between one's ears and the conversations among those with like minds. For instance, in a "prank" video entitled "John Oliver shoutout!" posted on YouTube in November 2016, members of MDE—Sam Hyde (aka "Sammy Gunz") and Charls Carol (aka "Judicious") are in a wooded area taking turns with various firearms, from pistols to automatic weapons.[2] The video might have been a response to Oliver's takedown of the National Rifle Association in an episode of his comedy show *Last Week Tonight* in June 2016. Regardless, MDE's taunt begins with the bogus disclaimer that all guns used were props and all explosions of targets were faked. It then proceeds with fast cuts of the men in action.

POE'S LAW AND MILLION DOLLAR EXTREME 49

Hyde invokes podcaster, comedian, and Ultimate Fighting Championship color commentator Joe Rogan when he announces his ability to kill animals with his bare hands. Carol fires off a few shots after suggesting that one should not mess with alpha males. Bang! Bang! Bang! Hyde announces that what we are seeing is essentially a lesson in self-defense, in peacekeeping (when a shot rings out, a haunting voice-over occasionally intones, "peacekeeping"). If Hyde is ever threatened while looking in someone's window or uncomfortable in a crowd, he will protect himself. He laughs. He won't be happy about any devastation caused by his gun violence, but he will be happy about saving his own life.

This theme of self-protection is subsumed in Hyde's underlying message when he fires rounds from a red submachine gun with the words "THIS MACHINE KILLS FASCISTS" emblazoned in white on the side, a mock tribute to folk musician Woody Guthrie. He laughs again and loads a weapon while the cameraman points a double-barreled shotgun at his face. At one point, a mock news banner runs quickly across the bottom of the screen, betraying barefaced sexism and racism. Then President Obama is set to issue an executive order making Khan Academy the "sole educator of Beast Image Youth." The "Mayo Saxon Tax" will be "expanded to include vouchers for getting nails did." Eventually the credits roll, but only for Carol to take some parting shots about what Ibram X. Kendi might call "the violent defense of white male supremacy."[3] Carol stands with a gun in each hand, pulls the triggers, and proclaims that neither gays nor strong black belts could survive "that kind of lead." Notably, Judicious is wearing a white T-shirt underneath an open camouflage jacket with the word "masculist" written in red letters. A masculist is one who embodies the typical attitudes of men and advocates for their rights. Various still images of Hyde have been lifted from this video and remade into memes that link him to mass shootings. In reflections on their comedy, Hyde, Carol, and a third member, Nick Rochefort, swear that MDE is an engine of entertainment. Many of their skits are absurd. Many of them are a bit mystifying. But the content represents a comic spirit of being "real" or at least giving the impression of authenticity in the face of a dominant US culture that has become too self-congratulatory. Cancel culture is a social and political machine for casting people out for illiberal transgressions. Wokeness, or demonstrable awareness of social, political, and other inequities, is a superficial performance. These are among the tenets of MDE and why the troupe aims to offend in its comic appeals.

This chapter unpacks MDE's comic spirit to establish how its excesses, absurdities, and even extremist beliefs make a comical anticomedy from knavish pranks and diabolical hoaxes. No such examination of MDE can proceed without some attention to the phenomenon of trolling. Beyond that, attention must be paid to the deep roots of MDE's use of comedy to demean the mainstream, the establishment, and more generally "liberal cultural norms and political correctness."[4] The troupe's sketches differ from standard comic fare (even as they resonate with the oftentimes cringeworthy material produced for Adult Swim by the likes of Tim Heidecker and Eric Wareheim, not to mention the dark jokes and "unfunny" humor associated with the Zoomers of Gen Z). But the comedy is not all that unique. In many ways, it follows from the infamous menace of talk radio, Rush Limbaugh, and feeds into the wellsprings of Trumpism. It is therefore embedded in a comic tradition that delights in a cruel world by clowning around.

MDE makes comedy a weapon of war in battles for cultural attention. As the ringleader, Hyde set the stage with a talk he gave for a TEDx symposium, entitled "2070 Paradigm Shift." Thereafter, a treasure trove of fool's gold amassed in the proliferation of "Sam is the Shooter" memes, circulated by trolls in the wake of numerous high-profile mass shootings and in the collection of YouTube videos cataloged on the channel Sam & Nick's Perfect Clips, since MDE's channel was taken down in 2018 for "violating community guidelines." The same goes for the short-lived television series *Million Dollar Extreme Presents: World Peace*, six episodes of which aired on Adult Swim in 2016 before it was canceled the same year for Hyde's presumed links to the alt-right and the troupe's aura of white supremacy (note that the logotype for the series integrates a symbol lifted from a page in the notebook of James Holmes, the perpetrator of a mass shooting at a movie theater in Aurora, Colorado, in 2012). Content is king in MDE's pranks and sketches, and in those memes. However, so is the shameless incorporation of anticomedic sentimentality in MDE's comic spirit, which—as Hyde contends—is all about the production of "funny stuff."[5] The sentimentality in MDE's dark humor prioritizes coarseness over nuance. A similar sentiment is manifest in the proclamations of comedians like Rogan, Dave Chappelle, Ron White, and others who stand up for the comic license as a hill to die on. For these reasons, the ambivalence of MDE's comedy needs to be better understood, but less in terms of its content and more in terms of the confusion it creates about which archetype the troupe most resembles: the Ox or the Frog.

COMEDY IS A JOKE

What is comic or not—never mind *how* it is comic or not—well, this is where Poe's Law comes in.

In an article for *WIRED* by Emma Grey Ellis, we find that Poe's Law is like Murphy's Law; it is more convention than legal code. It has its antecedents in digital creationists of the early twenty-first century. As Ellis tells it, a creationist who went by the name of Nathan Poe was "the first person to codify this particular digital phenomenon."[6] He did so when he contributed a somewhat comic attitude to an online discussion forum wherein people were "bemoaning how difficult it was to divine if participants were for real" in their remarks "about perceived flaws in the theory of evolution." "POE'S LAW," wrote Poe. "Without a winking smile or other blatant display of humor, it is utterly impossible to parody a Creationist in such a way that someone won't mistake for the genuine article."[7] Poe's remark is a joke. That there is some foundational act of intelligent design at the center of all things in the universe, Poe suggests, bespeaks a parody of religion predicated on religious paradox. It is hard to reconcile the folly in the hoax with the reality it ridicules. Some just believe. No joke.

There are important implications for comedy in Poe's Law. A decade after its codification, a controversial prank hailed as Gamergate showcased the transformation of online mockery into a culture of trolling and with it a platform for keen jokesters to invent extremist parodies meant to be mistaken for real, fanatical beliefs. Gamergate has been described as a harassment campaign. It began as a series of online threats against anyone advocating for more inclusion in the gaming community. It then evolved into what journalist Caitlin Dewey describes as a "freewheeling catastrophe/social movement/misdirected lynchmob."[8] Users across online forums trafficked in misogyny and white supremacy, suggested that feminism would lead to the "death of the gamer," and generally advocated for violence as a way of doing cultural politics. Gamergate impacted people in the real world. It got overdramatized by mainstream media. It made a mockery of social justice warism and wokeness, even as it made the troll into an internet trickster cut from a comic mold. Trolling is a comic way of turning the trick on comedy itself.

Conspiratorial message making and delight in duping mainstream reporters— these were staples of Limbaugh's rhetoric. Similarly, a principle of confusing what is real and what is not, and what is meant to be funny or taken seriously, is baked into Poe's Law. When he was a DJ at WIXZ in McKeesport, Pennsylvania, Limbaugh played a familiar prank. He called the electrical utility company Duquesne Light on air during one of his radio shows. On the call, Limbaugh pretended to be a man who just moved from Florida and wanted to know what it would cost to run fifteen thousand heat lamps on any given day. Why? Because, said Limbaugh to the Duquesne Light representative, he wanted to grow palm trees in his backyard. Ridiculous. But Limbaugh strung the representative along and set himself on what he later characterized as "the prank path."[9]

Along this path, pranks were often derived from cultural touchstones. Historical zeitgeists were comic foils. In the early 1990s, Limbaugh lured people in with something provocative, only to then instigate and harass them with the talking points of his conservative ideology. Global warming is "a hoax," he once declared. In fact, Limbaugh proposed, we are approaching another ice age—a "Global Cooling." His resident parody songwriter composed tracks like "Ball of Fire" to reinforce this idea. The hook for "Ball of Fire" is a joke on "ecowarrior" Al Gore sung to the tune of "Ring of Fire" by Johnny Cash. Shanklin sings as Gore, with lyrics pronouncing his cynicism about environmentalism and his true motivation to defend Earth for money and fame. Later, in 2008, during one of his recurring segments, "Global Warming Stack," Limbaugh opined that environmentalism is less about science-based arguments for "saving the planet" than totalitarian schemes for "taking away people's freedom." You are a sinner, he said to listeners, and can only atone if you "give up your freedom, make modifications in your guilty lifestyle," pay higher taxes, and thereby "feel better about yourselves."[10] Shanklin contributed a song so Limbaugh could better make his case. The song is simply a cover of "I Started a Joke" by the Bee Gees. Shanklin sings it.

> "I started a joke," goes the first verse, which started the whole world crying.
> But I didn't see that the joke was on me."

Limbaugh, writes Mary Harris in her trawl of an obituary for the talk radio host who died in February 2021, was an originary troll, doing his comic deeds "before there were internet message boards."[11] His tricks were meant to trigger the libs, and they were meant to forge a comic way of being.

Although many commentators and critics have addressed the contemporary issues with trolling, few have accounted for the comedy in its praxis. In *This Is Why We Can't Have Nice Things* (2015), Whitney Phillips identifies trolls as seminal troublemakers in the early days of the internet. The troll is "the main folk devil of the internet," says Richard Seymour.[12] Phillips locates in trolling a fundamental problem with human communication in the digital sphere. Interactions online privilege engagements with realities that garner attention, and that attention has long been driven by the pursuit of amusement. Phillips likens trolls to "mythological trickster figures" who make trouble "to make sense of what has happened."[13] Today, much troublemaking is done for the "lulz," or laughter at someone else's expense. It follows, then, that trolling can function as a comic trick, with trolls exploiting the conceit of comedy to bait a hook and catch fish in an "act of deception" that ends up being an act of "*self*-deception."[14] Trolls on platforms like 4chan, an image-based message board created by Christopher "Moot" Poole in 2003 on which anonymous users comment on specific topics without ever revealing their identities, can operate behind a comic mask. So, whereas communication on 4chan and elsewhere could foster honest communities of interest, it ends up inspiring rhetorical trickery, with truths as lies and lies as truths.

This does not mean that trolling is an outgrowth of what is now seen as cyberfascism or rightist extremism. Some like Matt Sienkiewicz and Nick Marx speculate that trolling could be the "most dangerous form of contemporary right-wing comedy."[15] After all, there is an overtly sadistic sensibility in the humor of trolls who keep up certain joke cycles to make fun from the suffering of others. There is also a disturbing attachment to comic *detachment* in trolling. For Phillips, this points to the ambivalence embedded in the comic praxis. And it points to why Seymour, in line with Sienkiewicz and Marx, finds in trolling a troublesome through line from "the traditional Right" to "the dark Right."[16] Once there were single men with microphones. Now there is anyone with the wherewithal in the digital machine. Do trolls embody everything wrong with comedy? The egoism of an individual acting out. A dispersed community of alter egos. All under the cover of comedy.

Comedy has cross-purposes in the lore of tricksters. Tricks are done "to tangle, lure, and snare."[17] Some of the earliest comic tricks are replete with tales of fish traps and captivating tunes put out from bamboo flutes. The previous chapter emphasized songs by Shanklin that helped make Limbaugh's radio show so popular. In a world made absurd by the likes of Shanklin and Limbaugh are comic seeds for "aggressive, adversarial humor" that, in Ryan M. Milner's words, renders a "world made meme."[18] This kind of comedy operates at "the boundary between where the troll mess ends and the mainstream begins."[19] The risk of "dirty tricks," "cruel jokes," and "terrible hoaxes" is inherent to comedy.[20] The point here is not to find some meta-comedy in the work of Hyde and MDE or any other troll. Likewise, it is not to bemoan either the loss of some comic ground or the notion that someone like Hyde is a bellwether for mainstreaming extremism. The point is to consider MDE for its comic dispirit.

THE CHARACTERS (AND CHARACTERISTICS) OF ANTICOMEDY

It is hard to know if Sam Hyde the troll has any idea that there is a Sam Hyde of American folklore. Maybe the mastermind of MDE knows that he shares his name with a legendary liar.

Traces of the apocryphal Sam Hyde (sometimes Sam Hide) can be found in accounts dating back to the seventeenth century. A mythic man of New England, he was known for tricking people with half-truths. In some tales, Hyde was a "Souldier faithful to the English" who kept tallies of people he "kill'd . . . on his Gun."[21] In others, he was a rambling everyman, going around doing pranks and playing tricks. In others still, he was a Native American prankster who, though blind late in life, could see the proverbial "light." He was a trickster, so much so that "to lie like Sam Hyde" was at once to allure some people with tricks and to repulse others.

The Sam Hyde of today likely fancies himself a trickster. He is surely what Bergson might call a *comic* character. In one of a series of articles about MDE, Buzzfeed reporter Joseph Bernstein characterized Hyde and his merry men as "court jesters of the alt-right, the pro-Trump movement that prizes offensive speech, believes white people in America are imperiled, and churns out memes at a metastatic pace."[22] Hyde repeatedly pilloried Bernstein for his reporting, especially after it was tied up with the cancellation of MDE's aforementioned television series. Ironically, he has also embraced many of Bernstein's prima facie characterizations. The members of MDE call themselves "misandrous comedioterrorists."[23] They traffic in hackneyed tropes about gender (e.g., men are superior to women), race (e.g., white supremacy is real), class (e.g., the elites are the root of all evil), and more. These tropes crop up across what Sienkiewicz and Marx term their "vital comedy," with "violent misogyny, racism, and anti-Semitism" as the troupe's prime rhetorical devices for "saying foolish, often vile things in order to evoke a predictable, performative response."[24] What is more, Hyde himself has various alter egos. He is occasionally known as Samuel Hydeburg, a name that gets used when he is the faux perpetrator of a mass shooting. As Samantha Hyde, he is a caricature of a white transgender person. When he is Samir Al-Hajeed, Hyde is a faux Muslim convert and, yet again, a gunman fabricated by meme makers. As of 2022 he was "the Candyman," a boxer who picks fights with other internet personalities under the auspices of the social media influencer company Happy Punch Promotions. In truth, Hyde is an imposing figure with round-rim glasses and a scraggly beard who owns his role as a comic provocateur and would undoubtedly accept Bernstein's sense that he has "a cult following on the internet and a reputation for being hugely offensive."[25] So, the tropes and the reactions to them substantiate many of the characterizations.

OK. So just what kind of comic character is Hyde? Comic characters, generally, are like children who divert themselves from the status quo by taking pleasure in "pushing the Jack-in-the-box, time after time, to the bottom of his

POE'S LAW AND MILLION DOLLAR EXTREME

box" so as to laugh in quasi-horror, again and again, when Jack suddenly re-emerges.[26] Children play with puppets, and enliven them, precisely so those puppets can be brought "to an ambiguous state in which, without ceasing to be puppets, they have yet become human beings."[27] Comic characters are child-like playthings. At best, they are tools for toying with "the illusion of life" in the "masquerade" that is our "mechanical arrangement" of the world.[28] They are the very stuff of childish (or childlike) pranks. At worst, they are—in a Nietzschean sense—illusions that we forget are illusions.

In October 2013, Hyde pranked TEDx. In the spirit of Technology, Entertainment, and Design (TED) and its well-known and widely circulated TED Talks, TEDx carries on the mission to promote "ideas worth spreading" with programs across the United States put on by volunteer organizers. In his mock TED Talk, entitled "2070 Paradigm Shift," Hyde disrupted this mission with a few ideas of his own. As with any good trickster act, no one is quite sure how the prank was pulled off. Somehow, Hyde was able to fool the organizers of a TEDx symposium at Drexel University into thinking that he was a video journalist and documentary filmmaker whose work has been aired on prominent television channels and featured in distinguished online and print publications. He was introduced as having "recently returned from Mogadishu, the most dangerous city on earth, where he shadowed the heroic *al-Mahamud* women on their quest to clean up the streets and restore humanity to their war-torn country."[29] In the first few minutes, it became clear that Hyde was there to make fun of TED Talks.

After his introduction, Hyde steps out from behind a black curtain and takes the stage set between two marble staircases in Drexel's main building. He is clad in a maroon jumpsuit with a matching beanie and armor resembling that of an ancient Roman centurion, including plastic greaves over his shins and a plastic bronze cuirass chest plate. Hyde waves to the crowd, then moseys to one of the staircases. He sits down, takes some deep breaths, sips water from a bottle, drops his lavalier microphone, and shuffles his notes. Hyde's opening statement is a request for the minute he just wasted to be put back on the clock. When he officially begins, Hyde is lounging on the marble steps. "Guys," he says, "pat yourselves on the back right now, OK?" He pats himself on the back and urges the audience to do the same. When it seems everyone is doing it, he tells them that it is for saving the world! "Worlds, world, worlds." He fumbles his words, grins, and praises the intelligence of an audience comprised mostly of college students, and it feels already that he is about to connect the fall of the Roman Empire to American decline and the collapse of Western civilization.

The paradigm shift presaged by Hyde is built on a parable. At a "second-tier" college, Hyde sat in on a class in which a professor was spouting some "horrible nonsense" about the legitimacy of women's rights and giving off that vibe of a self-righteous pointy-head who would get "extreme joy" in rebuffing any free-thinking undergraduate audacious enough to challenge him. Well, one student *did* speak up and, with "logic on his side," proved his point. That student, says Hyde, was Albert Einstein. This is some horrible nonsense, indeed. Hyde moves to make *his* point but fumbles over his words again, snorts out a laugh, and slaps himself repeatedly in the face. "That same sense," he continues once he has regained his composure, "of child-like play and innocence that we know from Albert Einstein—I can sense it in this room today." It is a ruse. It is a comic ploy. Hyde extends it with a meandering jumble of jests that all play on the vanity of those who might typify TEDx culture. Hyde quips about the importance of inspiration and links it to the need to educate Africans in JavaScript and the challenge of getting fresh water to Chinese people. "Get inspired!" He gestures to "great ideas," explains (with what he describes as reverence, not silliness) how 9/11—a terror plot concocted by eleven guys who had no weapons and "didn't even speak English"—shows us that sometimes "great ideas" are "horrible ideas" and, in so doing, lines up the "great ideas" of TED Talks with the "accomplishments" of terrorists. "Where are we at?" He offers some answers. We are addicted to fossil fuels. We are selfish. Our dominant cultural productions amount to a "sewer" of bad content. What to do?

Hyde has some more answers, all based on feigned studies and spurious data. Do away with individualism. Re-sign the social contract. Realize that the apocalypse is nigh and, with it, "big problems" like pollution and war. The world is on the brink. "Fix it!" he yells. "Now!" He misspeaks and fumbles through details. A screen behind him displays random slides of largely clip art. Try "sea farming." Create a "trash economy" using trash as money. Replace cities with "pleasure domes" for the neo-upper class. Fund the development of human lactation to deal with milk shortages. And get ready for Facebook profiles to double as birth certificates, robot police, gay men with reproductive capacities, and more. Some things members of the audience "are not gonna like," so he does not divulge. As the talk stumbles toward its conclusion, Hyde predicts race riots taking shape as what he calls the "Knockout Game"—a game white people "are gonna get tired of playing." A slide pictures an enraged mob next to an illustrated cover for *TIME* with white men in arms and a white family fleeing a burning building. He predicts that the elderly and disabled will not be cared for in the future. "We're just gonna kill 'em!" he shouts as he mimes a wrestler slamming someone to the ground. Gay marriage. "Surprise, surprise bigots," he intones. He crumples up a note and tosses it while announcing that gay people will be able to get married in 2070. "Makes me sick sometimes," he grumbles. Hyde ultimately reminds people to pat themselves on the back before wrapping up with a final prediction. Israel, he says, will be "straight up ripped off the map." "Bye! Bye! Bye-bye!" he screams while wildly waving one hand. The talk ends with his appeal for predictions from the audience. No one says anything. The emcee steps up. Hyde asks him what he thinks. "I think it's going to be better than what we have right now." "I think there can't possibly be anything *worse* than we have *right now*," Hyde replies, glaring at the audience. Then he leaves the stage.

Hyde's prank sparked unsurprising reactions in popular media. One blogger for the *Washington Post* named it "the most glorious TED Talk takedown."[30] A contributor for *HuffPost* saw it for what it patently was—a "Nonsense Buzzword Speech" that "was pretty fantastically entertaining" despite having "no discernible point."[31] Certainly, this nonsensical and entertaining "takedown" merged dog whistles with those buzzwords and made rubbish talk of racialized, misogynistic jokes. Criticisms with the benefit of hindsight determined that Hyde's "vitalist, Bronze Age Pervert–style rhetoric" had all the markings of a troll, not a trickster, as evidenced by the cavalier nature of his "energy, bravado, and moral recklessness."[32] A column on the *Atlantic* website widened the view on Hyde by representing a range of views about that "alt-right TV show."[33] For one person, MDE is "really not that political" if we stop to consider that "we need to be able to laugh at all societal aspects, including our own progressive causes and philosophies, instead of holding sacred cows." (This could be one of Limbaugh's Undeniable Truths of Life!) A self-identified Jew likened MDE's antisemitism to punk rock music; it is supposed to offend our sensibilities, like "flies in the ointment of popular culture." Another person praised MDE for the comic beauty that lies just beneath the surface ugliness of content that disrupts the borders of "humanity and inhumanity." Equal opportunity discrimination. Misogyny, racism, bigotry. Comedy is just a cover. These are cultural Rorschach tests.

To some extent, that supposition is neither here nor there. Hyde, and MDE in general, uses cheeky tropes as easy resources for pulling pranks. Think, however, about Kembrew McLeod's assertion that "pulling pranks" is "much like throwing a rock in the pop-culture pond."[34] The prank tells us less about any creator's true feelings than about the milieu in which those feelings are expressed. Our habit is to look at everything from the "silly hoaxes" to the "outlandish belief systems" that pop up in pranks as part and parcel of mischief-makers doing their deeds.[35] Hyde's prank should tempt us otherwise. We should consider his comic character, and the characters he creates to turn his tricks, for the outmoded truisms embedded in their comic appeals. The roles of men and women. Differences between Black and white people. Intrinsic laws of sexuality. Manifest Destiny. As per Bergson, the easiest comic spirit is one that "exercises its ingenuity on social actions of a stereotyped nature."[36] It is remarkable, too, if we admit that this comedy is funny to some *because* it is familiar and *because* it is contemptible to others. Hyde's point is partly that the world *is* made up of tribes. There *is no* common humanity. We are at odds with one another. War is peace, to borrow an Orwellian moralism. In the economy for MDE's comedy, this person's treasure is that person's trash.

NO PEACE FOR THE WICKED, OR ALL IS FAIR IN COMEDY AND WAR

My own engagement with Hyde begins with the infamous "Sam Hyde is the Shooter" meme (fig. 2.1). Before I knew him as a comic character, as a troll and a prankster, I knew him as the comic foil for an internet hoax.

Trolls on 4chan and elsewhere made it a routine to trick people into believing that Hyde was responsible for any number of heinous acts out there in the real world—namely, mass shootings. To wit, he was blamed for the shooting at Inland Regional Center in San Bernardino, California, in 2015. The shooting at Pulse, a gay nightclub, in Orlando, Florida, in 2016. At a music festival in Las Vegas in 2017. That same year, a US congressman got wind of the shooter's name soon after a gunman opened fire on worshippers at the First Baptist Church in Sutherland Springs, Texas. "Sam Hyde," representative Vicente Gonzalez told CNN anchor Ana Cabrera in an interview after the massacre. "That was the name I was given."[37] He was blamed for the shooting at Stoneman Douglas High School in Parkland, Florida, in 2018. In 2015, Hyde was linked to Gamergate. In 2020, on Facebook, Hyde was pictured as the man responsible for the spread of COVID-19 and thus the beginning of a global pandemic. In 2022, he was the "Ghost of Kyiv," an ace Mig-29 pilot for Ukraine in the war against Russia. Apologists for the meme makers argue that the real target of the punch line in this recurring joke cycle is the mainstream media. Wicked jokes are insensitive to those who suffer through mass shootings and other tragedies, perhaps. But of greater concern is the folly in how the media covers conflict and catastrophe in the first place. That folly can be found in a system of algorithms that ties advertising revenue up with attention as much as the exploits of trolls trying to mess with how mainstream content is propagated in and through digital platforms. That these memes sit somewhere along the lines of

Fig. 2.1. Screenshot of a still image that accompanies countless memes identifying Sam Hyde as a mass shooter.

"over-the-top-offensive" and "borderline-cringe" reinforces the ambivalence about an embodiment of the lone white gunman who doubles as a fool par excellence.[38]

This brings us back to the TED Talk. How does what Hyde is doing relate to the very spirit of his comedy? In his talk, Hyde says he is a number of things. An "important thinker." A "creator." An "innovator." An "artist." He even goes so far as to describe himself as an "idea"—or, what Bergson might recognize as a *comic* idea. At other moments in his talk, Hyde celebrates his own "child-like" passion. He reveals that, when you look at the data, you will find that we work hard but do not play hard enough. When we admonish children who are clowning around, we are often reminded by them that they are just playing, just having fun. That play is usually no holds barred, unfiltered. Hyde has said that his intentions are to "clown" the dominant institutions of culture and politics. This is why his comedy can come off as silly, self-indulgent, juvenile, and foolish. By these standards, Hyde's prank on TEDx was relatively tame. In what remains of available video clips on YouTube, one can see that Hyde's TED Talk was the tip of a comic iceberg that fits into an accumulation of what is, at base, MDE's comic spirit.

The videos are a mix of on-the-ground pranks in the real world and window-into-the-life-and-mind documentary shorts and sketches that feature rants and raves about everything from current affairs to content created by others.

60 WHEN COMEDY GOES WRONG

It might not be that MDE dwells in a "basement of the right-wing comedy complex."[39] Still, videos cataloged on the YouTube channel Sam & Nick's Perfect Clips look and feel as if they are recorded, quite literally, in a basement. But the editing in most of them is polished and intentional. There are trippy introductory graphics, almost video game-esque circa the 1980s. Cuts and transitions are composed of "subliminal blips and eye-straining text in service of subversive ends," which reinforce the "heinous views" that Hyde and his troupe espouse "in the service of a joke."[40] The form and the content create a sort of film version of tabloid journalism that merges with roughhewn reportage by devout iconoclasts. A lot of it is wonderful, in the true sense of the world. A lot of it is weird. All of it is the weaponry for a war of comic nerves.

PICKING BATTLES . . .

In early videos, Hyde is the main character in sketches, mockumentaries, and short biopics. One, entitled "Psycho Serial Killer (Documentary)," renders him a "reclusive loner" with "boyish good looks" who, in high school, drank at school, frequented boy bars, and earned the reputation as a "honey in the gay community."[41] Bogus school counselors and confidants are interviewees who play on stereotypes of mental illness to make a joke of true-to-life characterizations of lone wolves. Murder is the hook for an odd sense of self-aggrandizement and self-promotion. In a subsequent video filed under the category "HydeWars," Hyde addresses this subject matter while recollecting a visit by the FBI in relation to the "Sam Hyde is the Shooter" meme.[42] In it he walks and talks with friends answering questions about who he is in "real life." Hyde acknowledges the "mean-spiritedness" of his comedy but claims that it is a vehicle for creating alternatives to mainstream narratives. Even the FBI could not figure that out, he says. Then laughs. But what of that mean spirit and its role in his interest in stranger things?

Another video, cataloged as one of many Lil Shitposts, has Hyde the newsman going up to other newspersons under the pretense of wanting to help them cover breaking stories.[43] He approaches vans and introduces himself as a member of the Action 6 News team. It does not take long to realize that Hyde's goal is to mock how news gets produced and how newsworthiness is created. He harasses newspersons. He gets in their faces. "Did you hear about the guy who was keeping sex slaves in his basement?" he taunts one team. Footage shows Hyde jeering them until they pack up and leave. Some actually retaliate with their own profanity and insults. Interspersed with this footage are graphics related to jokes Hyde makes. One captures his comic angle: "News," "Hassle," "Hell."

These terms recur in other videos. This one ends with Hyde recording himself walking through a parking lot, the camera in his hand quavering as he approaches a car with a "RESIST" sticker on its bumper. An "ALERT" banner on the screen informs us that Hyde is a representative of the Resist Trump News Network. When he gets to the car, he points his camera at the woman behind the wheel. He needles her about her resistance to the Trump presidency while zooming in on her teeth. "Brave Woman Resists Trump with Teeth," some text tells us. Hyde walks away as the screen fades to black and gets replaced by a final graphic with a kaleidoscopic swirl of flowers and the words "SAM LIES."

Analogous videos turn the camera back on Hyde. In "Fuck-Drumpf-App," a mock public service video advocating for people to empower others against "the hate, the violence, the gore" turns into a rant that makes fun of liberal values, like empowerment, acceptance, and tolerance.[44] He pits himself against those who adopted a "Fuck Trump" or "Not My President" mentality and their adoption of euphemisms and glib affronts for affecting their cause. At one point, he puts his GoPro camera right in his face and lets out an uproarious, feverish scream, spewing spit from his mouth as he pleads for contributions from viewers to fund his own crusade. In "Beating Women," Hyde is once again the main character in a reaction video that has him almost sounding like Limbaugh with his diatribes about what he calls pretty princess astronauts who should work in flower shops, the stupidity of STEM education, and the glut of "dumb bitches" in the world.[45] Hyde sits at a desk in front of a laptop wearing a white hoodie. He calmly talks through his gripes, but occasionally flies into a rage as he rails against the concept of "equity" (which he defines as a demand for white men to "give up our shit"), impersonates Black speechifying ("How can we invest in society when we ain't got shit? You feel me?"), and ridicules popular opinions about gender normativity that have come to the fore because of things like the Harry Potter series. It is all "a fucking joke," Hyde proclaims.

There are too many videos like these to address and yet too many to ignore. What stands out in all of them is the overt confusion of what is "real" and what is meant to be Hyde's trademark "satire" and "absurdity." The prank is the comic ploy. Comedy lies in the trick of putting on a bold face. Another mockumentary from the summer of 2020 makes this clear. It came out during the COVID-19 pandemic. It is entitled "Women Stories."[46] Hyde is in a hotel room. He is dressed like a pimp, lounging on a garish bed, when he declares that it is time for a reality check. The Sam Hyde people think they know is a fabrication, a "comical farce." Hyde offers a look at his "true" lifestyle as he jumps up and down on the bed. One scene has him spread eagle in a tub announcing his plans for "squirting orgasms of wisdom," which end up being streams of consciousness about random topics from herbal supplements to life advice. A friend, named Agent X, joins him in conversation. They get room service. They eat (honestly, in the garden-variety YouTube videos on Sam & Nick's Perfect Clips and more recently Dollar Stream, Hyde is eating). They joke about how fun—and easy—it probably is to rape women. They laugh hysterically whenever they relay anecdotes about "dumb bitches." After they eat, the recording is interrupted with an alert: the COVID-19 protocols are too low! They sanitize their hands before Hyde quips that he "will kill a doctor one day." Good fun, in bad taste.

It makes sense here to connect this day-in-the-life video with a more polished and prepared sketch that is both a piece of comedy and a statement of comic principles. The sketch is called "Deal with the Devil."[47] In it, Hyde sits in a chair on a floor adorned with the Sigil of Baphomet. Hyde beckons the devil so he can make a deal. The devil or, as we discover, *a* devil emerges. He has an ugly face, one eye, and ram horns on his head. Hyde says he wants to sell his soul. Sure, the devil responds. The cost is a blow job. "That's so gay." Well, the devil responds, there are no "demonettes" around here. Hyde shifts the narrative and reprimands the devil for the bad work he is doing in terms of making "good" deals and spreading worthy evil around the world. Like a customer complaining in a retail shop, Hyde sends the impostor away to get the *real* Satan. The true Prince of Darkness is no better. Hyde expresses his willingness to trade his soul for riches and prestige and material possessions. Satan counters with an offer of a reliable car to get Hyde from A to B. The sketch is ridiculous. However, it illustrates a dark comic spirit that traverses Hyde's work with MDE, from his denigrations of the Black Lives Matter movement, "the hood," and "social retards" to other quasi-documentary accounts of his "descent into madness," all punctuated by his boxing match with TikTok star Jordan Thompson, aka THMPSN, and the death threats he later issued against Hasan Piker, or HasanAbi, a Turkish American and left-leaning political commentator on livestreaming platform Twitch. Following Bergson and those who also observe elements of caricature in comedy, the exaggerations and excesses are "more lifelike" than the real thing.[48] Angels look like devils in Hyde's comedy and vice versa. Bunco artists look like tricksters.

There is much to admire when a comic character freely indulges in conflict and controversy. Show me someone with a sense of humor who rejects this sentiment, and I will remind you of the playful insolence that has long underwritten what Conrad Hyers calls "the world of the circus clown."[49] This is the conundrum, no? The notion that a comic principle of clowning around is the countersign to a Clown World Order—an order defined by a "global society" in which "women are men, men are women, the schools teach propaganda

POE'S LAW AND MILLION DOLLAR EXTREME   63

instead of classes, left is right and right is left," and devotees of such tenets are "useful idiots for a leftist agenda."[50] Hyde could not have put it any better. The clownish world of MDE draws battle lines of cultural warfare. At the center of this clownish world, though, is Hyde's self-described "assault on comedic progressivism" as *the* "route to relevance."[51] Culture is not the only or even the most important battleground. Hyde and MDE have also picked a battle with the craft of comedy itself.

. . . AND WINNING WARS

When *Million Dollar Extreme Presents: World Peace* went into production, it did not take long for people to see it as a glimpse into "the mind of a far-right Twitter troll."[52] Sketch after sketch brims with "racism, sexism, [and] bigotry."[53] The official press release promises that if you watch, you can "unlock your closeted bigoted imagination, toss your inherent racism into the burning trash, and cleanse your intolerant spirit with pure unapologetic American funny_com."[54] It is tongue-in-cheek. It is honest. It is a lie, and it plays out in the numerous examples of comic transgression that led to its cancellation. In an interview with the *Hollywood Reporter* in December 2016 after *World Peace* was canceled, Hyde thanked the interviewer for an opportunity for "a racist like me . . . to spew my hate." "I'm kidding," he disclaimed.[55] Later in the interview, Hyde affirmed that the series was strictly a "comedy show." There was no partisanship, no cultural politicking, just funny content. The revilement of other comedians, and cancel culture more broadly, is what precipitated the demise. People mistook the extreme measures taken to garner laughter, joy, and clarity for malice and cruelty. Any suffering that people felt, said Hyde, was unintentional. Still, if sufferance is a by-product of a joke, so be it. Thus spake Hyde.

Such sentiments give the impression that *World Peace* was made to be a losing battle. Was cancellation an unintended consequence of the comedy? Was it the culmination of a quintessential exercise in trolling? Was it the end goal? Lose a battle? Win a war?

The rest of the press release seems to offer some clues. The series, it says, "is a super pure tragicomedy rosary of pious prayers bringing unity, joy, and excellent living to the people of all sizes, sexualities, and colors."[56] Do not, however, expect *easy* viewing. For it is only the "naïve slob" who "expects hemlock medicine to taste of milkshake." Anyway, the creators have no plans to be martyrs. But if they end up dying, and if by apparent suicide, then blame "CIA_MOSSAD." Two intelligence agencies in cahoots: the Central Intelligence Agency of the United States and Mossad, the Israeli counterpart. MDE

64 WHEN COMEDY GOES WRONG

speaks for the new age silent majority. Comedy is the troupe's blunt object for breaking the fourth wall of the Fifth Estate. "PRAY FOR WORLD PEACE," goads the press release.

Why? The proof is in the poison pills of each episode.[57]

In a sketch called "Fitness Zone," a gym bro exchanges glances with a woman. He seems to be a military man, confident and cocky. But when he tries to do his first set with weights, he collapses to the ground. After he lifts his shirt and presses a "Fozzy Contin" button affixed to his abdomen, he is able to reboot. And reboot he does, as a madman with bulging eyes encased in swollen red skin. His face resembles Pepe the Frog, a cartoon insignia of the alt-right that was originally the face of a character from *Boy's Club*, a comic series created by Matt Furie. The face exists in countless memes. Pepe the Frog has been labeled a "hate symbol" by the Anti-Defamation League, since the frog's catchphrase "feels good, man" has been aligned with phrases like "kill Jews, man." As Alexander Blum puts it, Hyde "embodies the spirit of Pepe in all its dark and comical allure," playing as he does on notions of a "gutless, feminized politically correct male population," an embrace of "the chaos" and the "failure of progress" brought about by "progressive busybodies," and the deployment of the comic mask as "a sign of its own total despair, designed to ward off its predators, and make others fear the same forces that inspired men to become frogs."[58] This sketch ends with the frog-man staring back at the woman as she tries to continue her own workout on a step machine. She is clearly uncomfortable and scared. A wide-angle shot of their standoff cuts to psychedelic imagery with peace signs countervailed by the sounds of what can only be the woman's voice, shrieking.

The sketches only get better (or worse) from there. In one, Hyde plays a reporter for News 17 who portrays bullies as "social watchdogs," extols "the value of juvenile mistreatment" in schools, and pronounces the "sad truth" that "the path from beaten social pariah to school shooter is both inevitable and hilarious." A young Black boy who was bullied by a classmate and nicknamed "Chicken Nugget Schoon" is profiled as a beneficiary. Another sketch, which unfolds across three installments about "Male Hookers," portrays young women with sexual fantasies about stereotypical jocks, gay men, and deadbeats who conspire to indulge in them only to get arrested by aggressive cops who handcuff them on their beds and inundate them with verbal abuse regarding their bad behavior. "The Wall Show" conjures up a motley game show for undeserving women in their late twenties who are looking for sugar daddies. Hyde is one of two foppish cohosts with terrible British accents leading contestants to the conclusion that their delusions are "complete rubbish." In another sketch,

POE'S LAW AND MILLION DOLLAR EXTREME 65

Hyde is a stereotypical "wigger" (a term he has used to describe a few of his comic characters, and the epithet for his handle on X, formerly Twitter), walking out the front door of his girlfriend's house (a contrivance used on other sketches, i.e., "Backseat Girl") and getting dumped. Hyde raps a response to his girlfriend in mock Black dialect, likening himself to a puppy free to go to the "pound house" and find "another bitch" and threatening to put her "motherfucking ass through the wall." The bulk of the sketch has Hyde listing off what people call him. Peanut Arbuckle. The Silver Bullet. Argon. Dark Child. Night Master. Peabody. Doorway. Pink Dress. His grin widens as he adds to his list of sobriquets. His girlfriend grins too, and he concludes by saying, "Bitch, I'm angelic." He screams, and his body lifts up and out of view.

As with so many MDE sketches, these are all variations on themes. In "Guy Heaven," for instance, Hyde drinks milk while he works out like a maniac, puking as he pushes himself to the limit and dreams of a "guys-only" gym. In "Teacher," Rochefort plays a "silly," slovenly, white "dinosaur man," Mr. Jones, who feeds into the standard curricula for teaching the Holocaust and Black History Month. He is harassed by students who are smarter than him and who act up in class by clowning around and hitting him with wads of paper. The sketch ends with him absolving himself of any guilt for making kids stupid (parents and the government have done that) and taking abuse until he finally snaps, slips a noose around his neck, and lifts off as a rock band made up of students takes over a stage above the classroom. It's all on brand.

One other sketch does stand out as particularly egregious, though, which is likely why it never aired. The sketch is entitled "Thank You, White People." Hyde is wearing a jacket and slacks, with a flat cap on his head. He is pushing an enormous boulder up a hill, like Sisyphus, except that the boulder represents the progress of Western civilization (fig. 2.2). "Listen up and listen good," he implores viewers as he pushes. "Since the beginning of recorded history, the white man has been coming up with technologies, cultures, civilizations worth keeping, worth saving, worth giving a damn about." A narrator for the documentary film BLACKLISTED (2018) describes what unfolds: "Along the way he encounters a succession of minorities thankful for the historical contributions to societal advancement by white people."[59] He occasionally stops to accept their gratitude. Toward the bottom, a Black man reads from cue cards, thanking the white man for inventing "the computer, the microwave, medicine, electricity, sanitation, theory of evolution, the radio, the pencil," et cetera. While he recites the accolades, Hyde stands in the backdrop, propping up the boulder, chewing on . . . something. He moves on to an apparent Mexican man with bizarre mutton chops and a small sombrero who thanks white people for

Fig. 2.2. Screenshot from sketch "Thank You, White People," created for *Million Dollar Extreme: World Peace*, unaired but viewable on YouTube.

"creating a society where people don't shit in the street" and for letting wetbacks "use your pristine clean emergency rooms." The man offers a final, emphatic thanks for "all the free money," tips his hat to Hyde, and shares an aside that he is "one-eighth Hopi Indian." "I don't give a fuck about that," Hyde replies and keeps pushing the boulder. He "[skips] past an Asian man," as if to pay respectful disdain to "the intellectual superiority of sneaky panheads" and perform his hardheartedness toward intercultural exchange. Eventually, Hyde "reaches the top only to be distracted by a woman standing next to the hill."[60] She calls up to Hyde, thanking him for giving women the vote. While Hyde's attention is diverted, the minorities steal his boulder. A Hasidic man emerges from behind the hilltop. "What happened to your boulder, goy!?" he jeers. "I don't know," Hyde responds. "I wasn't looking and the next thing I knew my boulder is gone. I guess I'm a stupid goy!" The man adjusts his fedora, chuckles like a happy merchant, titters like a laughing Jew, and disappears behind the rocks.

There is a way to interpret *World Peace* that does more than acknowledge that MDE is "not *just* joking."[61] There is also a way to avoid the conclusion that MDE's comedy is "of a piece with the lulz competition."[62] It requires a stretch of the comic imagination that makes possible a stretch of the very idea of comedy and the spirit that inspires it. Two resources for imagining this comic way come to mind.

One has to do with what Hyers calls the traditional "props" and "tricks" of the clown.[63] Consider the "bang" gun. This prop has long been a weapon for

POE'S LAW AND MILLION DOLLAR EXTREME

practical jokes. In a "typical routine," a clown will point the toy gun at his audience, pull the trigger, and fire out a funny flag on which is written "BANG."[64] The gun creates a moment of tension and discomfort. Loaded humor leads to comic relief with the trick of an unloaded gun. Because, as Robert Westwood wonders, "what if, when the clown pulls the trigger, the brains of the nearest five-year-old are splashed into the crowd? Then we have not comedy, but horror."[65] It is all fun and games until someone gets hurt. This is the conventional wisdom that motivates DC Comics supervillain the Joker to keep the "bang" gun as a key piece of equipment in his arsenal. Toward the end of *Batman: The Killing Joke* (1996), a graphic novel by Alan Moore, the Joker exchanges blows with Batman. The Joker gets knocked to the ground. He lies there, prone. But when he rolls over, he has an evil grin on his face. Batman reaches for him. The Joker sits up, pulls a gun from behind his back, points it at Batman and pulls the trigger. "CLICK CLICK CLICK." "God damn it," he mutters in seeming dismay. "It's empty!" Did the Joker actually want to kill Batman? Was the prank gun all part of his plan to make, well, a killing joke? The scene ends with the Joker descending into a fit of laughter, his madness belying the punch line of a joke he tells Batman about two madmen escaping from an insane asylum, one of whom tricks the other into leaping to his own death. His fracas with the Dark Knight sparked the Joker's memory of the joke. Both the prank and the killing joke can be taken to comic extremes.

The other way builds on this setup and requires us to revisit the comic spirit of the clown. So much of clowning around revolves around childish pranks. Sometimes they are silly. Sometimes fantastical. Sometimes riotous. The joke, though, is almost always that in those pranks and other comic machinations is "nothing fantastic at all. That is the trick," says Hyers, "the joke."[66] Members of MDE are clowns. They "play the fool, indulge in silliness, enjoy nonsense, act with childlike abandon, and deliver themselves to the caprice of the instant."[67] They do this to rebuff officialdom and destabilize any established order. And they do so to ensure that if anything done amounts to a crime or a sin, these are *comic* crimes, *comic* sins.[68] What is comic, says Bergson, comes from what is lifeless about a way of being. From what is "rigid," or "ready-made," or "mechanical" in the conceits of those who imagine themselves to have a handle on the larger human comedy. What Hyde misses about his comedy is just how much ready-madeness and mechanistic qualities are at play in it. This omission could be intentional. MDE could very well be a ruse. If, however, in the "struggle between two stubborn elements"—one of which is "simply mechanical" and the other pliable, stretchy—what is mechanical makes a "plaything" of what is not, then MDE is not a frog that boils itself in water.[69] MDE is a frog that puffs itself up until it explodes.

68   WHEN COMEDY GOES WRONG

Back, then, to *BLACKLISTED*. Perhaps more telling about the comic spirit of MDE than *World Peace* or any of the videos and pranks and hoaxes examined in this chapter is this professionally produced and superficially cogent documentary film by Porsalin that turns the pages of the playbook. Here are some highlights.

The comic spirit of MDE is "ironic, satirical, and prank-like." The troupe's comedy is intentionally "equivocal" in its representations of dominant culture. Much as Hyde's TED Talk satirized the "smug self-affirmation" of those who invest in their own thoughts and feelings with "unchecked egos," so is a sketch about necessary gratitude for white people a vital "commentary on the rapid shift in Western values through forced diversity" that uses "extreme means to ridiculously decorate the point." The pettiness is profound. MDE sketches are also designed to stand against the formulaic comedy of "shitcoms" made by Jewish producers and other "entertainment elites" and created by people whose names usually end in either -stein or -berg. In various moments throughout the film, Hyde is the voice-over in a mock narration on the cancellation of *World Peace*—a narration that undercuts the rest of the film's self-styled objectivity. On screen, as the voice-over plays, film reels show black-and-white footage from the Nazi era. Hyde speaks with a German accent. Subtitles clarify what he says. They are written in the Fraktur font. *World Peace*, says Hyde, was canceled because of "the downward trend of increasingly low-testosterone and non-white content" in comedy. The narrator agrees.

The content MDE creates is derived from the perceived pomposity and pretensions of the Left and the progressivism of libs. What the narrator points out to be "unwarranted feminine victimhood" in sketches like the one with the game show for contemptible women is proof positive. So is any sketch that mocks the "Leftist Hipsterdom" so prevalent in shows like *Always Sunny in Philadelphia* and the comedy gone wrong in caricaturist turned mainstream lackey Stephen Colbert. Mainstream critics revel in their castigations of Hyde as a "pig in shit," doing comedy like someone with a camera, a following, and the energy of "Trump-enthused mob outrage." His comic spirit is petulant. His sketches are tantrums. On the contrary, Hyde does comedy how it *should* be done, and his comic spirit hearkens to a time when the show *Politically Incorrect* was forced off the air and Fox News was experiencing a meteoric rise under the directorship of Roger Ailes. The "elucidations" in the content are little more than "progressive stereotypes" made even more absurd. It is telling just how familiar is Hyde's contempt.

The meaning of the comic for MDE is the manufacture of conflict with "over-the-top hyperbole"—that is, "by design, an elaborate troll." Moot points

POE'S LAW AND MILLION DOLLAR EXTREME

are purposeful, witting. The aim is to present something comically problematic in order to leave people guessing about the possible solution. If comedy corresponds to "the mechanical encrusted on the living,"[70] it can also be found in phenomena like cancel culture and wokeism. "Whether the comic emerges from the mechanical encrusted on the living," in Lisa Trahair's words, "or from the contingent reality that messes up the operation of the mechanical is a moot point."[71] Herein lies the possibility for perfectly sensible nonsense, festive cruelty, the nastiness and scatology of pranks. Are Hyde and his compatriots comic heroes or comedy hacks? Does MDE do right by comedy or do it wrong? Without doubt, MDE approaches culture as a battlefield. Hyde is a leading cultural warrior. Comedy is his weapon of choice. The documentary ends with Hyde speaking in his German accent and footage of Nazis marching in lockstep on screen. Hyde talks of brotherhood, of ancestral ties, of making meaning of the comic as if one is serving in the military. Entertainment elites and Adult Swim executives can win battles with their forcible bowdlerization of content that does not fit with the mainstream. But they will lose the war.

This, in effect, is what MDE makes clear about its purpose. The troupe is weaponizing the comic spirit. Hyde says so in an interview with the maker of *BLACKLISTED*.[72] The interview is chockablock full of recognizable topics. Hyde and his brethren are antiestablishment provocateurs who have become victims of their own whiteness and targets of the woke mob. Why? Because white males are, at all times, supposed to behave in an "appropriately apologetic" way. Hyde refuses. He makes this obvious when he and his interviewer share a hearty laugh at examples of women they deem "unrapeable" accusing men of sexual violence. They also agree that mainstream comedy is "nonsense" and that "women are not funny." Female comedians should be imprisoned, says Hyde and then "jokes" that there should be a police force tasked with putting their heads in burlap bags, beating them into submission, and prosecuting them as witches. The sentimentalization of misogyny is the joke. Just as Limbaugh used to joke about "sluts" and "unattractive women" and "rape police" and just as he proclaimed over and again that—of all people—Caucasians should have no "guilt" about slavery or really anything, Hyde sentimentalizes a politics of resentment and white grievance that he vehemently denies is actually the basis for his comedy. Like so many other acolytes of the alt-right, he "idealizes offensive speech as a principled transgression against a censorious liberal culture."[73] He and his apologists pat themselves on the back by being so identitarian that they demonstrate the full extent of how put upon they feel. The interviewer gets MDE. He gets the jokes. Hyde embodies a rightful comic spirit.

If this is the case, then Hyde's comedy represents the sling and stones in a clash between David and Goliath (his terminology), even as it feels like the sword of Damocles. Comedy is a way of fighting cultural wars, says Hyde. To "make funny shit" is to supply "our side" with rhetorical arms against "enemies." The David in this comic situation wins not by fighting but rather by being funnier. I say "necessarily" because of a "joke" Hyde makes at the end of the interview. His comedy is not meant to encourage anyone to create "elaborate mail bombs" or "pipe bombs with nails in them" or any other weapon that could be used to "attack government buildings." But if someone *wants* to, then so be it. Or, to say it as Hyde said it in conversation with fellow contrariant comedian Shane Gillis, jokes against perceived enemies are funny when they are transformed from comic ideas into "physicalized opinions."[74] Cue the laughter.

CONCLUSION

It is one thing to get a joke. It is another thing to find it funny. It is another thing still to push a joke to the end of the line such that it becomes a principle of cultural warfare and politics by other means. Simply, we should take a lesson from young Frogs.

Remember that in Aesop's fable, it is the adult who ends up bloated and blown to bits. Despite admonishment from her children, Mother Frog puffs herself up so much that she explodes. As a parable about the conceits of comedy, Mother Frog laughing off the harbingers of young Frogs reveals something about going to comic extremes. There is an alluring death drive in such comings and goings. The young Frogs have the imagination enough to temper the temptation to take things too far. By the same token, they have a *comic* imagination enough to pursue an outcome that lets each other live. Hyde prefers killing jokes. In 2016, the same year *World Peace* was canceled, he and his MDE compatriots published a book. The title is *How to Bomb the U.S. Gov't.*[75] It is billed as a "guide to the collapse of Western Civilization," with tips for protecting oneself from "Unarmed Bl_ck Men," "Overweight Women," "Child Molesters," "E.L.F. Weapons," and other elements of Toxic Hellworld Culture™. Its comedy is compelled by what the troupe calls "a time of psychic-spiritual bombings of The Soul." In Aesop's fable, Mother Frog meets her own demise. Hyde and MDE want others to come along with them. Poe's Law becomes a Law of Calculated Indifference, marked by "raw primo content" that is oriented toward "CLEAN laughs." Funny. Comedy based on some common humanity is about due care. Comedy based on common enemies is about collateral damage.

POE'S LAW AND MILLION DOLLAR EXTREME   71

Multiple times, Hyde and Rochefort have imagined what a second iteration of *World Peace* might look and feel like. They are their own broadcasters, and their own publicists, with MDE.TV. They still post most of their content on YouTube. In one video they kick around some ideas for sketches.[76] They sit in a studio filled with television screens and laptops. It could be a set from *Videodrome* (1983). There are a few small displays behind where Hyde and Rochefort sit. Two are static, with the words "APPLAUSE" and "ONE WAY." Another display has banner text that changes every few seconds with sentiments like "miserable sociopath," "I Fake Cry a Lot," "I Wish You Could Tell Me What It Feels Like to Do," and "I'm Gay and I'm Obsessed with [Your Name here]," along with catchphrases of "words that kill," such as "Clown Cult," "Conspiracy," "Credible Threat," "Assault," "Speech," "Retarded," and "Advertiser-Friendly." Hyde and Rochefort assert their commitment to comedy that riles up people who get "butt hurt" and pushes back on "media hit pieces" against them.

So, picture this. A busy road and a bodega in an inner city. Overlooking the scene is a crowd on bleachers, and a panel of judges to determine who among the various Black people can get across "as flagrantly, badly as possible." The sketch is a game, entitled "The Olympics of Black People Crossing the Street." Hyde pitches it, first with his mockery of Black men sucking their teeth at drivers, fixing their lips, and almost getting hit by cars. As they cross the street, commentators remark with deadpan reactions and awards of faux-style points. Banner text in the backdrop reads "Gangstatalking Is Only the Beginning" as Hyde characterizes "a dummy dressed up like a pimp getting hit by [a] van and slamming into the windshield." This tees up the impression that a "real" pimp gets dragged by the vehicle and ultimately earns no points for his effort. "DQ for the Baltimore native," Rochefort chimes in. Hyde laughs and repeats the punch line. A Korean woman wins. But the game does not end there. In a follow-up event, in the interest of being "fair" and "not hateful," Hyde proposes a game of white people crossing the street with looks of embittered irritation on their faces.

The two go from one extreme to another as new banner text traverses the screen behind them. "Treat Her Right." "I Am Going to Kill You." "Whore." "Ball Buster." "PERFECT GUY LIFE!" (The handle for their YouTube channel, by the way.) Hyde has another pitch. Stereotypical women are looking to buck the established wisdom of the patriarchy by making it OK again to drink alcohol during pregnancy. One woman will do a spiel about the chauvinistic antifeminism in this medical advice. A Chinese male narrator will then advertise a "pregnancy beer," TenChen (the namesake of an imaginary, Amazon-like company), with the slogan "We don't care if this cunt has a retarded kid" and a jingle to go along with it. New and different banner text reads "How to Become a Fucking Fucked Up Freak." Rochefort then pitches a mob sketch wherein a Black guy gets into an altercation with an Italian mobster and the mobster uses it to magnify his braggadocio. Hyde ups the ante with a sketch about a confrontation between a guy in a wheelchair and a typical gym bro. The one threatens fisticuffs. The other pulls out firearms, one of which has an inscription: "my E.L.F. weapon." This is the same inscription that was on a shotgun used by the shooter at the Washington, DC, Navy Yard in September 2013. It means "extremely low frequency" and refers to the gunman's suspicion that he was being manipulated by electromagnetic waves. All of it ends up being a prank designed for the man in the wheelchair to win over a girl. The last idea Hyde has is to simply hire some "smoking hot girls" and film them getting catfished. So, his principle holds: Lure people in under false comic pretenses. Set up a joke. Go in for the kill.

These are not exceedingly clever setups. In Bergson's terms, they put forth an "absurd idea" and contain it within ready-made frames of racial difference and categories of masculism.[77] The characters are stock characters. Hypersexual gangsters. Karens or emblems of privileged white womanhood. Vengeful white men. There is no real comic heroism in the tricks. While there might be hints of what Hyers describes as "flexibility, freedom, compromise, playfulness, lightheartedness, childlikeness, celebration of life, survivability," Hyde and his compatriots are inclined toward real battles waged by characters who *are* "eager to die" and *are* wont "to propose hanging-trees for themselves and others."[78] They are not comic heroes. If they do have weapons, comic heroes turn them into tools for humanizing comedy. Swords get dulled or misplaced. Spears get turned into fishing poles.

There is a coarseness, by contrast, to the sham heroics of Hyde and MDE, and the comic effects of how they arm themselves. Similar to Hyers's sense that comic heroes complicate matters is Bergson's contention that "many coarse comic effects are the direct result of a drop from some very subtle comic element." Vanity, for example. "We look for it if only to laugh at it."[79] When the act of looking out for simple ways to frame cultural problems and categorize people becomes a habit, or a principle, we find easy means for exploiting laughter to anticomedic ends. We delight at the image of "a short man bowing his head to pass beneath a large door; two individuals, one very tall the other a mere dwarf, gravely walking along arm-in-arm, etc."—an image that requires minimal comic imagination to see "that the shorter of the two persons seems as though he were trying *to raise himself* to the height of the taller" much "like the frog that wanted to make itself as large as the ox."[80] Much like the frog. MDE gets bent on easy comic imagery. Hyde's characters are built for coarse comic effect.

We should take a lesson from young Frogs.

NOTES

1. "The Ox and the Frog," in *The Fables of Aesop* (New York: Hurd and Houghton, 1865), 100.

2. MillionDollarExtreme2, "John Oliver Shoutout! Joke Video Political Commentary," YouTube, November 26, 2016, https://www.youtube.com/watch?v=nCN-JE8of5Q.

3. Ibram X. Kendi, "The Violent Defense of White Male Supremacy," *Atlantic*, September 9, 2020, https://www.theatlantic.com/ideas/archive/2020/09/armed-defenders-white-male-supremacy/616192/.

4. Ishmael N. Daro, "Reddit Banned a Page That Trafficked in White Supremacist Content, but the Problem Is Much Bigger," *BuzzFeed News*, September 11, 2018, https://www.buzzfeednews.com/article/ishmaeldaro/reddit-sam-hyde-million-dollar-extreme-ban.

5. Seth Abramovitch, "Sam Hyde Speaks: Meet the Man behind Adult Swim's Canceled 'Alt-Right' Comedy Show (Exclusive)," *Hollywood Reporter*, December 8, 2016, https://www.hollywoodreporter.com/news/general-news/sam-hyde-speaks-meet-man-behind-adult-swims-canceled-alt-right-comedy-show-954487/.

6. Emma Grey Ellis, "Can't Take a Joke? That's Just Poe's Law, 2017's Most Important Internet Phenomenon," *WIRED*, June 5, 2017, https://www.wired.com/2017/06/poes-law-troll-cultures-central-rule/.

7. Ellis, "Can't Take a Joke?"

8. Caitlin Dewey, "The Only Guide to Gamergate You Will Ever Need to Read," *Washington Post*, October 14, 2014, https://www.washingtonpost.com/news/the-intersect/wp/2014/10/14/the-only-guide-to-gamergate-you-will-ever-need-to-read/.

9. "El Rushbo, the Prankster, April 1, 2021," *The Rush Limbaugh Show*, April 1, 2021, https://www.rushlimbaugh.com/daily/2021/04/01/april-fools-el-rushbo-the-prankster/.

10. "The Global Warming Stack," *The Rush Limbaugh Show*, April 8, 2008, https://www.rushlimbaugh.com/daily/2008/04/08/the_global_warming_stack/.

11. Mary Harris, "Rush Is Dead, but We're Still Living in the World He Created," *Slate*, February 18, 2021, https://slate.com/news-and-politics/2021/02/rush-limbaugh-republican-party-conservative-media.html.

12. Richard Seymour, *The Twittering Machine* (London: Verso, 2020), 118.

13. Whitney Phillips, *This Is Why We Can't Have Nice Things* (Cambridge, MA: MIT Press, 2015), 50.

14. Michael Chabon, foreword to *Trickster Makes This World: Mischief, Myth, and Art*, by Lewis Hyde (New York: Farrar, Straus and Giroux, 1998), xi. Emphasis added.

15. Matt Sienkiewicz and Nick Marx, *That's Not Funny: How the Right Makes Comedy Work for Them* (Oakland: University of California Press, 2022), 142.

16. Seymour, *Twittering Machine*, 126.

17. From a verse quoted in Hyde, *Trickster Makes This World*, 285.

18. Ryan M. Milner, *The World Made Meme: Public Conversations and Participatory Media* (Cambridge, MA: MIT Press, 2016).

19. Phillips, *This Is Why We Can't Have Nice Things*, 136.

20. Conrad Hyers, *The Spirituality of Comedy: Comic Heroism in a Tragic World* (New Brunswick, NJ: Transaction, 1996), 193.

21. "Notes and Gatherings," *Bulletin of the Society for the Preservation of New England Antiquities* 13 (July 1922–April 1923), 94.

22. Joseph Bernstein, "The Underground Neo-Nazi Promo Campaign Behind Adult Swim's Alt-Right Comedy Show," *BuzzFeed News*, September 13, 2016, https://www.buzzfeednews.com/article/josephbernstein/neo-nazi-promo-adult -swim-million-dollar-extreme.

23. Fruzsina Eordogh, "How 4chan Tricked the Internet into Believing This Comedian Is a Mass Shooter," *Forbes*, June 2, 2016, https://www.forbes.com /sites/fruzsinaeordogh/2016/06/02/explaining-the-sam-hyde-as-mass-shooter -meme/?sh=205c67211270.

24. Sienkiewicz and Marx, *That's Not Funny*, 157, 156, 158, 159.

25. Bernstein, "Underground Neo-Nazi Promo Campaign."

26. Henri Bergson, *Laughter: An Essay on the Meaning of the Comic*, trans. Cloudesley Brereton and Fred Rothwell (New York: Macmillan, 1914), 73.

27. Bergson, *Laughter*, 69.

28. Bergson, *Laughter*, 69, 43.

29. deez, "Sam Hyde's 2070 Paradigm Shift," YouTube, January 28, 2014, https://www.youtube.com/watch?v=KTJn_DBTnrY.

30. Alexandra Petri, "The Most Glorious Ted Talk Takedown You Will Witness before 2070," *Washington Post*, October 14, 2013, https://www.washingtonpost .com/blogs/compost/wp/2013/10/14/the-most-glorious-ted-talk-takedown-you -will-witness-before-2070/.

31. Ross Luippold, "Comedian Sam Hyde Pranks TED Talks with Nonsense Buzzword Speech," *HuffPost*, October 11, 2013, https://www.huffpost.com/entry /comedian-sam-hyde-pranks-ted-talks_n_4086129.

32. Sienkiewicz and Marx, *That's Not Funny*, 157.

POE'S LAW AND MILLION DOLLAR EXTREME

33. David Sims, "The Battle over Adult Swim's Alt-Right TV Show," *Atlantic*, November 17, 2016, https://www.theatlantic.com/entertainment /archive/2016/11/the-raging-battle-over-adult-swims-alt-right-tv-show/508016/.

34. Kembrew McLeod, *Pranksters: Making Mischief in the Modern World* (New York: New York University Press, 2014), 26.

35. McLeod, *Pranksters*, 4.

36. Bergson, *Laughter*, 45.

37. BNO News, "Congressman Vicente Gonzalez just told CNN that the Texas shooter is Sam Hyde. This is false, it's an internet hoax," Twitter, November 5, 2017, https://twitter.com/BNOFeed/status/927300884417204228 ?lang=en.

38. Eordogh, "How 4chan Tricked the Internet."

39. Sienkiewicz and Marx, *That's Not Funny*, 173.

40. Christian Williams, "Take in the Work of the Comedy Provocateurs in Million Dollar Extreme," *AV Club*, April 23, 2013, https://www.avclub.com/take -in-the-work-of-the-comedy-provocateurs-in-million-1798237780.

41. The video has been removed from YouTube.

42. Sam & Nick's Perfect Clips, "Sam Hyde—FBI & Shooter Meme [HydeWars_040]," YouTube, August 4, 2019, https://www.youtube.com/watch ?v=ILTR3DKFfws.

43. Sam & Nick's Perfect Clips, "Sam Hyde—Action 6 News [HWD_e04]," Sam & Nick's Perfect Clips, YouTube, May 16, 2019, https://www.youtube.com /watch?v=Zom56GOLlVo.

44. Sam & Nick's Perfect Clips, "KSTV2 EP. 2—Fuck-Drumpf-App [Sam Hyde]," Sam & Nick's Perfect Clips, YouTube, June 19, 2019, https://www .youtube.com/watch?v=w8XuNsSnXUE.

45. Sam & Nick's Perfect Clips, "Sam Hyde—Beating Women [KSTV2 EP.4]," Sam & Nick's Perfect Clips, YouTube, December 20, 2019, https://www .youtube.com/watch?v=cOG5ypoX_Dw.

46. Sam & Nick's Perfect Clips, "Sam Hyde—Women Stories [HW_047]," Sam & Nick's Perfect Clips, YouTube, August 5, 2020, https://www.youtube.com /watch?v=Q9yyeNG68g4.

47. Sam & Nick's Perfect Clips, "Sam Hyde—Deal with the Devil [TOA Cut]," Sam & Nick's Perfect Clips, YouTube, July 16, 2019, https://www.youtube .com/watch?v=wB5KKdkRyfg.

48. Bergson, *Laughter*, 27.

49. Hyers, *Spirituality of Comedy*, 152.

50. "Clown World," *Urban Dictionary*, June 10, 2020, https://www.urban dictionary.com/define.php?term=Clown%20World.

51. Porsalin, "Sam Hyde Interview Blacklisted," YouTube, October 31, 2018, https://www.youtube.com/watch?v=EwvgDXfBxic.

52. Sims, "Battle over Adult Swim's Alt-Right TV Show."

53. Jon Blistein, "Adult Swim Cancels Controversial Show 'Million Dollar Extreme,'" *Rolling Stone*, December 6, 2016, https://www.rollingstone.com/tv -movies/tv-movie-news/adult-swim-cancels-controversial-show-million-dollar -extreme-118787/.

54. See Megh Wright, "Adult Swim Orders 'World Peace' Series from Million Dollar Extreme," *Vulture*, March 3, 2016, https://www.vulture.com/2016/03 /adult-swim-orders-world-peace-series-from-million-dollar-extreme.html.

55. Seth Abramovitch, "Sam Hyde Speaks: Meet the Man behind Adult Swim's Canceled 'Alt-Right' Comedy Show (Exclusive)," *Hollywood Reporter*, December 8, 2016, https://www.hollywoodreporter.com/news/general-news /sam-hyde-speaks-meet-man-behind-adult-swims-canceled-alt-right-comedy -show-954487/.

56. Note: the press release has been removed from Adult Swim's website as well as other outlets that reported on it.

57. To watch each episode of the series, see "Million Dollar Extreme Presents: World Peace (Uncut)," archive.org, January 14, 2020, https://archive.org/details /worldpeaceuncut/World+Peace+Uncut.

58. Alexander Blum, "Pepe the Frog: The Roots of a Symbol," *Merion West*, November 5, 2017, https://merionwest.com/2017/11/05/pepe-the-frog-the-roots -of-a-symbol/.

59. Porsalin, "Blacklisted a Million Dollar Extreme Documentary," YouTube, October 29, 2018, https://www.youtube.com/watch?v=8cugXJ84CMw.

60. Porsalin, "Blacklisted A Million Dollar Extreme Documentary."

61. Sienkiewicz and Marx, *That's Not Funny*, 168.

62. Julie A. Webber, "Conclusion: 'You're Fired!' Neoliberalism, (Insult) Comedy, and Post-network Politics," in *The Joke Is on Us: Political Comedy in (Late) Neoliberal Times*, ed. Julie A. Webber (Lanham, MD: Lexington Books, 2019), 301.

63. Hyers, *Spirituality of Comedy*, 152.

64. Robert Westwood, "Theory as Joke: A Hysterical Perturbation," in *Humour, Work and Organization*, ed. Robert Westwood and Carl Rhodes (New York: Routledge, 2007), 50.

65. Westwood, "Theory as Joke," 50.

66. Hyers, *Spirituality of Comedy*, 152.

67. Hyers, *Spirituality of Comedy*, 85.

68. Hyers, *Spirituality of Comedy*, 57.

69. Bergson, *Laughter*, 70.

70. Bergson, *Laughter*, 37.

71. Lisa Trahair, *The Comedy of Philosophy: Sense and Nonsense in Early Cinematic Slapstick* (Albany: State University of New York Press, 2007), 143.

POE'S LAW AND MILLION DOLLAR EXTREME 77

72. Porsalin, "Sam Hyde Interview Blacklisted."

73. Bernstein, "Underground Neo-Nazi Promo Campaign."

74. Sam & Nick's Perfect Clips, "Shane Gillis & Sam Hyde Talk MillionDollarExtreme & World Peace," YouTube, November 30, 2023, https://www.youtube.com/watch?app=desktop&v=7DTVGnkSxjA.

75. Sam Hyde, Nick Rochefort, and Charls "Coors" Carroll, *How to BOMB the U.S. Gov't: The OFFICIAL Primo*™ *Strategy Guide to the Collapse of Western Civilization* (self-pub., 2016). See also a digital version at https://theroyalstudio .com/How-To-Bomb-The-US-Gov-t-Dummy.

76. Sam & Nick's Perfect Clips, "WORLD PEACE 2: Sam Hyde & Nick Rochefort REVEAL Sketch List," YouTube, January 5, 2023, https://www.youtube.com/watch?v=uSdVDNFb1X8.

77. Bergson, *Laughter*, 112.

78. Hyers, *Spirituality of Comedy*, 65.

79. Bergson, *Laughter*, 175.

80. Bergson, *Laughter*, 175.

THREE

—w—

KILLING IT

Joker and Comedy beyond Recognition

IMAGINE IF IMPOSTOR SYNDROME WAS a comic affliction. If, for instance, a comedian who is not funny still finds funniness in his observations of the world and because of that is deemed laughable by society. Or if human folly indicated some kind of fraudulence or glitch in the ability to decide when to laugh, what to laugh at, and what laughter even means when it seems to be misapplied. Might this make laughter less a symptom of some malady than a warning sign? Might this make comedy itself more dubious?

Smile. Put on a happy face. That was the advice Arthur Fleck received from his mother. "She told me I had a purpose," says Arthur, played by Joaquin Phoenix, as he fantasizes about being recognized in the audience of his favorite television show, *Live with Murray Franklin*. He is watching the broadcast from a small room in his dilapidated apartment, and yet he is on the set as he announces his adoration for Murray (played by Robert De Niro) in the middle of the host's monologue. "I love you, Murray," he shouts. "I love you, too," Murray replies. The audience looks on as Arthur stands up, in the spotlight, and chats with Murray. Arthur tells Murray that he lives with his mother. The crowd laughs. Murray defends him by sharing that, growing up, he was also the "man of the house." Arthur smiles, takes pride in his role as caregiver, and then elaborates on his purpose "to bring laughter and joy into the world." Murray likes that. He says as much. Then he invites Arthur to the stage as the show cuts to a commercial break. The audience applauds. Murray hugs Arthur and tells him in confidence that show business is essentially a farce. What matters is human care and connection. The two embrace like father and son. It is a cheerful scene. But it is a sham.

To watch this early scene in Todd Phillips's controversial film *Joker* (2019) is to witness just how laughable it is that one such as Arthur might feel like a fraud

Fig. 3.1. Screenshot of Arthur Fleck in *Joker* alternating between forced smiles and irrepressible tears as he puts on a clown face.

as he lets his imagination run riot in an obvious foreshadow of horror to come. After all, this faux exchange of camaraderie with a famous late-night compere sets the stage for the scene of a crime. Arthur had a traumatic childhood. He is a troubled man. We know this. The film opens on him sticking his fingers in his mouth to force a smile while he does up his face like a clown. Arthur looks at himself in the mirror, white paint illustrating the false appearance of humor on his skin, bright red lips, tears in his eyes (fig. 3.1). Later, while in full clown regalia doing his act as a sign spinner trying to coax cosmopolites and city dwellers into a shop, Arthur is assaulted by a group of kids. They make fun of him, steal his sign, and run down an alleyway. Arthur gives chase only to be whacked with the sign by one of the louts and then laughed at while the group members thrash him. We know from the get-go what his boss, Hoyt, eventually tells him. Arthur is a "fuck-up." Worse than watching Arthur fool himself is imagining along with him that there is some humor in the fact that he is an utter failure even as he holds on to the possibility of making it. We'd be right in thinking this way. Arthur, a man unfunny by most standards, fantasizes about becoming a comedian. He has visions of making people laugh for all the right reasons. He stokes his desire to be loved, to fit in. What a joke.

The joke, though, is on our very standards of what constitutes comedy. Opinionators were quick to label *Joker* a "political parable," revealing a broken culture (and, sure enough, a popular entertainment industry) and reveling in white male resentment.[1] Before the film even hit theaters, people on social media and, more prominently, on the dark web celebrated it and used its conceits as source material for espousing misogyny and promoting violence. Trolls threatened critics who did not like the film.[2] Security was heightened at venues where it was screened. Some Landmark Theaters banned costumes and masks among moviegoers, hearkening to the haunt of shootings.[3] Years later, some in academic circles have doubled down on the idea that *Joker* is a big joke about contemporary lived experience, and—whatever that joke is—it is not funny.[4] Still, *Joker* is less a parable about the corruptibility of cultural politics or the perils of psychopathology (let alone ostracism and persecution) than it is a paradigm case for scrutinizing the conditions for comic judgment. Arthur is the shadow character for Joker—that infamous comic book fiend who has long haunted our collective psyche with his mix of violent anarchism and clownish defiance of societal norms.

In *Joker*, this unsettling mixture forms the basis of a character study wherein imposture is to the comic mask as villainy is to the figure of the fool. Fleck is delusional. If he is a funnyman, he is a fraud. This is not entirely his fault. As a grunt for Ha-Ha's, a sort of comic talent agency, he is a second-rate clown-for-hire who does his act by spinning signs in front of pawnshops and cavorting about at kids' birthday parties. In the real world, though, he cannot shed the clown label. He is a clown insofar as he is foolish, except not on account of his own comic devices. His comic imposture is imposed on him by society. Arthur is a weirdo, a freak. He looks and acts out of humor. He is socially awkward. He suffers from pseudobulbar affect—a condition that provokes irrepressible fits of laughter that neither reflect his true feelings nor correspond with the circumstances. As a result, he is a subject of laughter or an object of ridicule for those who clown around at his expense. His painted face therefore epitomizes a comic mask, especially when he cracks up even as he appears to be crying on the inside. In short, Arthur—and Joker besides—is not a familiar loner or outcast or psychopath but rather an embodiment of comedy gone wrong.

There has been much ado about how *Joker* portrays mental illness.[5] There has been much ado about the film's glorification of violence too.[6] Prior to its release *Joker* was labeled a failed attempt at adapting parts of Alan Moore's graphic novel *Batman: The Killing Joke* (1988). Relatedly, it was branded a regretful response on the part of Phillips to make a statement about the death of comedy. As one reviewer put it, *Joker* is little more than "a bitter and humorless work."[7] Perhaps, but only because so-called woke culture has killed our sense of humor. That, at least, is Phillips's take.[8] While some have lamented the fact that

Joker is no laughing matter in large part *because* it lacks comic relief, others have called it out for what it really is: a film not about mental illness or martyrdom or mania but about the need for empathy.[9] Be that as it may, this chapter does not deal with these controversies, and it does not really deal with the evil omens of ill humor. This chapter takes the comic elements of *Joker* seriously in order to entertain what can happen when egoistical, moralistic cultural politics make comedy into a vehicle for backsliding instead of regeneration and real social change. The problem is not with Phillips's (or Phoenix's) portrayal of the Clown Prince of Crime or with this or that personification of some public health crisis. It is with what we recognize as comedy and what we do not.

This chapter therefore begins with the historical situation of a US culture that is riven by quarrels about what passes for a joke, what topics should or should not be subjects of humor, and what is apt for a comic guise. The figure of the clown poses a specific problem in this setup. There is a certain egoism, if not egocentrism, that accompanies the act of playing the fool.[10] Joker has a recognizable penchant for crossing the line of what makes one capable and competent and commendable *as a comic figure* and then again as one who is culpable (or not) for intemperate jest. Some of the things he does are funny because they are not funny. Some of what he says is humorous because it is so true. Much of what he enacts and, to be sure, responds to is the role that sufferance plays in so many comic arts of making fun. Joker's own artfulness is intimately tied to the rhetorical craft of killing it. To achieving comic triumphs. To telling jokes and getting laughs. But also to stoking literal, murderous violence and ultimately a coup de grâce for how we recognize comedy. If we do not so much get the heroes and villains we need as we get those we deserve, the same might just be the case for clowns.

WHAT'S SO FUNNY?

"Why so serious?" This was the infamous and creepy line associated with Heath Ledger's portrayal of the Ace of Knaves in *The Dark Knight* (2008). He uses the line after fabricating an origin story just before killing a mob boss. In many ways, it was meant to be a joke. The phrase encapsulates his drive to be a self-described agent of chaos. Joker, as played by Phoenix, begs a different question: "What's so funny?" In *The Dark Knight*, the Joker is a criminal mastermind. He is cunning and vile. In *Joker*, the freakish clown is much like the leper that Ledger's character references when he confronts Batman about the badness (never mind the madness) that lurks in all people. Arthur Fleck is an object of ridicule. He laughs out of time. He finds the "wrong" things funny. He is not amused by what amuses the masses. Eventually, he snaps and makes a joke of his newfound sense that murder will out. In both cases, the outcast status warrants a comic license to kill. What differs is the motive and thus the comic (dis)guise.

In early 2022, actor Willem Dafoe disclosed his idea for a sequel to *Joker*. The follow-up film, in Dafoe's imagination, would feature a "Joker imposter."[11] This is a fascinating concept not only because of its allusions to the "copycats" that pretend to be Batman in the beginning of *The Dark Knight* or because it would have Dafoe as the mock bad actor but also because it implies a character donning a comic mask in order to be a faux laughingstock. There is a sequel to *Joker*. It is called *Joker: Folie à Deux* (2024), and it features Lady Gaga as Harley Quinn, a psychiatrist at Arkham Asylum who, in the DC Universe, falls in love with Joker and eventually becomes his partner in crime. There might not be an impostor, but there is very much folie à deux: the folly of two. Characters share guilt by association with delusions of comic grandeur.

This designation alone goads us to grapple with what is taken seriously as a joke and, as such, how and where and *why* we laugh. The devil is an impostor par excellence. Joker is the devil's advocate, in part because he personifies seemingly pure evil and in part because he is "the archetypal fool."[12] Joker is the devil wearing a comic mask. When that mask is removed, we realize "that what we had assumed to be the face" of seriousness, or of funniness, is "a façade."[13] The comic mask puts the rhetorical function of comedy on display. Hence Glasgow's sense that recognition itself is the sine qua non of comedy.[14] To get a joke is to be in on something. To take a joke is to demonstrate something about your character. To *be* a joke—well, that is something else entirely. The masking and unmasking that comes with comedy exposes the tensions inherent in cultural politics and social life. It is integral to comic judgments about "not having a function and not fitting in."[15] These tensions make fertile grounds for orthodoxy as well as transgression. The grounds of concealment and revelation are dangerous grounds. They are "carnival grounds" too.[16] The clown mask tarries with the comic spirit just as it tarries with violence. As a clown-for-hire and later as an unhinged killer, Arthur paints the comic mask directly on his face. Fanatics are ardent followers who wear plastic face coverings. They are pretend clowns. Joker is the real thing.

Joker is also a recognizable enigma. To recognize is to categorize and to put in place. It is to acknowledge. It is to "get" something in accordance with patterns and principles that let us judge matters. To recognize is to identify with. By the same token, it is to *dis*identify. Recognition is built on what is normal just as it is built on what is deviant. To be recognized is to be seen, to be accepted (if not praised), to fit in. Comedy taps into familiarities. By normative standards, the comic mask serves its purpose when it reminds us what is funny and what is not. So many jokes rely on formulas and cycles, and there is glory to be had when you are in on those jokes. There is likewise a "gesture of self-applause" in laughter.[17] Comedy, on these terms, boosts the ego. However, it also determines who should be admitted and who expelled.

When *Joker* shifts from why people are so serious to what is so funny, it shifts the very standards of comic judgment. As Ledger's clown prince would have it, what does not kill the one behind the comic mask only makes him stranger. Arthur, as Joker, makes this strangeness seem familiar. However, he can only endure so many killing jokes until a familiar strangeness makes his comedy *wronger*. Before getting to what happens when we send in the clowns, it is therefore crucial to acknowledge the milieu of cancel culture in and around the monstrous egoism of Joker, and the misrecognition of comedy that Arthur makes flesh when his very being testifies to what's (not) so funny.

Cancel Me This

Activities among early denizens of the internet "to ferret out information about objects and figures" quickly turned into what the Chinese at that time labeled *renrou sousuo,* or the "human flesh search." These searches constituted an "ad hoc detective agency" by which vigilantes would seek out "supposed wrongdoers" in order to expose them as undesirables—as bêtes noires.[18] The impetus to expose those who are presumed to be morally deficient is as ancient as the will to use tragedy as a tool for imagining crime and punishment. We might all be foolish, but some of us have flaws that let slip our bad judgment and even risk our downfall. Kenneth Burke says as much in his categorization of both tragedy and comedy as frameworks for sizing up situations and arbitrating human conflict. The difference is that tragedy tends to ritualize the purification of what has gone bad. Comedy is a carnival of revelry in our shared stupidity. In twenty-first-century US public life, this dyed-in-the-wool regime took on a specific identifier. We call it cancel culture.

While it has its origins in genuine interests to root out injustices on the bases of racial prejudice, gender stereotypes, and discrimination, cancel culture typifies an age of outrage wherein a spirit of humiliation often trumps any sincere aim for truth and reconciliation in the name of accountability. In his acceptance speech for the Best Actor award at the 2020 Oscars, Phoenix delivered what one commentator describes as "a sprawling sociopolitical epic" on "racism, queerness, misogyny, animal rights, personal sacrifice," his own past mistakes, and—yes—cancel culture.[19] The speech kept with the Oscars tradition of actors using their platform to set forth a diatribe. Regarding cancel culture, Phoenix proclaimed that comedy had become a lightning rod. In late 2019, director Todd Phillips had grown weary of making comedy films. A cultural politics of offense meant that films like *Old School* (2003) and the *Hangover* series (2009, 2011, 2013) were too irreverent, too male-centered, too ignorant. They were, as one moniker suggests, mere "dick flicks"—hilarious to some yet hurtful to others, with their unapologetic sexism, homophobia, and chauvinism. According to Phillips, the constant threat of cancellation makes it impossible to be funny, let alone honest. Famed comedian John Cleese of the Monty Python troupe vehemently reinforced these sentiments by arguing that cancel culture takes the fun out of life and thereby justifies vengeful "woke jokes."[20] In that vein, Phillips used *Joker* to play around with anticomedy in a sort of full-circle account of how foolish pride can lead to vindictiveness and spite.

Cancellation foments its own kind of funny-not-funny egocentrism when it motivates us to look out for shameful individuals. This is how Phoenix put it in his speech when he declared that comedy provokes too many disputes about wrongful behavior and tolerable cruelty. Numerous comedians and comic actors have been canceled, at least nominally. Stand-up comedian Louis C.K. was among the most high profile, earning backlash after multiple allegations of sexual misconduct in 2017. Celebrated TV personality Ellen DeGeneres ended her wildly popular talk show in 2022 after nearly two decades when it was made known that she fostered a toxic workplace. In 2017, Kathy Griffin made a joke of then president Donald J. Trump when she posted a picture of her holding what looks like Trump's bloody, severed head. Thereafter, in her own words, Griffin was not canceled; she was "erased." Self-proclaimed GOAT of stand-up Dave Chappelle used his Netflix special *The Closer* (2021) to carry on his habit of making transphobic jokes a centerpiece of his act and situating himself as a victim, not an aggressor. In some instances, comedy is "wrong" when the jokes are bad (or, alternatively, it is "bad" when it features the wrong jokes). In some instances, comedy is not right when it is replete with moral deficiencies. It is easy to understand how members of the trans community might take Chappelle's comedy as a form of festive abuse. It is easy to feel that Griffin might have gone too far. Ellen was outwardly funny but utterly unfunny behind closed doors. And so on. The through line to *Joker* exists in the fact that it is no longer acceptable for comedy to be the thing that lets people get away with distasteful, and at times disgraceful, behavior. That old defense of "just joking" is no longer a license for comic offense. Or is it?

Comedy is an unsettling thing. If we imagine that the comic way is the way of laughter, then *Joker* contends that our expectations are wrong. Comedy is not

KILLING IT   85

just in the jokes of recognizable comics. It is also in the affective relations that trouble the very bonds that tie victimizers to victims, and jokers to the targets of jokes. A comic spirit can inspire, and perhaps even promote, ordinary malice in the wiles of dominant culture. Who cares *that* we air grievances, either from the center of public discourse or from the margins? What matters is *how* we do so, and what we expect of those comedic airings. In spectacles of cancellation wherein this or that public figure is recast as a sacrificial figure, onlookers are reminded to remain "woke." Elsewhere, though, people are inundated with malicious content that is often masked by a comic façade. What is "wrong" on the face of it draws attention. The tragic circumstances of those who are unable to get in on the action, let alone the joke, do not.

In complicated circumstances like these we continue to figure out ways to send in the clowns. The significance of this propensity is taken up in the next section. Before going there, though, it is worthwhile to more firmly establish the situation of *Joker* as a comic appeal to comedy gone wrong.

Coming to Comic Judgment

At one point in the film, Arthur is riding the subway. He is headed home after performing at a children's hospital. Something went wrong. In an earlier scene, Randall, a fellow clown at Ha-Ha's, gives Arthur a gun. It is for protection if Arthur gets jumped again. The gun grows on Arthur. He fondles it in his apartment, imagines using it, accidentally fires it. He also brings it along with him when he performs, which we discover when it falls out of his pant leg and onto the hospital floor during a gamboling rendition of "If You're Happy and You Know It." The children look on in surprise. The nurses gape with horror. Arthur tucks the gun into his long white coat and puts his pointer finger to his lips as if to smilingly suggest that no one saw it. Arthur pronounces to his boss that the gun is just a prop, just a part of his act, but the joke is lost. "What kind of a clown carries a fucking gun?" his boss shouts through the phone as he berates Arthur, who stands dejected in a phone booth after getting fired. Arthur rests his head against the glass. Then he *slams* his head against it. Next, Arthur is sitting in a subway train, alone, except for three dark-suited men at the other end of the car. They are clowning around.

Still clad in his clown getup, Arthur watches two of the so-called Wall Street bros (who just happen to work for Wayne Enterprises) stand at the end of the car and bicker over whether or not a woman one of them had been dancing with that evening was interested in him. "She was in love, bro," one says to the other, who laughs at the idea. "She couldn't wait to get away from you," he retorts before the braggart summons the third one of the group to come to his defense.

"Ryan," he says. "Tell him what you saw." Ryan is busy. He is sitting down, clearly drunk, and waving a bag of french fries at a woman seated across from him. Arthur looks on with his own degree of interest. "Helloooooo?" Ryan intones. The woman acknowledges Ryan but declines the offer. She tries to ignore his taunt, but the other guys get in on the fun. Ryan tosses a fry at the woman. His bros laugh. She looks down the car at Arthur, who appears to grimace as he grins through his painted lips. He sniggers, rolls his eyes, and looks away. Ryan continues to toss fries. His bros continue to laugh. That is when Arthur joins in with a belly laugh that might as well be a bawl. To borrow words from D. Diane Davis, he "wants desperately *not* to laugh," but he is possessed, out of control.[21] Laughter takes hold, like it does in so many scenes that precede this pivotal one. Arthur is stricken with laughter, strangely amused, although downright aghast. He is a clown coming to judgment. Arthur is becoming Joker.

It is, of course, the bros who carry out their own form of retributive justice. The guys are amused by their irksome "joke" on the woman. They are *not* amused by Arthur's laughter. It is almost as if a clown is laughing at *them*. "Is something funny, asshole?" the braggart shouts down the car, his piercing gaze directed at Arthur. The woman gets up and walks away. Arthur attempts to gesture that nothing is funny, but he cannot stop laughing. "Isn't it rich?" The braggart sneers and starts singing the first line of Stephen Sondheim's song "Send in the Clowns" from the 1973 musical *A Little Night Music*. "Are we a pair?" he continues as he makes his way toward Arthur, listing a bit down the aisle and then swinging his body around slowly as he clutches a pole grip. "Isn't it bliss?" he croons as he leans in toward Arthur. His bros approach. "Don't you approve?" Arthur is shaking his head, laughing through tears. The lights go in and out as the subway barrels through the tunnel system. Ryan sits next to Arthur and removes his wig. The braggart hangs from the ceiling straps. He stares Arthur down while Ryan adorns the wig and mocks him with his own laughing fit. "So, buddy, tell us," says the braggart. "What's so fucking funny?" Arthur cannot contain himself. Nothing, he tells them, while attempting to disclose his condition. Before he can, though, the braggart lifts him up, forces him into Ryan's clutches, and punches him in the face. Arthur falls to the floor. "Stay down, freak!" Arthur stays down, and the three guys start kicking him.

One popular opinion is that *Joker* lacks any real regard for the spirit of the times. It is essentially "a misguided commentary on mental illness and sociopolitical rage, a glorification of incels, an antidote to 'woke' culture, etc. etc."[22] It confuses the laugh with the caterwaul. It makes the clown a target for our own cultural predilection to derive pleasure from the pain of others and, worse, to find it either fun or funny—or both. Funniness is a standard of comedic activity such that to be funny is to be liked, to sustain the approval of others. As a symptom of comedy gone wrong, laughter is manifest in the paroxysms of a sad clown that cannot control how he expresses his feelings or makes sense of things. There is more to this moment, however, than these weighty matters.

In a previous scene, Arthur sits in a comedy club and watches a stand-up comic doing his act. Tellingly, he watches the audience, too, and tries to learn what gets a laugh. As he listens and watches, he makes notes in his ragged journal—the same one we get a glimpse of when, after the show, Arthur sits shirtless at a table in his home and writes. *Why are poor people always confused?* Punch line: *they don't make any cents.* Simple wordplay. Hardly sophisticated. Yet it is followed by another expression that is comic in its framing but perhaps not in its finale. *What is the worst part of being mentally ill?* Punch line: *people expect you to act as if you are not.* When Arthur finally finds himself on stage at the comedy club, Pogo's, he bombs. He can barely utter any of his jokes. He is a picture of stage fright. He comes off as someone who laughs at his own jokes and makes a fool of himself. He is a depraved and ghastly glory seeker. He is a clown.

What's funny-not-so-funny here is that Arthur exposes an ego function of comedy that is built on the misrecognition of standards for comic judgment. What do you get when you laugh at those with cultural privilege? In the lyrics of "Send in the Clowns" are notions of bliss, approval, freedom of movement. The Wall Street bros are, in a sense, the clowns. They are showmen fulfilling their roles as uppity financiers and enacting a kind of fiendish privilege that comes with being among those who control the course of laughter. When Arthur lies on the floor of the subway car as the three guys kick him and laugh, he is the embodiment of what happens when you mess with the standard-bearers for clowning around. When he rolls over and shoots two of the guys dead—well, then he enacts a version of comic retribution. Arthur is a clown gone mad. His killing joke ends with the guys being stopped dead in their laughter. The original pesterer tossing fries at a woman in the subway takes off down the aisle, moving to another car and eventually onto the platform where he runs for the stairs. Arthur gathers his belongings and follows him. The guy limps as he goes because he was shot in the leg. "Hey!" he screams in a desperate call for help. The platform is empty. Arthur closes in on him with a death stare in his eye, his arm outstretched, gun in hand. One shot takes the guy down just before he reaches the bottom of the stairs. Three more shots kill him. Two clicks of the gun reveal that Arthur would have done even more if he could have. Arthur pauses for a few seconds before he runs up the stairs and out of the subway.

Fig. 3.2. Screenshot of Arthur Fleck in *Joker* admiring himself in the mirror after dancing alone having just murdered three bullies in a subway.

In darkness, Arthur hurries down the city street with a childlike looseness. He eventually takes refuge in a squalid bathroom in an alleyway. He locks himself in beneath a flickering light. Then, with nothing but a cello moaning along with some other strings in the background, Arthur moves from an air of anxiety and anguish to a freewheeling, if not graceful, dance. He is liberated. He is free (fig. 3.2). He is transformed by retributive violence that doubles as a wickedly blissful brand of reckoning. He is the comic justice of "just joking."

Until this point, Arthur has perceived his laugher as a symptom of something that is wrong with him. He sees the systems and the structures of a city infested with rats, of his apartment building and its rickety elevator, of the alleys filled with trash, of tough conditions all around. He observes the well-to-do and those of the in-crowd who are all, seemingly, in on the jokes, and he imagines himself a victim of his environment. Then he becomes Joker. Arthur leaves his job, but only after he literally punches the time clock on the wall of the workplace and crosses out the words "forget to" on a sign posted above the stairs on the way out. The sign reads, "Don't forget to smile!" He laughs hysterically on the floor of his home when he discovers that his childhood was one of abandonment and neglect, that his mother was delusional and psychotic. Soon after the subway incident, Arthur becomes a suspect. The police try to question him when he goes to visit his mother at the hospital where she is in bed with a stroke that she suffered after the police questioned her. He evades them by sidestepping their suspicions and slipping through the sliding glass doors marked "Exit Only." Arthur enters his mother's room. He sits at her bedside, smokes, and ruminates aloud about his life. His mother is stretched out, catatonic. I always hated my name, Arthur tells her. I always thought something was wrong with me. I have always been unhappy. "You know what's funny?" he says as he stamps out his cigarette and stands up. "You know what really makes me laugh? I used to think that my life was a tragedy. But now I realize it's a fucking comedy." Arthur takes the pillow from under his mother's head and suffocates her with it.

To call Arthur's life a comedy is to establish its embroilment with normative standards for what's so funny and what it means for comedy to go wrong when the clowns are sent in or cast out. What kinds of jokers get comic license to make fun? Who do they get to make fun of, and why? What forms of humorous cultural production are validated and accepted? What is the relationship between jokes that are killed and jokes that kill? One of the hooks in that captivating yet peculiar tune "Send in the Clowns" is that culture is all bread and circuses, that society—however high or low—is a charade. "Don't you love a farce?" goes one of the lines. "Send in the clowns / Don't bother, they're here." Some clowns are sent in insofar as they are already among us, clowning around. Some clowns are sent in when the very function of comedy is called into question.

SENDING IN THE CLOWNS

The Joker is a fascinating character. Aside from a lineage that runs from the figure of the beggarly madcap in tarot card decks through Shakespeare's fools to the emergence of a court jester representing the topmost trump card in games like euchre and into the narratives from Batman stories as we know them, his transformations across time are in themselves as beguiling as what he tends to represent. That is, once a wild card or free spirit, the Joker is now variously a witty jokester, a pitiless killer, a frenetic prankster, a lurid mobster, a cartoonish criminal, a cruel anarchist, and a sociopathic madman. And because he is depicted as a *comic* by-product of his historic moment, he is never without mystery and intrigue. This is not the space to carry out a genealogy of the Joker.[23] But it is fitting to outline the principles of clownery that underwrite his role as a funnyman who kills, with laughter out of place and, seemingly, comedy out of humor.

One recent version of the Joker, which has already been mentioned, is particularly pertinent as a starting point. It is the version played by Heath Ledger in *The Dark Knight*. Therein, the Joker betrays a psychopathy combined with unnerving intelligence, vile cunning, and strange charm. This clown prince is an image of madness that far exceeds "comic criminality."[24] The Joker in *The Dark Knight* is noticeably detached from the carnival character of other iterations (for instance, in Cesar Romero's televisual portrayal from the 1960s as well as in numerous comic books and in Jack Nicholson's rendition for Tim Burton's 1989 film, *Batman*). He is less a dandy or a caricature of human wickedness and more a despicable personification of malice. He is a social outsider who exploits the vulnerabilities of society's institutions. He orchestrates wildly elaborate and illicit misdeeds. Moreover, the Joker as played by Ledger lives without rules, without empathy, and without regard for the established order of things.

Like so many other Jokers, the character of Arthur Fleck is born into laughter by an absentee, malingering father and a mother mired in lunacy. His childhood leaves him with unresolved traumas. Additionally, like the clown that he is, Fleck is so utterly familiar because his strangeness as a fool-for-hire and as a "freak" in everyday life represent the lines between "order and chaos, mask and face," acceptance and rejection, "play and reality," the sacred and the profane.[25] In other words, Joker blends "clown violence" with "joyful transgression."[26] He shows us when comedy is right and when it is wrong according to the difference between making jokes on "us" and making jokes on "them." We tend to be fine with clowns who make fools of themselves. We laugh at them. They perform their folly for us. The foolish egoism in Joker's desire to be part of the in-group, to conform, and to earn acceptance is in keeping with our expectations of clowns. A clown is a clown, after all, precisely because he can "dramatize the fragmented and alienated character of our individual and social existence, yet at the same time offer a kind of resolution of it."[27] Clownish Wall Street bros usually get away with their comic antics. So do stand-up comedians, despite how many lament their inability to joke about the very topics that crop up in their jokes. And clowns who make fun of kings. Joker is different. He traverses the social context for what's so funny into the realm of what's so serious about comedy when he resorts to crime and violence. Joker is no "gay monster," in Mikhail Bakhtin's words.[28] He is not some variety of a "bad clown" like Pennywise.[29] He is not just a misfit. He is not just "laughter incarnate."[30] In *Joker*, he is something of a clown's alter ego sent in as an incarnation of comedy beyond recognition.

Clowns indicate status and privilege. Embedded in their weirdness is "a defense of the ordinary."[31] They are enigmatic, no question. They are allowed to be. The folly, buffoonery, and jests of clowns make up the essence of comedy most overtly when tormentors tolerate them. We revel in the clown's capacity to bring our societal misdeeds "into the open so we can see where we have gone wrong" precisely *because* we who are not conventional clowns get to decide

KILLING IT 91

what it is to set things right—or not.[32] So, even though a clown can temper our egoistic tendencies, the comic otherness that mirrors our sense of self, there is in clownery a "crude basis for the pride, pleasure, and permanence of culture."[33] Clowns are recognizable *as clowns* when they mock convention and regale us with their embrace of the profaneness in the sacred, stagger and trip and dance out of step. They reinvigorate life and restore laughter and remind us of the nonsense in our condition when they revel in their own situation as comic personages. Clowns operate within certain parameters. They are guided by arbiters of cultural dominance and exploit a comic license that is bestowed on them. What happens, then, when a clown takes issue with the ordinary, revolts against the world, and upends convention?

Joker is what happens when the clown is sent into a new comic situation. In *Joker*, clownery occurs as the mischief-making of bullies—of tyrannizers—and the material of professional comedians and late-night talk show hosts like Murray Franklin. Joker, the clown, embodies "comic ridicule," a target for jokesters who harness a "collective ego" to make fun of, to terrorize, to oppress.[34] Ledger as the Joker makes dark comedy out of disorder, anarchy, and chaos. Phoenix, in *Joker*, plays the victim and the fool. He is the dupe who clowns around in reaction to those who make a clown out of him. The teenagers on the street who steal his sign and give him a beatdown. The bros on the subway. His boss. And, eventually, Murray Franklin. Joker becomes a comic egoist who tries to escape his identity as a clown who is not funny. His laughter is pathological. His death drive thrives on a principle of comic pleasure. This means that what David B. Morris dubs its "pain-killing effect" cuts both ways.[35] Comedy of this kind reorients standards of what should or should not be associated with monstrosity, with attraction or repulsion, with who or what is weird. It would be easy to see Joker as a "harsh, cruel, malicious, boring, depressing, hateful, violent, destructive" clown.[36] Joker challenges us to imagine the clown as scapegoat, as miscreant, even as some foolish messiah of the mentally ill. But his comic spirit of harshness, cruelty, and malice comes from the very society that either reveres or rejects him.

This is how *Joker* serves as an object lesson in the overlap of comedy and cancel culture. The conventional wisdom about comedy is that in everything from slapstick run amok to jokes taken too far, we expect "violence without violent consequences."[37] Can't take a joke? You're either a victim or one of the weak willed. Want to "slay" an audience with your comic wit and wisdom? Then "kill it" on the comic stage. In these ways, *Joker* is a character study that doubles as a cultural indictment of the "mocking ritual of humiliation" that predetermines exchanges with social, political, and other outsiders.[38] Throughout the film, comedy is "a symptom of the very same disease it pretends to diagnose."[39] It is not the way of dealing with madness or doing away with human follies. It is not the means for breathing new life into the human condition. It is the footing for retributive violence, the vehicle of pent-up rage, and a resource to exact revenge. It can be argued that "comedy exists in the terrain where boundaries are recognized and then transgressed without harming people who don't deserve it. When boundaries are transgressed and people who don't deserve it are harmed," says Danielle Fuentes Morgan, "it is no longer comedy—it's horror."[40] Joker makes a comic blend of these boundaries. To call back to the previous chapter, he trades the toy gun for a real one, pulls the trigger, and renders comedy a loaded gun.

One scene in particular captures Joker in his transformation of comic violence from a supposedly inconsequential part of the clownish act to a grave part of the materials that make up those boundaries. Arthur is once again shirtless in his apartment. He is standing in the dark, hunched over a small shelf in the kitchen, his gaunt torso lit only by a dim light that illuminates the space from another room. The phone rings. Arthur lets the machine pick up. A police detective leaves a message as Arthur opens the door to a refrigerator and removes its contents—food, racks, everything. Arthur weeps as he listens to the detective requesting a callback regarding the subway murders. The detective hangs up. Arthur crawls into the fridge and shuts the door.

In the scene immediately following this one, the phone rings and the machine again picks up. This time, the caller is Shirley Woods, a booker for *Live with Murray Franklin*. The room is brightly lit. Arthur emerges from the blurred backdrop. He is lying on his bed, wearing only white underwear and a red shirt. On the wall beside the phone are clippings from the newspaper. They reflect images Arthur saw on the streets soon after he killed the Wall Street bros. Headlines pronounce the dirty deeds of a "killer clown," a "clown vigilante." In and around that same moment, Arthur saw others donning clown masks, first in isolated instances and later all throughout the subway and across Gotham. He even saw himself on television when Murray featured a clip from his stand-up act at Pogo's during the opening editorial for a show. Arthur is visiting his mother in the hospital when he sees Murray's bit. He is looking up at a television on the wall and holding his mother's hand while she rests in bed. Murray works through his editorial. It is about how only some are fit for comedy. We live "in a world where everyone thinks they can do my job," Murray jeers. Then he plays a clip of Arthur doing his joke about not heeding his mother's advice to enjoy school. He does not need to enjoy school, the comic Arthur tells his mother, because he'll never be someone who actually works for a living; he'll be a comedian. Arthur stands

KILLING IT 93

up, horrified to see himself on screen. However, after he hears his own joke, he laughs. The camera cuts back to Murray, who snickers and quips that Arthur should have listened to his mother. Murray then adds insult to comic injury by playing another clip. Arthur is back on stage disclosing how everyone laughed at him when, as a boy, he disclosed his dream of being a comedian. "Well," says Arthur in a riposte, "no one's laughing now." Murray smirks. "You can say that again, pal." In the hospital room, the look on Arthur's face is piercing as he glowers at the television. The studio audience claps and laughs.

The show booker for *Live with Murray Franklin* is leaving a message about the "amazing response" from viewers that followed from the clips Murray played of his stand-up when Arthur gets out of bed to pick up the phone. Shirley reiterates her comments about the public reception of Arthur's comedy and invites him to be on the show. Arthur can't believe it. "Isn't that great?" Shirley exclaims. She then says that Murray would like Arthur to do some of his act. Arthur takes a drag from a cigarette with a blank stare on his face and then accepts the invitation.

In this moment, Arthur has made it. Unlike the clowns who, in Thomas Wayne's words, fail to "make something of themselves," Arthur has become a recognized comedian. What Murray and others do not know is that he is also Joker—the one who still understands that he is the butt of jokes in dominant culture. In "making it" by getting onto Murray's show, he does not actually get a hold of what Bakhtin calls that "gay and free laughing aspect of the world."[41] Only as Joker does he do that. This is the dark side of the carnival. Ordinary acts of comic violence get folded into the normal course of things. Comedy forces some people to put on a happy face, some to laugh at others inflicting pain on the undeserving, some to accept the comic act as that which reinstates the hierarchy of the establishment. The rhetorical force of comedy comes from the power to pass judgment on people for what they laugh at, for who they laugh with, and for when they laugh through everyday, ordinary injustices. Arthur is an example of how change and renewal are not always comic goods. As Joker, he is living proof of what can happen when comedy goes wrong by sending in the clowns.

CONCLUSION: KILLING JOKES

"Knock, knock," says Joker.

He is sitting in a chair at the place of honor right next to Murray's desk on the set for *Live with Murray Franklin*. Joker is dressed in a blood-red tuxedo suit with a deep yellow waistcoat and a floriated emerald shirt. His hair is dyed garishly yet grotesquely green. His face is painted, crudely, with blue triangles above and below his eyes and exaggerated lips and nose, both colored to match his suit. He appears at ease, cross-legged, as he reads from his joke book. Murray makes fun of him for needing notes to remember a knock-knock joke. Joker continues, and Murray plays along.

"Who's there?"

The audience laughs.

"It's the police, ma'am," says Joker. "Your son has been hit by a drunk driver." Joker looks up from his notebook and chuckles. "He's dead."

One of the musicians from the band plays that familiar "wah-wah-wah" on his trombone to express disappointment. The audience groans.

"No, no, no," interjects one of the other guests on the show. "You cannot joke about that."

"Yea, that's not *funny*, Arthur," Murray agrees. "That's not the kind of humor we do on this show."

Joker nods and apologizes. Then he discloses how tough it has been for him since he "killed those Wall Street guys."

"OK," says Murray, dubiously. "I'm waiting for the punch line."

The assumption is that Arthur is doing a bit.

"There's no punch line," Joker replies, shrugging. "It's not a joke."

Murray's showrunner gestures off screen for the host to end the interview by waving his hand underneath his throat. The audience groans again. Murray scowls and presses on. He cannot believe that Arthur is serious. Joker dispenses with this disbelief, grins, and with an air of insouciance proclaims that his life "is nothing but a comedy." Death is akin to the outcome of a killing joke. It is "the system" that decides to what extent this or that is "right or wrong," in Joker's words, whether or not it is "funny." Joker is flippant as he speaks. His tone is embellished when he utters words like "funnyyy" and when he addresses "Murraaayyy" by his first name. That same system, in which Murray is the king of comedy, determines what constitutes clownery and what makes for madness. But Joker rebuffs the notion that he is crazy. After all, his motive makes sense. He killed those Wall Street bros because, as he announces with fervent delight, "they couldn't carry a tune to save their lives." Now, that's a joke!

The host and his devotees disagree. Joker then outs them all for their hypocrisy. Murray only brought Arthur on, says Joker, for a good laugh—to make fun of him. Murray's aim was to get more laughter at his expense and extend a joke that killed with the audience during an earlier editorial. Arthur was never meant to provoke laughter with his own comic material. He was meant to be the laughingstock. Murray does not like this suggestion or the assertion by Joker that he and all his fawning fans are "awful" and moves to shut down

Fig. 3.3. Screenshot of Arthur Fleck in *Joker* shooting late-night TV host Murray Franklin as the punch line of his joke on mainstream comedy.

the interview. The place of comedy is disrupted. Murray's position is fraught. Joker is fuming.

Still, he interposes with one more joke. "What do you get," he asks while commotion takes hold on the set and a haunting drumbeat begins to intensify in the background, "when you cross a mentally ill loner with a society that abandons him and treats him like trash?" Murray wants the police to be called. He tries to wrap things up. Joker, however, wants to deliver his punch line. "You get what you fucking deserve!" Joker pulls out his gun and shoots Murray in the head (fig. 3.3).

Everyone screams.

The other guests cower.

Joker laughs.

Then, with fresh blood on his face, smiling, he stands up and shoots Murray again before cavorting his way to one of the cameras as the set falls silent. "That's life!" he attempts to proclaim to viewers, but the live feed is killed.

—⁂—

During a podcast conversation with Edgar Wright of *Empire* magazine, famed filmmaker Quentin Tarantino made a case for why the ending of *Joker* is so powerful. In the end, Tarantino argues, audiences are on Joker's side. They *want* him to blow Murray's head off. He is such a typical "talk show guy," which is to say "an asshole comedian." It is more than that, though. Maybe Murray did get what he deserved. Regardless, the darkly comic effect of Joker is that, according to Tarantino, he subverts the system by getting people to think and feel and imagine what it is to be "a fucking lunatic."[42] Yes. Sort of. Joker does fulfill our expectations and perhaps even satisfies our desires. His motive makes good sense, even if it is perverse. All the same, what matters is that a killing joke crosses the line to make comedy itself the focal point for comic judgment. By Murray's standards and those of "the system," it is not funny when comedy gets its pleasure from the pains of others. When Arthur laughs uncontrollably or fails to win a crowd over with a joke, that is funny. But it is not funny when Arthur as Joker is amused when other people suffer. Joker is neither a monster nor an anomaly. He is an incarnation of that comic tendency to laugh at someone else's expense, pushed to the end of its line.

In this weighty scene, Joker calls Murray's bluff. Comedy is about fine lines and loose borders. It traffics in the all-too-real circumstances of cultural fantasies and the phantasms of so-called real life. Joker is a comic vigilante. He is a clown. Yet he is no less a wannabe comedian who comes to change the tune of comedy. When comic laughter is made into "capitalist laughter," Kenneth Burke once wrote, comedy is corrupted. This is because what's so funny gets tied up with forms of "patronage," making the core human act of recognition— of identification and division—into a matter of buying in or opting out, of rendering something good or evil, of drawing lines between right and wrong.[43] Killing jokes are judged according to a spectrum of "slain-notslain." All the while clowns like Arthur, like Joker, remain targets of comedy with little regard for how, or if, such clowns will suffer any "fundamental harm."[44] We see this perhaps subtly in Murray's misrecognition of Joker as Arthur. In the dressing room before the show, Murray inquires about Arthur's choice of wardrobe. He wonders if it is appropriate given all the chaos that had been provoked by the antics of that "killer clown." Riots broke out. Posses of frenzied clowns in masks were attacking police and overwhelming the city. In such a city, Arthur was not an outsider. He fit in—even *blended* in. Joker called the tune. Ultimately, he emerges as the patron saint of clowns. Comedic performances are patronizing in systems of patronage and censorship. They move us to reject some forms of wrongful comedy in order to accept others. They require a distinction between the clown of privilege and the parasitic clown. The question is therefore not *if* but *how* we expect our clowns to do our dirty work. Some of those clowns are kings. Some of them are just ordinary people. Some of them are criminals.

Lest we forget what can happen when the clown exceeds the carnival, when he loses his comic aspect. A culture of comedy that takes clowns and crowns

KILLING IT

them as kings or kicks them to the gutter risks riddling itself with opposition, conflict, and resentment. Granted, this "prophetic riddle," as Bakhtin calls it, is built on the presumption of an "established hierarchy" that accommodates clowns and kings in the name of maintaining order. When mutual recognition of clownery and kingliness breaks down, there can be joy in the comic image of an Old World being destroyed. To make jokes is to play a dangerous game. It is to condense a "formula of life and of the historic process" into plays of "fortune, misfortune, gains and loss, crowning and uncrowning."[45] When Joker kills Murray, he transforms the regenerative and gay spirit of comedy into a formula for "complete destruction."[46] This is why the film carries so much weight in an era of cancellation, retaliation, and—unnervingly—comic tradition.

At the end of the film, we find Arthur in Arkham State Hospital. It is an asylum. The view on him comes as the screen fades in from black. He is laughing, hysterically, and not trying to control himself. The camera cuts to a close-up of Arthur's face. His hair is no longer green. It is black, slicked back. He is not wearing any makeup. Just the countenance of a man seemingly amused with himself. His laughter stops. He smiles and takes a drag from a cigarette. Arthur is handcuffed and dressed in what looks like a white straitjacket. He is sitting across the table from a mental health professional who is studying him. Not a Harley Quinn, not a harlequin, not a comic servant—not yet.

"What's so funny?" she asks with a straight face.

Arthur says that he is just thinking of a joke.

Preceding this scene is one wherein Joker is taken away in a police car, smiling in the back seat as he disappears into a night of riotous unrest. In the same instance, one of his clown acolytes follows Thomas and Martha Wayne into an alley as they attempt to flee the theater. The clown hails them in the darkness, proclaims that they get what they deserve, and then shoots them dead. Their son, Bruce, gets his mother's blood splattered across his face as he witnesses their murder. In the flurry of the bedlam, some other clowns sabotage Joker's arrest by causing the police car carrying him to crash and slide across the street. Joker is knocked unconscious. When he comes to, he spits blood from his mouth before climbing atop the car and reveling in the warm reception of a clown mob that is chanting and cheering all around him. He smiles. Then he realizes the blood in his mouth. He puts his fingers to his lips, gets them wet with blood, and pushes them into his cheeks as he smiles wider.

In the hospital, Arthur laughs even harder at the recollection of this "joke."

"You want to tell it to me?" asks the doctor.

Arthur smiles with his fingers pressed softly against his bottom lip, a cigarette burned almost to the butt. He looks askance. "You wouldn't get it."

98 WHEN COMEDY GOES WRONG

Arthur looks at the doctor and grins as he sings along with Frank Sinatra's "That's Life" while it plays in the background. "That's life, funny as it may seem." He mutters as Sinatra swoons about puppetry and poesy and pauperism and piracy, about pawns and kings. The things that make this "fine old world" go 'round. And as Sinatra continues to sing, we watch as Arthur walks alone down the white halls of the hospital, leaving bloody footsteps as he goes. By the time he gets to the end of the hall, basking in the light from the window to the outdoors, he is dancing, and his hands appear to be uncuffed.

Some comedy deals in remorselessness, indifference, irresponsibility, and violence. Some feeds into egoism and the identitarian crises of both individuals and communities. In *Joker*, comedy is struggled over, but not for its capacity to avert catastrophe or avoid brutality or affirm humanity. Rather, it is struggled over for its normative principles. Joker is a clown, reimagined. He is a figure for comedy that turns the riddle into a comic disaster. What is more, Joker is a provocation to work through what happens to the laughing aspect of our world when we send in the clowns and they get us to laugh at the wrong things. Plainly, if we take Joker seriously, we need to ask ourselves: What's so funny?

A POSTLUDE: FROM ALTER EGOS TO ALTERNATIVE ENDINGS

What if Joker was nothing but a figment of Arthur Fleck's imagination?

With character studies like this—dabbling as they do in Freudian nightmares of psychobabble, sexualized fantasies around family and fame, childhood traumas, physic retentions, and violent releases—it is hard not to suspect that everything from Arthur's first cogitation about going on *Live with Murray Franklin* to his final comic act is a fabrication. There are numerous hints that he never actually had a relationship with a Black female neighbor that he essentially stalks for most of the film. That he invented a romance with her, which he appeared to consummate soon after killing the Wall Street bros and capped off when it looked as though, toward the end, he butchered her daughter. Even his pseudobulbar affect might have been a lark, however tied it was to the repressions that reified a childlike narcissism that Arthur never outgrew. Not only does laughter reinforce what we find either funny or disturbing (or both), but it also "exposes an/other way of seeing, an/other way" of accounting for what we might "have been unable to ac/count."[47] Figments of imagination and Freudian fantasies and all jokes aside, what matters here is not what comedy *means*. What matters is what comedy *measures*.

KILLING IT 99

Soon after *Joker* came out, rumors circulated about an alternate ending. That ending centers on the moment when Bruce watches his parent die. In it, the mad clown shoots Bruce dead too. For enthusiasts of the DC Universe, such an ending would have created a problem: no Batman. At least, Bruce Wayne would not grow up to become the Dark Knight. There is more, though. In the rumored alternative, the murderer would not be some anonymous assailant from the gang of clowns. It would be Joker himself. He would still laugh and mull over the "joke" while sitting with a doctor in Arkham State Hospital. The difference, as actor and comedian Kevin Smith described it on his *Fatman Beyond* podcast, is "it was [Joker] killing Thomas and Martha Wayne and the boy was screaming and crying and he turned to walk away and he turned back, shrugged, and shot the kid. Credits."[48] Yikes. Talk about humor of the "bang" gun devolving into horror. Or try these other alternatives, which are readily available as bits of fan fiction on YouTube. After proclaiming that Joker's knock-knock joke is not funny, Murray pulls out a gun and shoots him. Alternatively, instead of killing Murray, the just desert Joker supplies when he fires his gun appears as a red flag emblazoned with the word "bang" in all-black capital letters. True to form, Murray doesn't find *this* kind of humor funny either.

There are many reasons why such endings probably wouldn't have been well received. The first one in particular ruins the origin story of Batman. It is gratuitous in its casual slaying of a child. It is lacking in even partial closure for the fate of Joker. And it perverts the comic trope of getting the last laugh at the same time as it reasserts the real justification in being repulsed by questioning, honestly, what is so funny about what Joker has done. The others? Well, either too in line with fait accompli or simply too tongue-in-cheek. However, there is another alternate ending that is toyed with in the film just before Joker's ill-fated appearance on *Live with Murray Franklin*. It comes when Arthur meets Murray backstage before the show. Murray's showrunner, Gene, expresses concern about Arthur going on as a guest. He is worried about the clown getup. He is worried about Arthur's indifference to the mayhem in the streets. Murray assuages Gene and urges Arthur to follow some simple rules. "No cursing," Murray insists. "No off-color material." *Live with Murray Franklin* does "clean" comedy. Arthur agrees and makes a stipulation of his own. In the episode when Murray made fun of Arthur, he called him a "joker." Arthur adopts the label and asks that Murray introduce him by that appellation. Gene and Murray leave, and Joker leans back in a chair where he will wait to go on. The camera moves in above him, zooms in on his face, and displays Joker staring at the ceiling, pointing his gun at his chin. This was not the first time he harbored delusions of grandeur in committing suicide as an act of playing the fool—indeed, of getting the last laugh—on live television. Before he goes to the studio, Arthur appears in his apartment playing a rerun of a Murray Fanklin show. He practices his entrance and pretends to be a guest. After taking a seat on his couch, he imagines himself telling a joke. "Knock, knock," he says. Then he pulls out his gun and feigns firing it at his chin. The crowd claps and cheers, and he leans back, smiling, with his head hanging off the couch.

If Joker kills Bruce before he becomes Batman, the conditions of comedy are not so much the concern as what Burke might brand the "rival structures of authority" at play in the DC Universe.[49] Comedy would not really be appreciated or even abhorred if these rival structures did not turn on crude depictions of "necessary evils."[50] The rebuffed comedian would simply be another piper who insists on the right to call his own tune. Relatedly, if Joker kills himself in a spectacle of comic madness, the act would only affirm his guilt, prove the rightness of a tragic system and its standards for making and taking jokes, and substantiate that a criminal vigilante is wrong. In this monstrous version of a murder-suicide, Joker would situate comedy out of history by relinquishing his position as one who might spoil the fun in "normal" ways of doing things. Joker would be a victim of his own crimes. A sociopath. An egoist. A clown gone bad.

These alternate endings therefore stand as wake-up calls for the rhetorical force of the actual one. There are limits to the comic spirit. But comedy can be taken to extremes. Nowhere is this more in our faces than when the other clowns, an amalgam of comic masks, laugh right along with Joker as the kill emerges as the crux of clownishness. This is what can happen when comedy in bad faith precludes the restorative possibilities of gay laughter. Or when the ambivalence of a carnival gets turned into a source of viciousness and violence, and ritual decrownings derive their joy from comic acts that are at base vengeful and vindictive. Joker, though, is not the only one with dirty hands. The Wall Street bros exceed the limits of comedy when they harass the woman on the subway and hit Arthur only to continue hitting him while he is down. Murray, impelled as he is by that capitalist laughter, is also unable to recognize the various ways that comedy can cross the line. In the case of Joker, one is left wondering just how far we are willing to let jokes go. The same goes for those of us who might be concerned about some of the clowns and clownishness in our midst.

NOTES

1. Jeff Yang, "'Joker'—A Political Parable For Our Times," CNN, October 6, 2019, https://www.cnn.com/2019/10/06/opinions/joker-political-parable-donald-trump-presidency-yang/index.html.

2. Alissa Wilkinson, "Joker Has Toxic Fans. Does That Mean It Shouldn't Exist?," *Vox*, October 3, 2019, https://www.vox.com/culture/2019/10/3/20884104/joker-threats-cancel-phillips-art.

3. Keith Coffman, "Landmark Theaters Bans Costumes at Screening of Upcoming 'Joker' Movie," Reuters, September 26, 2019, https://www.reuters.com/article/film-joker/landmark-theaters-bans-costumes-at-screening-of-upcoming-joker-movie-idUSL2N26I00L/.

4. See volume 19, issue 1 of *New Review of Film and Television Studies*, a special issue from 2021 devoted to *Joker*, https://www.tandfonline.com/toc/rfts20/19/1.

5. See Annabel Driscoll and Mina Husain, "Why Joker's Depiction of Mental Illness Is Dangerously Misinformed," *The Guardian*, October 21, 2019, https://www.theguardian.com/film/2019/oct/21/joker-mental-illness-joaquin-phoenix-dangerous-misinformed. See also Bryan Alexander, "How Accurate Is 'Joker's Portrayal of Mental Illness? The Answer Is Complicated," *USA Today*, October 23, 2019, https://www.usatoday.com/story/entertainment/movies/2019/10/23/what-joker-movie-gets-right-wrong-about-mental-illness-violence/3978028002/.

6. See "'Joker' Opens to Controversy over Film's Depiction of Violence," *All Things Considered*, NPR, October 4, 2019, https://www.npr.org/2019/10/04/767339474/joker-opens-to-controversy-over-film-s-depiction-of-violence. See also David Sims, "Untangling the Controversy over the New *Joker* Movie," *Atlantic*, October 3, 2019, https://www.theatlantic.com/entertainment/archive/2019/10/joker-movie-controversy/599326/.

7. David Sims, "The Comic That Explains Where *Joker* Went Wrong," *Atlantic*, October 7, 2019, https://www.theatlantic.com/entertainment/archive/2019/10/killing-joke-and-joker/599512/.

8. David Mack, "Todd Phillips Blamed 'Woke Culture' for Killing Comedy and Leading Him to Make 'Joker,'" *BuzzFeed News*, October 1, 2019, https://www.buzzfeednews.com/article/davidmack/todd-phillips-joker-woke-culture-comedy.

9. See Anthony Lane, "Todd Phillips's 'Joker' Is No Laughing Matter," *New Yorker*, October 7, 2019, https://www.newyorker.com/magazine/2019/10/07/todd-phillips-joker-is-no-laughing-matter. See also Samantha Dale Fox, "JOKER: A Plea for Empathy," *Medium*, December 26, 2019, https://medium.com/@samanthadalefox/joker-a-plea-for-empathy-c25b7a70976f.

10. R. D. V. Glasgow, *Madness, Masks, and Laughter: An Essay on Comedy* (Madison, NJ: Fairleigh Dickinson University Press, 1995), 161. See also Conrad Hyers, *The Spirituality of Comedy: Comic Heroism in a Tragic World* (New Brunswick, NJ: Transaction, 1996), 145.

11. David Taylor, "Willem Dafoe Has Fantasised about Playing a 'Joker Imposter' Opposite Joaquin Phoenix's *Joker*," *GQ*, June 8, 2022, https://www.gq-magazine.co.uk/culture/article/willem-dafoe-joker-sequel.

12. Glasgow, *Madness, Masks, and Laughter,* 198.

13. Glasgow, *Madness, Masks, and Laughter,* 109.

14. Glasgow, *Madness, Masks, and Laughter,* 47.

15. Michael Taussig, *Defacement: Public Secrecy and the Labor of the Negative* (Stanford, CA: Stanford University Press, 1999), 162.

16. Taussig, *Defacement,* 50.

17. Glasgow, *Madness, Masks, and Laughter,* 42.

18. Ligaya Mishan, "The Long and Tortured History of Cancel Culture," *New York Times,* December 3, 2020, https://www.nytimes.com/2020/12/03/t-magazine/cancel-culture-history.html.

19. Aja Romano, "Joaquin Phoenix's Oscars Speech Was a Sprawling Sociopolitical Epic," *Vox,* February 10, 2020, https://www.vox.com/culture/2020/2/10/21130778/joaquin-phoenix-oscars-speech-awards-season.

20. Rollo Ross, "Cancel Culture Takes the Fun Out of Life, Says Comedian John Cleese," Reuters, July 21, 2020, https://www.reuters.com/article/us-people-john-cleese/cancel-culture-takes-the-fun-out-of-life-says-comedian-john-cleese-idUSKCN24M2QV.

21. D. Diane Davis, *Breaking Up (at) Totality: A Rhetoric of Laughter* (Carbondale: Southern Illinois University Press, 2000), 22.

22. Dan Reilly, "What *Joker* Gets Right bout Stand-Up Comedy," *Vulture,* October 15, 2019, https://www.vulture.com/2019/10/joker-gary-gulman-sam-morril-stand-up-comedy.html. See also Alex Abad-Santos, "The Fight over Joker and the New Movie's 'Dangerous' Message, Explained," *Vox,* September 25, 2019, https://www.vox.com/culture/2019/9/18/20860890/joker-movie-controversy-incel-sjw.

23. See Robert G. Weiner and Robert Moses Peaslee, introduction to *The Joker: A Serious Study of the Clown Prince of Crime* (Jackson: University Press of Mississippi, 2015), 15–31.

24. Ashley Cocksworth, "*The Dark Knight* and the Evilness of Evil," *Expository Times* 120 (2009): 541.

25. Glasgow, *Madness, Masks, and Laughter,* 155, 206, 212.

26. Louise Peacock, "Battles, Blows and Blood: Pleasure and Terror in the Performance of Clown Violence," *Comedy Studies* 11 (2020): 74.

27. Hyers, *Spirituality of Comedy,* 137.

28. Mikhail Bakhtin, *Rabelais and His World,* trans. Hélène Iswolsky (Bloomington: Indiana University Press, 1984), 400.

29. Benjamin Radford, *Bad Clowns* (Albuquerque: University of New Mexico Press, 2016).

30. Hyers, *Spirituality of Comedy,* 132.

31. Hyers, *Spirituality of Comedy,* 154.

32. Beatrice K. Otto, *Fools Are Everywhere: The Court Jester around the World* (Chicago: University of Chicago Press, 2001), 41.

33. Robert M. Polhemus, *Comic Faith: The Great Tradition from Austen to Joyce* (Chicago: Chicago University Press, 1980), 206.

34. John H. Towsen, *Clowns* (New York: Hawthorn Books, 1976), 9.

35. David B. Morris, *The Culture of Pain* (Berkeley: University of California Press, 1991), 98.

36. Hyers, *Spirituality of Comedy*, 163.

37. Morris, *Culture of Pain*, 101.

38. John Semley, "Corrupted Headspace: *Joker* and the Vacuity of Influence," *Baffler*, October 7, 2019, https://thebaffler.com/latest/corrupted-headspace -semley.

39. Semley, "Corrupted Headspace."

40. Danielle Fuentes Morgan, "Dave Chappelle the Comedy Relic," *Vulture*, October 21, 2021, https://www.vulture.com/article/dave-chappelle-the-comedy -relic.html.

41. Bakhtin, *Rabelais and His World*, 83.

42. Zack Sharf, "Quentin Tarantino Analyzes 'Joker' Climax: It Forces Viewers 'to Think Like a F*cking Lunatic,'" *IndieWire*, February 4, 2021, https:// www.indiewire.com/features/general/quentin-tarantino-analyzes-joker-climax -subverison-1234614892/.

43. Kenneth Burke, *The Philosophy of Literary Form: Studies in Symbolic Action* (Berkeley: University of California Press, 1967), 225, 229.

44. Burke, *Philosophy of Literary Form*, 343.

45. Bakhtin, *Rabelais and His World*, 235.

46. Bakhtin, *Rabelais and His World*, 237.

47. Davis, *Breaking Up (at) Totality*, 2.

48. Nick Reilly, "Kevin Smith Says Batman Was Killed Off in Alternative 'Joker' Ending," *NME*, December 31, 2019, https://www.nme.com/news/film /kevin-smith-says-joker-had-a-seriously-dark-alternative-ending-2591803.

49. Burke, *Philosophy of Literary Form*, 233.

50. Burke, *Philosophy of Literary Form*, 229.

FOUR

FOOLS ON THE HILL

Trumpsters and the Capitol Insurrection

THOSE WHO LAUGH ON THE gallows are usually the ones who are about to be executed. Sure, some undoubtedly take pleasure in tying the hangman's knot. But the fact that a scene of horror and distress can be made into a comic spectacle has to do with a kind of humor that comes from someone who sets their own laughable condition at a distance. Laughter here can function as an outburst of fear and trembling in the face of death. It can ring forth like peals of protest. More crucially, though, it can embrace sealed fate with *self*-mockery, and thereby laugh off certain doom by laughing at whoever may be the embodiment of Jack Ketch. And yet this proved not so at the US Capitol on January 6, 2021, when members of an insurrectionist mob erected a makeshift gallows as an apparent symbol of populist fervor in what amounted to a coup attempt in the wake of a legitimate presidential election.

Much has been said of Insurrection Day. What began as the fulfillment of a congressional duty to codify votes cast by the Electoral College morphed into a riotous scene. Hordes of supporters wishing to "stop the steal" and reject Joe Biden's victory over Donald J. Trump rallied on a promise to "save America." By midafternoon, as a joint session of Congress settled in the Senate Chambers to count the votes, the rally had become a riot and the People's House, the carnival ground for a violent attack on the Capitol. With particular attention to Confederate iconography, flags and figures of chauvinistic nationalism, conspiratorial ideologies in QAnon imagery, and an aura of white supremacist terror, many critics and commentators portrayed the insurrection as a culmination of the Big Lies and Lost Causes that fomented a rise of Trumpism in the first place. According to journalist Michael Sean Comerford, the Capitol siege represents the ultimate realization of a "dark carnival," with its dependence on a political culture made up of "alibi flimflam" and a "mingled sense of unreality and desire."[1] Similarly, historian Nancy Isenberg wrote about a gleeful embrace of "violent fantasies" that accompany Trumpism—fantasies that are rooted in "feelings of grievance, revenge, and alienation."[2] To simply assert that all of the rallygoers were insurrectionists in a furious mob is to miss the point that the crowd contained a mix of regular, cut-from-the-cloth Trumpsters (who, as it happens, were regulars at earlier Trump rallies), "white-supremacist warriors," and Christian nationalists goaded by a range of reasons for patriotism and pride.[3] It is also to ignore that the Capitol Insurrection was as much a moment of foolish festivity as political and cultural folly.

Indeed, an emphasis on the carnivalesque should give us pause. Beginning with Trump's now infamous descent down that escalator in the atrium of Trump Tower to announce his presidential candidacy in June 2015, the idea of a Trump presidency and with it the notion that a movement such as Trumpism could ever take hold was, for many, a joke—a fool's errand. On the campaign trail, Trump was a carnival barker. In everything from journalism to late-night television, he was depicted as a clown, and eventually an "insane clown president."[4] Famed comedian and "Most Trusted Name in Fake News" Jon Stewart hailed Trump as Fuckface von Clownstick when the two were embroiled in a social media feud. At the time of writing, Trump's candidacy for a second term along with the range of criminal indictments looming over it is widely regarded as a clown show. The thing is that these sentiments capture a much more widespread sense among political elites and media personalities and ordinary citizens that while Trump and Trumpism are a "big joke," the origins (and now outcomes) of the dark carnival are anything but.[5] Insurrection Day was, for some, a 1776 moment. It was a glimpse of the Second Civil War, if not a Second American Revolution. Worse, it was a *cruel* day of celebration. As Emily Nussbaum argues, candidate Trump originally couched his cultural politics of racism, chauvinism, isolationism, misogyny, and more in "the thrill of hyperbole" and the comic delight "of treating the extreme as normal" when "the shock (and joy) of seeing the normal get violated" becomes a pretext for revelry.[6] Trump could therefore go after comedy as an inapt frame for dealing with *him* while utilizing a they-are-laughing-at-us scheme to provoke resentment and rage and ascend to the presidency as the Insult Comic in Chief.[7] In the words of Lawrence Grossberg, the carnival antics got where they got under the cover of chaos. For my part, if the chaos and cruelty and carnivaelsque festivity of the Capitol Insurrection (never mind Trumpism and the persistent MAGA [Make America Great Again] movement) are to be taken seriously, we must understand how they developed under the cover of comedy.

Insurrection Day is a prime example of comedy, and its carnivalesque footings, converted into a mainstream resource for doing politics by "killing" perceived adversaries. As detailed in previous chapters, there is a politics of comic display at work in the exploits of cancel culture to kill comedy and in the retaliations of some comedians. In the case of Trumpism and the Capitol Insurrection, a carnival spirit constitutes the comic foil for an element of authoritarian populism that runs deep in the US American tradition.[8] The appearance of that jarringly recognizable frame for performing executions, complete with a crossbeam and noose, necessitates our attention to a *comic* tradition that makes the so-called Death Cult of Trumpism make sense.[9] To focus on the comicality is to focus on how and why the Capitol Insurrection looked like a homegrown plot against America in the name of a "carnival king" even as it felt like a prank.[10]

This chapter begins with a look at the Capitol Insurrection as a carnival of comic expression and a demonstration of carnivalesque merriment pushed over the proverbial line. Costumes were cultural and political disguises. Vulgarity and vigilantism were vehicles for a strange mode of virtue signaling. Violence was a perversion of what Mikhail Bakhtin might describe as "narrow-minded seriousness and intolerance" and a substitute for the sort of "gay laughter" that counteracts any barefaced enjoyment in the sufferance of others.[11] The argument therefore moves toward an inquiry into the carnivalesque in US comic politics, especially as it relates to the maneuverings of political leaders and the paroxysms of rather undemocratic mobs. Finally, the conclusion establishes a basis for working through the lex talionis, the law of retaliation, baked into comedy that seems to be so prevalent in and around the age of Trumpism.

THE GROUNDS FOR CARNIVAL AND THE US CAPITOL AS CARNIVAL GROUNDS

In a carnival, the image of a person in the throes of death can constitute what Bakhtin might call a "comic gesture."[12] Let's put this in more historical terms. Hanging was the dominant form of capital punishment in colonial America and the only means of execution from the American Revolution through the end of Reconstruction. It was also a means of entertainment. Particularly in Boston in the 1760s, ordinary citizens would carry out "mock executions," mainly of Loyalists and British officials. People at these festive public events would delight in "liberty trees, liberty poles, hanging effigies, pulling down houses, tar-and-feathering, Indian disguises—the whole kit and caboodle of popular revolutionary rituals."[13] Hardly ever, though, did these ritualistic fetes feature

Fig. 4.1. The makeshift gallows erected during the Capitol Insurrection, with protesters gathered around. Photo by Sarah Sicard, senior editor for *Military Times*.

the image of a living political figure put to death, or a figure that might actually be "in their midst."[14] Such a feature would be too much like the real thing, as it was in the "carnivals of death" that emerged from a spectacle of racial violence with the lynching of Black people in the late nineteenth and early twentieth centuries.[15] And it would tempt the sanctimony of officialdom that lurks in the shadows of the carnivalesque. Carnival executioners are supposed to maintain a "laughing tone."[16] Outside the carnival, and absent a carnivalesque spirit, executioners do not laugh; they bark. Furthermore, images that betoken death throes in a mood of merry triumph betray revelry with serious comic flaws. So it was when clownish protesters stormed the Capitol, and when a coincident clownery motivated would-be insurrectionists to send political enemies to the gallows.

As the rally-turned-riot was ramping up, a gallows was erected near the reflecting pool (fig. 4.1). The wooden beams were clearly prefabricated. The noose was created from orange broadcasting cables that were pilfered from the Associated Press.[17] "Execute the traitors!" shouted one member of the crowd.[18] Others pretended to be a death mob. Eventually, there arose a chant that gestured to the assassination of the vice president. "Hang Mike Pence!"[19] The gallows was not just a stage for some mock execution. It was part of a staged festival—planned largely online through fringe social media outlets—for the ritual killing of anyone in power who was unwilling to overturn the 2020 presidential election and reinstall President Trump. Countless images from photojournalists reveal the gallows as the wooden frame for seeing the People's House in the backdrop. This framework became the site for a photo opportunity. People took turns posing on the structure. One person was draped in a Trump 2020 flag, grinning. Another held the noose with one hand and the Gadsden flag in the other. Yet another stood with her hand through the noose and a smile on her face. Another still kneeled on the platform with the noose around his neck and his fingers pointing to the sky. These were open-air gestures to criminality. The gallows was a perversely comic gesture. "Executing politicians?" wrote one commentator in response to the glibness with which so many in the crowd seemed to get on board with taking liberty by giving death. "Lulz."[20] Fun. Laughter. Amusement. Comic delight in the suffering of others. A carnival mystique.

Here's the trouble: the gallows was imagined as something more than a rhetorical means for the threat of violence. It was conceived as art. A white sign was affixed to the base of the scaffold. A statement stenciled in black letters read "THIS IS ART." The statement is laced with ironic conceit. According to cultural anthropologist Marilyn Ivy, it insinuates that "this is not really a machinery of execution," and "we aren't really going to hang Mike Pence, and by the way, what we say goes (and it's fun!)."[21] The perception of fellow feelings in the name of vigilante, terroristic enjoyment is commonplace among those who witnessed the "roiling festivities" that radiated from the gallows.[22] By one account, these were feelings of "half mutinous rage, half gleeful excitement."[23] The insurrectionists, like their seeming counterparts in the mock executioners of the American Revolution, were bound together as a "group of laughers" attempting to take down the "frauds and imposters" who dared to deny the will of the people.[24] Motives varied. Some were "eager for a spectacle." Others were "spoiling for a fight."[25] Regardless, the dark carnival was a source of power and fun.

Art like this is deathly ridiculous and yet seriously deadly. Specifically, *comic* art can feel like an act of "making a joke while watching a murder" when it appears in the midst of political crisis and cultural upheaval.[26] The irony in this art, as Bakhtin might remind us, is that it is too "devoid of true gaiety," too driven toward "*reduced* laughter."[27] What is more, the comic artfulness undercuts a carnival spirit when it perverts "the borderline between art and life."[28]

FOOLS ON THE HILL

Never more so than when it is couched in comedy, art is "active in expressing and conveying a system of values."[29] Carnival is a lived spectacle. Comedy can be a framework for political action. The stakes are changed when violence takes on a comic element such that fools and clowns imagine themselves as actual executioners and kings. The first trick, though, is to look the part.

A Travesty of the Carnivalesque

When Bakhtin imagined the "great power of travesty," he did so with the idea that comic distortions of a body politic and literal costume changes (i.e., a clown adorned in the regalia of a king) rendered people more humane, and playful, by making "the world more carnal."[30] Costume play, or cosplay, was rampant at the Capitol Insurrection. There were Marvel superheroes galore. People bedecked in MAGA merchandise. Some wore plastic face masks of Trump. Some wore camouflage. There were cavemen, gladiators, and men dressed up in colonial garb. An older gentleman dressed as Uncle Sam shouted directives through a megaphone. Others were clad in the aura of frontiersmen, hunters, and warriors. One man was dressed as Captain Moroni from the Book of Mormon. Collectively, they created "a thrilling juggler's fair with fluttering flags, caps and knitted hats (quite a few with pompoms), helmets and flak vests, masks (but not too many), hockey sticks and flagpoles, zip ties and bullhorns, baseball bats and nooses."[31] And this festival of fun turned into what those who are now called "coupologists" remember as a faux revolutionary moment that was ultimately undercut and—sadly—reinforced by calls for executions, the visible array of zip ties that could be used by insurrectionists to restrain politicians named traitors, Kevlar vests, and "a truck full of rifles, shotguns, and bomb-making supplies parked outside the RNC [Republican National Committee] headquarters" in the aftermath.[32] There is great power in travesty.

The thing is that a carnivalesque clown is supposed to be "disguised as a king" but then "travestied" so as to become a clown once again. "The abuse and thrashing" that Bakhtin delimits "are equivalent to a change of costume, to a metamorphosis," which "is the king's uncrowning."[33] During the Capitol Insurrection, disguises actually unmasked the facade of a carnival spirit in the act of keeping up false pretenses, with the comic guise serving as a *dis*guise for what ultimately became a "license for mayhem."[34] Insurrectionists left urine on the floors and fecal matter on the walls. Notwithstanding the aggression and cruelty that animated so much behavior outside, bodily functions of those who breached the Capitol became a resource for desecrating their own house. The costumes and the travesties did not make the political world more carnal. They made it, perversely, *more carnival.*

No one was more carnival*ish* than the self-styled QAnon Shaman, also known as the Yellowstone Wolf. His real name is Jacob Chansley, aka Jake Angeli. Once a navy man, he gained infamy as the QAnon Shaman when he made himself into something of a mascot for the Capitol Insurrection. In what are now widely circulated images, he can be seen with face painted red, white, and blue; a fur headdress with horns and coyote tails; and a shirtless torso that displayed a variety of tattoos. While there is much to be said about the comical co-optation of Native American iconography in Chansley's getup, just as noteworthy is the ink on his skin that showcased Thor's hammer, Mjölnir; the Norse world tree, Yggdrasill, which represents the organization of the cosmos with branches that stretch to the sky and roots that reach to the depths of the underworld; a Sonnenrad, or sun wheel, which has been used in Nazi imagery; and a valknut, comprised of three interlocked triangles to symbolize the glory of death in battle (hence its literal translation as "knot of the slain"), used by white supremacists as a symbol for what Trump's personal attorney, Rudy Giuliani, seemed to call for in his own speech at the initial "Save America" rally: "trial by combat."[35] When he entered the Capitol, Chansley wielded a spear and spouted conspiratorial slogans about liberty and republicanism. He yelled "freedom" at the top of his lungs when he stood in the Senate Chamber. He led fellow insurrectionists in a prayer to condemn what he called "the tyrants, the communists, and the globalists." They prayed at the dais, where Pence would traditionally sit. Chansley took the vice president's seat, announced that Pence is a "fucking traitor," posed for a picture, and then scrawled a note on the desk that read, "IT'S ONLY A MATTER OF TIME. JUSTICE IS COMING!"[36] Elsewhere, people were gleefully calling for the execution of reporters and the hanging of traitorous "motherfuckers."[37] A Bakhtinian carnival, a "second world," can certainly be a shit show. This incident was that and more.

As numerous accounts suggest, the QAnon Shaman and so many others looked "ridiculous" in their costumes.[38] One cultural critic saw in the QAnon Shaman a clownishness that mirrored that of Jack Napier when he transmogrifies into the Joker.[39] Another reporter maintained that Chansley, the shoddy spiritual leader, walked and talked "like some kind of racist Party City Viking."[40] Under the not-so-subtle cover of this ridiculousness is the replacement of political activism with violence and comicality with vulgarity in cultural politics. There are parallels to the early history of Ku Klux Klan (KKK) rallies when members would kit out with "animal horns, fur, fake bears," and those iconic "pointy hats," all making for "homemade costumes that drew on traditions of carnival or Mardi Gras."[41] There are resonances of southern pride and paramilitarism, Lost Causes and pretend heroics, with Proud Boys and

Oath Keepers and even suburbanites living "the life of the carnival square, free and unrestricted," blaspheming, profaning, debasing, and being obscene.[42] Hence a tendency in some circles is to see the costumes as comic masks for racism, white nationalism, and extreme right-wing politicking and to imagine the festive space of the Capitol Insurrection not as one for popular revelry but rather as a realm of Old Americanism and nationalistic heritage masquerading as democratic protest. These vestiges of Indigenous war cultures and of animism as some exoticized form of American mysticism and of the colonial frontier undergird what is really a subculture of "Violent Trumpism."[43] It is no surprise, then, that the costumes resemble a "comic deniability" in the sartorial rhetoric of the KKK.[44] The "wild comedy" that unfolded was an extension of "the ludicrous culture inside the Oval Office" and the foolish absurdities of stolen elections and other Big Lies.[45] The dark carnival *became* officialdom.

It would be one thing if the Capitol Insurrection really was a festive ritual and really was a second life for comedy outside the mainstream. But it was not. The costumed insurrectionists were not denying anything. They may have since expressed their remorse and regret in the face of lawsuits and jail sentences. However, there was no denial of anything other than the legitimacy of a democratic process. The carnival spirit was the inspiration for a corruption of comedy into uncritical civic engagement and antidemocratic wildness. This spirit was everywhere in the costume party coup, including the religious imagery (i.e., large wooden crosses, placards with depictions of Jesus wearing a red MAGA hat, a "Jesus Saves" sign on display near the gallows) that evoked a Christian nationalism still on the rise and shot through with "assumptions of nativism, white supremacy, patriarchy, and heteronormativity, along with divine sanction for authoritarian control and militarism."[46] It was a motivating factor for the comic violence of insurrection. In addition, it was an impetus for a carnival mob to do harm.

The Fuck-Yous and Middle Fingers

Watch any number of live streams and social media posts and videos uploaded on microblogging platform for Far Right extremists and conservative conspiracy theorists Parler, and you will quickly discover that "fuck you" and "fucking" this or that and "motherfucker" are among the most prevalent expressions that came from the crowd on January 6, 2021. There is a pretext and catalyst in the "politics of white rage" that Trump broadcast throughout his "Twitter Presidency."[47] By the end of his first year in office, the daily routine seemed as abhorrent as it was predictable: "Another day, another vulgar Trump tweet."[48] In the lead-up to the Capitol Insurrection, Trump tweeted with anything that could be confused as a riddle wrapped in an enigma. At rallies, he urged supporters to "take back" what was lost in the election. He advertised a "big protest." He tweeted incessantly about election fraud. In mid-December, his message on Twitter about January 6, 2021, was simple: "Be there, will be wild." There was going to be festivity, but there was also going to be a fight to accompany all the fighting words. This bore out with the sheer volume of individuals who flipped off Capitol officers, gave the bird to the sky during photo opportunities, and generally flashed a one-finger salute at anything that could be a target for their comedy and contempt.

In some ways, this sort of vulgarity should be expected in a carnival atmosphere. Obscenities and abuses are familiar in these contexts, and they are blended with what is otherwise sacred. The vulgar profanities here overlap with oaths, which—as Bakhtin reminds us—can be similar in origin as well as "ideological and artistic function."[49] The carnival of the Capitol Insurrection was not about festivity in joyfulness or a regenerative comic mood. It was about promoting some version of American greatness that confused not only the cultural but also the comic frame. With a wildness and looseness and revelry once common in the carnival theatrics of antebellum mobs, countless participants shouted out for Republican congresspersons to keep their oaths. One rationale stood out: "1776, bitch."[50] The proclamations and profanations spiraled out from there.

Even before the Capitol was ransacked, the crowd chanted things like "America first!" and "Bullshit!" People railed against "fucking cocksucking Commies!" Politicians who were going to codify Biden's election were "scumbags," an affront that proved itself a precursor to cries about betrayal and calls for ritual hangings. A couple of months earlier, following violence that broke out at the Million MAGA March from Freedom Plaza to the Supreme Court, then president Trump tweeted that it was "ANTIFA SCUM"—or contemptible followers of a loose-knit antifascist protest group—who were really to blame for any postelection unrest, not Proud Boys or Oath Keepers or any right-wing death squads selling the revolution, as it were. On Insurrection Day, there was a generalized "fuck you spirit" that gave a sense of merriment to the menace.[51] Counterprotesters slung their own insults, calling insurrectionists brainwashed Nazis and lambasting them for supporting the will of a wannabe dictator. These insults and lambastes were largely dismissed or, at least, overwhelmed by exclamations like "Fuck Black Lives Matter" and by the exploits of Far Right white nationalists, so-called groypers, shouting profanities as they channeled the online activism and provocations that overlap with the internet meme Pepe the Frog.[52] To profane here was to keep a solemn promise—and to have fun.

In that spirit, there seemed to be an oath among many insurrectionists to see that House Speaker Pelosi meet her comeuppance. Members of the Oath Keepers were actively trying to find Pelosi as they stormed the Capitol. "We want to hang that fucking bitch," one woman yelled from the crowd.[53] Soon after he breached the gates and entered the building, self-avowed white nationalist and QAnon devotee Richard "Bigo" Barnett made his way to Pelosi's office, took a seat in her chair, and kicked back with his feet on her desk. Her office then became a festal space for the carnivalesque. Another insurrectionist parroted Jack Torrance, the demented caretaker of the Overlook Hotel in 1980s horror film *The Shining* (1980). "Nancy, I'm *ho-ome!*" he jeered.[54] Others took pleasure in stealing "shit" from her office.[55] Bigo wrote what he later described as a "nasty note." "Nancy," it read, "Bigo was here, you bitch." He left it on her desk. After leaving the building with pepper spray on his face, laughter on his breath, and a piece of Pelosi's letterhead in his hand (which he said he paid for by leaving a quarter behind), Bigo "stood outside the Capitol, his shirt ripped open and his chest bared to the cold, loudly bragging about how he had broken into the speaker's office."[56] Bigo was arrested days later and ultimately charged with federal crimes. As part of his defense, he tried to claim that he did not write "bitch" in the note; he wrote *biatd*—a "made-up sillytime word" that, in the argument, did more to mock the gravity of his actions than to absolve him of guilt.[57] He even solicited money from followers on his personal website by selling signed photographs of him sitting at Pelosi's desk. The pretense was to raise funds for his legal fees. True enough. Although a vast majority of the crowd wreaked havoc on the Capitol with antidemocratic joyful abandon, many others could be seen just "milling around."[58] A carnivalgoer is as a carnivalgoer does. The wrongheadedness of the carnivalesque stands out most for its mockery of re-generation and renewal with overt bigotry and resentment.

Consider what this mockery communicates. It is a comic virtue to make use of personal liberties in the act of vigilantism as a collective expression of national character. It is a comic virtue to transform the perilous rage that comes with deep-seated umbrage and bilious anger as expressions of some traditional aesthetic of US Americanism. This rage is an outgrowth of old-world orderings that urge people to begrudge change and get charged up by a new birth of freedom in Trumpism. There are undoubtedly a great many believers in the idea that the 2020 presidential election was tainted by fraud. Yet it is much more the case that so many who stormed the Capitol did so under the comic guise of self-defense, not convinced of any real fraudulence but rather strong in the conviction that some vision of America, some ingrained idea of the American Way, was being lost—indeed, stolen.

Such a comic guise goes well beyond any withdrawal of support for people or things deemed unjust, which is typified by cancel culture. It gets into the realm of rhetorical appeals to who and what belongs; to institutionalized cultural politics that have been codified in media systems and that are still basking in the long shadow of the fairness doctrine; and to centuries of racial, ethnic, and other forms of intolerance. The vulgarity that emerged out of the mock solemnity during the Capitol Insurrection represents an American tradition, no question. This tradition is likewise a comic tradition, albeit not in any classical sense traceable to the founders. This tradition lies in the ideals of rebels who revel in the carnival of revolution, what Bakhtin might see as the "avarice, jealousy, stupidity, hypocrisy, bigotry, sterile senility, false heroism, and abstract idealism."[59] It culminates in violence as a last resort and as a last laugh for those pronouncing their faith in a civil religion. But what of violence as part and parcel of sacrificing something on the altar of comedy?

The Violence, Stupid—That's the Trump Card

Well before the Capitol Insurrection, it was widely reported that Trump was serious whenever he "joked" about inciting violence.[60] His threats to political enemies as slobs and losers and sons of bitches were commonplace. This was no less the case throughout his bid for a second term in 2024, except those ramped-up threats to prosecute and imprison political opponents. He had no problem announcing to a crowd of supporters his own desire to punch rivals in the face when they showed up at MAGA rallies. On Twitter, the president would spin reporting of anything deemed bad about the goings-on at the White House with cartoonish videos, such as one he circulated in condemnation of the Fake News Network, FNN (a play on the Cable News Network, CNN) that "featured old footage repurposed for a new world" with a "pre-White House Donald Trump engaged in a bit of theatrical violence that played out during a 2007 WrestleMania event" wherein "the pre-president . . . body-slammed and then repeatedly punched another man" whose face was masked by the CNN logo.[61] In late March 2024, amid his bid to retake the White House, Trump posted a video on his alt-tech digital media platform, Truth Social. The video captured a pickup on Long Island, the tailgate of which contained a decal with a photorealistic image of President Biden, looking as if he was hog-tied in the bed of the truck. Beside the decal was a bumper sticker with the acronym FJB: Fuck Joe Biden. Within this framework, insurrection is part appeal to the ultimate political sacrifice and part play on comedic violence.

The violence, though, was very real. There is an online FBI archive for videos and images of violence at the Capitol from that day. There is evidence of

FOOLS ON THE HILL

unlawful entry, destruction of property, and vandalism. More disturbing are the accounts of insurrectionists fighting with cops and counterprotesters and of officers responding by firing rubber bullets and deploying tear gas. Countless people were injured, including over one hundred members of the Capitol Police. Nearly ten people died. One rioter was shot and killed. An officer was beaten to death. Others were trampled. As many people were equipped for battle as they were geared up to be "overgrown children play-acting as revolutionaries."[62] It was enough to render the carnival grounds of the Capitol a quasi-combat zone. In the comic tradition, satire regularly melded with outrage in the carnival image of American revolutionaries "tarring and feathering and carting along figures in effigy" as acts of protest.[63] These protests were projections of violence. By and large, the real weapons and true war footings were reserved for the battlefield.

There is good reason to highlight the overlap of comic frameworks with violent festivity in this political carnival. Prior to the event, online organizers urged attendees to bring guns and ammunition. Social media platforms advertised the enlistment of a "Pepe army." In Parler forums, posters presaged the execution of traitors. Even before the immediate buildup to January 6, the cumulative effect of Trump rallies had the (comic) effect of a call to arms. What ultimately unfolded might be described as symbolic violence in the wild desecration of the People's House, with insurrectionists shitting on democracy. These same people added insults to injuries by deriding officers as "filthy rats," echoing Trump's claim in July 2019 that the Baltimore district represented by renowned civil rights advocate Elijah Cummings is a "disgusting, rat and rodent infested mess."[64] The violence was thus a by-product of the purification rite that appeared to be a prime mover for costumed rioters to act as if they were reliving a revolutionary moment, reviving the Lost Cause of the Confederacy, or even restoring the acceptability of a KKK parade.[65] No wonder there was a sense that one might go to one's reward in a fit of laughter that could trump the fit of rage.

Violence is the Trump card here not because it represents the lengths to which insurrectionists would go or the political might (and sense of cultural righteousness) they held in reserve. It is the Trump card because of its attachments to comedy and consequence. Cruel humor is integral to the carnivalesque. As the last chapter demonstrated, though, clowning around risks the danger of wrath when paired with wretched sociopathy in a comic mood.

This is not a sentiment meant to be taken lightly. Trump is (and was) widely regarded as a clown president—even an *insane* clown president. During his presidency and up to and through his bid for a second term, he has been referred to across media platforms, and from a variety of intellectual vantages, as a sociopath.[66] Countless critics and commentators, as well as legal professionals and scholars—to say nothing of former cabinet officials and political loyalists—call him a man with narcissistic personality disorder. In the wake of Trump's own proclamation that if he took back the White House he would be a dictator on day one, ghostwriter for *Trump: Art of the Deal* (1987) Tony Schwartz warned that Trump was trying hard to turn Trumpism into Red Caesarism.[67] Schwartz issued a similar warning before Trump took office.[68] A member of Trump's own family, niece and clinical psychologist Mary Trump, pronounced that sociopathy was a trait passed on down from his father and that it had long led relatives to see Trump as little more than a "clown."[69] George Conway, who is a lawyer, an anti-Trump activist, and former husband of strategist, pollster, and senior adviser to Trump Kellyanne Conway, actually started the playful but serious Anti-Psychopath Political Action Committee in 2024 to highlight the forty-fifth president's narcissistic sociopathology as a means of forestalling his return to the White House. These sentiments are manifest in principles that motivate a comic basis for doing things and the manifestation of those principles in practice.

Any references to violence and cruelty and clownishness should therefore be taken seriously, especially given some of their referents. In a skit entitled "Welcome to President Trump's Reality," which appeared on *The Daily Show* in January 2017 soon after Trump gave his first exclusive interview to ABC News, host Trevor Noah suggested that the president should don Joker makeup (à la Heath Ledger's depiction). Why? Because of the president's dire rhetoric about the world being "an angry place" and his supposed insinuation that the American people are his hostages.[70] In November 2019, President Trump screened *Joker* (the version with Joaquin Phoenix as the Clown Prince of Crime) at the White House and professed his enjoyment of the film. It reflected, he said, his own criticism of Hollywood elites and the liberal establishment.[71] Avowed white supremacist Paul Miller soon thereafter grew fond of dressing up like the Joker and producing social media content on Bitchute and Telegram to promote race wars and advocate for violent political activities in line with the so-called boogaloo movement, underwritten by the antigovernment "joke" that a second Civil War would be the new Electric Boogaloo. Far Right conspiracy theorist and onetime editor-at-large of Alex Jones's site *InfoWars* Paul Joseph Watson trumpeted *Joker*'s message. "The movie," he declared, "holds up a mirror to how a society that humiliates, shames, and disenfranchises people is itself responsible for generating violence."[72] This aligns with premonitions that the sequel, *Joker: Folie à Deux*, would make the Far Right and the Far Left into mirror images of each other. It is also in line with Trump being named by satirist and comedy writer Andy Borowitz the 2019 Person of the Year for *Popular Sociopath* magazine.[73]

Some of this amounts to a joke. Some of it is deadly serious. Regardless, it is not funny that the egoistic tendencies inherent to Trumpism bleed into the violent behaviors of those who, at times, seem to be carrying out rather clownish politics. At the Capitol Insurrection, this egoism revealed itself as the crux of political and cultural in-groupness. Call it a mob mentality. Call it mass mobilization. Call it a cult of personality. Whatever the signifier, insurrectionists appeared much like comic actors capitalizing on their license to say and do whatever they want without responsibility—and yet with seditious aims exhibited as at once "fundamentally unserious and deeply dangerous."[74] This is the theme that runs through Trump's speech that incited insurrectionists to action. It is the theme of coupologists and participants in the movement Justice for J6. It is the theme of any dismissal of January 6 that belies the gravity of what could have happened had the coup attempt succeeded, including Trump's 2024 campaign appeal to imprisoned J6ers as "hostages." And it is the freedom of comedy, and the comedy of freedom, that should make us wary of the carnivalesque when it is seen through a comic lens, darkly.

SOMETHING COMIC THIS WAY COMES

The very structure of political and cultural feeling just described has its own comic tradition. Beyond the gallows, people sported "combat gear, MAGA hats, star-spangled hoodies, coonskin hats, superhero costumes, ghillie suits, [and] flag capes," and they flashed symbols and slogans that ranged from Uncle Sam to QAnon and from the Confederate flag to mantras like "Trust the Plan."[75] Tellingly, when faux news anchor for *The Daily Show with Trevor Noah* Jordan Klepper recounted what he saw at the Capitol Insurrection, his observations and interactions were decidedly similar to those from his earlier attempts in a recurring segment to "finger the pulse" of Trump supporters at MAGA rallies. Klepper noted a certain "charge" in the crowd's energy.[76] This charge can now be understood, in part, as what we call "charged humor," repelling detractors but attracting those who want to flip the script on comedies of cultural difference and promote social dominance, entitlement, and even prejudice as key characteristics of belonging. One man was wielding a pitchfork. Klepper asked him why. Because it is an "iconic representation," the man replied. For agriculture, I suppose. Still, when Klepper pressed him on what the pitchfork might represent in a moment of insurrectionary action, the man elided any hints of

Christian symbolism and devilish forces (despite the white flag with the words "AN APPEAL TO HEAVEN" hanging from the farming tool), not to mention a brand of populism that coincides with angry mobs on witch hunts. Klepper confronted another man who was racing toward the Capitol on a self-balancing electric scooter. "Is this the last stand?" Klepper shouted as he ran alongside the man. "They say it is!" he replied. Klepper could not help but make fun of the comic dissonance of a man ascending the Capitol steps as a victim of the very democratic edifice on which he was mounting an attack.

The (comic) appeal to a last stand is fitting. At the height of Trump's presidency, columnist for the *New York Times* Roger Cohen detected a fateful sense that the combination of defensiveness and aggression in attitudes about nationhood, cultural identity, whiteness, and other touchstones of the MAGA movement is underwritten by a defiant feeling of true Americanism.[77] Call it Trump culture. Call it Trumpland. Its framework is built on a fight-to-the-death form of defiance. In the words of sociologist Arlie Russell Hochschild, it relies on a "dreampolitick realm" wherein realistic fantasies of democratic politics and cultural life can be played out as fantastical realities.[78] The comic extremes of this political phantasmagoria predate the insurrection. In May 2020, for example, hundreds of people gathered outside the Michigan State Capitol building to rail against Governor Gretchen Whitmer's support for coronavirus restrictions. A man in the crowd protested with a fishing pole that was strung with an American flag and a brunette doll—obviously an effigy of Whitmer. The doll was hanging from a noose. Similarly enraged protesters in New York called for Dr. Anthony Fauci, the president's chief medical adviser, to be hanged. Throughout his presidential candidacy, what many saw as Trump's protofascism was nonetheless interpreted as carnival barking. From these seemingly farcical reenactments to the misfortunes of the Capitol Insurrection, Trump was a kingly fool acting as a foolish king. Over and again he hailed those railing and rallying against stay-at-home measures as liberators. No matter how vile or vicious his rhetoric, it was always shown forth with the willfulness of someone who is as unwilling to bend to the will of his critics as he is to break from the carnival spirit.

Herein lies the rhetorical force of cruelty in his comic appeal. There is real anger in Trumpism. Real outrage. Real resentment. A real sense of loss. Of ownership. More disturbing is that Lost Causes, Big Lies, criminality, and more have been tapped as resources for making fun. The rallies that typified a MAGA carnivalesque long before January 6, 2021, are replete with much of what defines Trump's comedy: "the insults, the mean jokes, the apocryphal stories about killing Muslims with bullets dipped in pigs' blood or humiliating Mexico by forcing them to pay for a wall on the southern border."[79] As journalist Adam Serwer puts it, for all of its nationalistic politics and cultural warmongering, Trumpism is by and large a "spectacle of cruel laughter" that thrives on "the suffering of others."[80] This changes what it means to "get" jokes (or not) when objects of ridicule are excluded by default or brought into the comic frame only as specimens of mockery and scorn. It allows jokes to insulate nonjokes. It makes the moniker of a mob boss that much more apt as a comic designation. It makes a "carnival atmosphere" that might have begun with at least some "merriment and foolery" end in all the seriousness and piety of bad blood, bad faith, and bad humor.[81] Evidence of this appears in the black flags with pirate skulls and crossbones and the words "give us liberty or death" together with "1776" that flew alongside red MAGA flags. They flew in the same air as Kekistan flags, which look like Nazi war flags except that they are green with a Kek logo in the middle emblematizing a satirical religion contrived by white nationalist Trump supporters to mock left-wing movements by promoting praise for a frog-headed "god of chaos and darkness."[82] Remarkably, Kek is synonymous with LOL, laugh out loud. Attach Kek to a cultural or political message and you get a joke based on the conversion of an ancient Egyptian deity, Kek, into a cartoon frog. The art of comic fealty.

Like the gallows "art," such cruel artfulness serves as a foil for the kingdom of Trump. Neither is very far removed from phrases like "Let's Go, Brandon," an epigram to suggest that President Biden should go fuck himself, nor from the rallying cry to "Hang Mike Pence." After all, at the same time as the fantasy of literally uncrowning a vice president looked as though it could become a reality, President Trump reportedly "joked" that hanging Mike Pence might not be such a bad idea.[83]

We should have seen this coming. As with the arrival of Mr. Dark to Green Town in Ray Bradbury's fantastical novel, *Something Wicked This Way Comes* (1962), so with the descent of then candidate Trump down that elevator. When the carnival comes, Bradbury writes, it comes with "death like a rattle in one hand" and "life like candy in the other."[84] Fear gives way to festivity, rage to folly, the strange to the familiar. Carnival worlds are not simply exaggerated parodies or lampoons of the "real" world. They are by-products of that world. They are part of it. They exist only in their interanimation. To think this or that dark carnival is some punctuated event is to miss the point that the carnival "goes on—and on and on."[85] A month before the anniversary of January 6, the city of Phoenix hosted AmericaFest. One commentator described the four-day event as "a carnival of right-wing nationalism" and "fun-filled fascism."[86] The thing is that these carnival spirits do not only come with particularly American ways of deploying "propaganda [and] demagoguery" or of "intimidating, and fearmongering" to encourage people "to repudiate their country's foundational principles."[87] With Trump, they come with the "comedic trick" of provoking laughter as grease to the skids of "sign-waving, fist-pumping, [and] rabble-rousing roars."[88] These are features, not bugs, of cruel humor, and they come with a particular comic tradition.

Carnival Beginnings and Ends without Endings

Throughout America's history, people have predicted the death of democracy. It is hard to imagine that many of those living through the American Revolution thought democracy might be dead on arrival. When citizens watched Washington burn during the War of 1812, it would be easy to think that they thought democracy, too, might be set afire, and yet it sparked the Era of Good Feelings. In the early twentieth century, in the long shadow of world wars, American democracy "staggered, weakened by corruption, monopoly, apathy, inequality, political violence, hucksterism, racial injustice, unemployment, even starvation."[89] The revolutionary spirit is in part a *comic* spirit. Then again, we are accustomed to dealing with comedy that deploys humor to upset and interrupt human folly, not ignore it. The carnival element here might beckon what Henry Carlisle once pronounced as "the death of the comic spirit in America."[90]

The kind of "death" being summoned here is "a regenerating and laughing death."[91] It is the kind that keeps carnage out of comedy and clowns away from cults. Unfortunately, any spirit—of 1776, of a wartime triumphalism, of the comic—can be co-opted. Consider the Trump administration's 1776 Commission. Consider the twenty-first-century iterations of "Don't Tread on Me" and the Gadsden flag and the persistent Lost Cause of the Confederacy. Consider "Trump the Man" vis-à-vis "Trump the Spirit."[92] Consider Project 2025 and what Batya Ungar-Sargon described during an appearance on *Real Time with Bill Maher* as its ironic promise of political revenge, uncivil religion, and autocracy.[93] These are the makings of a comic tradition that needs to be better understood, especially since its carnivalesque features were decades in the making. From the rise of Rush Limbaugh and conservative talk radio in the late 1980s through to the age of Trumpism, carnival itself has been variously used as a term of abuse and as a comic appeal to American greatness made grotesque.

Revolution is no carnival. It is, however, a time of change and disorder and confusion in which everyone's bearings are a bit off. The American Revolution was an obvious boon for democratic self-governance. Even more, it established the basis for a collective egotism that, in a democratic society, seems foolish.

FOOLS ON THE HILL

Yankee Doodle was a rugged individual. He was also a comic figure of mockery, used by British soldiers to deride their American counterparts. He was, as his name testifies, a doodle—a fool. Similar notions of self-reliance and individualism appear in later figures like Rip Van Winkle, who embodies a comic spirit that takes delight in democratic messiness and the folly of shared governance as a means to express the gall to laugh, together. These sentiments persist in ongoing rural and urban divides, paranoia about government overreach, and tensions between things like progressivism and globalism. Revolutionary moments instigate clashes between old worlds and imagined frontiers. The carnival "is revolution itself," says Bakhtin.[94] Carnivals can help society circle back to *what was* in the process of working out *what could be*.

These are crucial founding principles. They provide a way to understand the comic tradition from a dark side of the American revolutionary spirit. The clownishness, showmanship, opportunism, egomania, and megalomania of Trumpism are deeply rooted in American history. In the antebellum South, for example, a "comic diabolism" pervaded the Peculiar Institution, particularly the festive atmosphere of the slave trade.[95] At auctions, slaves put on a spectacle of sufferance that was overshadowed by "fun and frolic," from their own singing and dancing to the "comic antics" of auctioneers.[96] In the 1920s, the KKK had gone mainstream, as had Christian fundamentalism and ideologies of America First. While the twentieth century saw a rise of the New Woman and the New Negro, it also saw by the 1950s a rise of the New Right. Conservatism became a tool for being political without any ordinary engagement in public affairs. The first chapter outlined how much these other means had to do with media institutions and cults of political personalities. The spiritedness of this movement made a sense of authoritarian individualism into the collective power for reducing American traditions to friend-enemy relations. This spiritedness reveals the fact that in the midst of what was widely deemed the golden age of political comedy (i.e., the reign of Jon Stewart and Stephen Colbert), the comic impulses of carnival became the motives for everyday politicking.

The Life and Death of Comedy

The problem here is twofold. On one hand, there is the homegrown specter of folly in Ugly Americanism. It is a truism that comedy, at least in the United States, is a tradition of the Left and one that animated a so-called Stewart-Colbert Effect. In that tradition is a slew of jokes about conservatives as "narrow minded, book banning, truth censoring, mean spirited; ungenerous, envious, intolerant, afraid; chicken, bullying; trivially moral, falsely patriotic; family cheapening, flag cheapening, God cheapening; the common man, shallow, small, sanctimonious."[97] These "real" Americans, these holdovers from the two Americas, are a laughingstock. They are conspiratorial thinkers. They are dupes. They are the Trumpsters who carried out a carnivalesque feast of indulgence, impropriety, and vulgarity, with a president as their carnival king and comedy as a façade for conducting politics in bad faith.

This leftist tradition continues in various comic responses to the Capitol Insurrection, like a satirical commemoration produced by *The Late Show with Stephen Colbert* on January 6, 2022, that mimicked the song "Seasons of Love" from the Broadway musical *Rent*.[98] The commemorative video, entitled "Abhor-Rent," puts new lyrics over the musical number, with a mournful chorus singing about the 525,600 minutes it has been "since feces were smeared" and dissidents like "one Viking Shaman" and "defectors," "infectors," "huge douchebags," and "asswipes" staged an "unsuccessful coup." The condemnatory lyrics are accompanied by still images of the insurrection, with the video culminating in a punch line that makes fun of the "real" traitors: complicit politicians and one scum of a president. *The Daily Show with Trevor Noah* did something similar when it put up temporary monuments in New York City to commemorate "Heroes of the Freedomsurrection." Far from doing any real comedic work of revaluation, these responses perpetuate the familiar comic effect of preaching to the choir, which might be why there seemed to be such trouble in making fun of Trump and his supporters in the first place. Truthiness in the age of Trumpism became Trumpiness, or a condition in which something doesn't even need to feel true to be acted on as truth, and people ran with it. They embodied "comic victims," killing the laughter of their assailants with the foolhardiness of their own "dogmatic laughter."[99] How do you deal with a democratic populace made up of an in-group that refuses to take a joke and yet personifies a comedy of antidemocracy that celebrates grudges and rancor and severe dislike for those supposedly on the wrong sides of cultural and political disputes? And how do you deal with comedy like this when it cuts both ways?

One approach is to recognize that we have gone wrong with our conceptualizations of comedy and grown too comfortable calling something comedy or not. Scholars who wrestle with what is comic and what is humorous, in addition to countless thought leaders in popular culture, tend to draw unexceptional conclusions about comedy and humor. Dannagal Goldthwaite Young, for instance, recently examined how irony and outrage have represented competing political aesthetics. According to Young, it makes sense that Rush Limbaugh, Bill O'Reilly, Sean Hannity, Ann Coulter, and others on the Right came from the same political and cultural conditions that merge politics and entertainment as Stewart, Colbert, Samantha Bee, Noah, and others on the Left. Still, she concludes that one aesthetic (irony) is comic while the other (outrage) is not. Young therefore makes the consequent claim that even if he is a quasi-comedian, and even if he makes jokes, Trump is "noncomic."[100] The sense of humor that defines Trumpism is really a sense of humorlessness. It is the comic sense of an agelast. Young makes a good case. Others do, too, like James E. Caron when he suggests that something should only be deemed comic if it contributes to a public sphere wherein laughter is provoked so as to rouse honest debate and real opportunities for changing minds.[101] Still, such conclusions are limited by the unwillingness to accept irony and outrage, or what Caron calls "the domain of the laughable," with regard to not only different iterations of comedy but also iterations that meet in the same comic space. Comedians in the Trump era are outraged. More and more apologists for Trumpism pawn off expressions of their politics and policy preferences as jokes. Here again we discover why there is such a struggle to treat Trumpism comically (because of how comical are some of its tenets) and to treat the outrageousness of its adherents as comedic. The celebrated comedy of "fake news" furnished by Stewart and Colbert is the conceptual, truly the cultural and political, fodder for the operationalization of "fake news" in the age of Trumpism.

There is more. In *Irony in an Age of Empire* (2008), Cynthia Willet suggests that comedy retains the resources to "combat oppression and instill cooperation" in society.[102] The limits of freedom are the limits of comedy. As such, we need to bolster what Willet renders the "libidinally charged obligations of the comic realm" if we are to make good democratic use of irrationality and conflict.[103] Willet makes good use of Bakhtin and the carnivalesque in her conceptualization. We need to recognize, though, that Trumpism—and, more evocatively, the Capitol Insurrection—does precisely what "good" comedy should do. It turns the tables. In Bakhtin's words, the "carnival crowd" is one that puts its comic freedoms to the test by playing on political and cultural decrepitude by breaking with "the usual norms of social relations."[104] This act of "breaking with" defines a certain freedom of comic expression. At the Capitol Insurrection, a crowd took liberties to violate and do violence in the name of crossing lines but also rejuvenating or regenerating a preferred world order. The cruelty and chaos on display were festive. Those who feel oppressed, and who grow resentful and, shall we say, "libidinally charged," can come in their own comic ways "to prefer an authoritarian government of *their own people* over authentic freedom."[105] Put differently, if carnival can turn the tables of political cultures and cultural politics, then comedy, too, can turn the tables on the fools and follies of carnival. What might otherwise lead to charged humor can then lead to a perversion of the comic spirit.

None of this is to suggest that Caron, Willet, Young, and others are alone (let alone wrong) in their attempts to redeem comedy. Neither is it to cast judgment on in-groups or out-groups of Trumpism. The fact that comedy since ancient times has been looked on for its capacity to humanize and humble us is a reminder of just how valid our shared interest is in taking stock of the ugliest aspects of ourselves. Ugliness in the carnivalesque signals something that is messy and incomplete. Any wrongheadedness comes from this messiness, this incompleteness. We might therefore need to operate less on a concept of what comedy could or should be than on how it is operationalized as a real-world idea.

Let us start by making some connections to reckonings that do not begin with comedy. Grossberg, for instance, argues that the Trump presidency established how what he sees as the "Reactionary Right" presumes "the possibility of an insurrectionary-civil-war" that is "based on a politics opposed to the national government derived from the states' rights, strict constitutionalism and white supremacism," and "no small amount of laughter."[106] In other words, all the paranoia, racism, misogyny, xenophobia, and conceit that often get attached to "real" Americans are tied up with "forms of 'carnivalesque' behavior" that enables people to turn feelings of resentment and rage into political acts of humiliation.[107] Henry Giroux argues similarly when he observes that Trump's most impressive rhetorical feat was to reduce politics itself "to a carnival of unbridled narcissism, deception, spectacle, and overloaded sensation."[108] Recall how often Trump would proclaim that *they* are laughing at *us*. Recall, too, his tendentious goad to make *them* into a joke. This gets at what I meant earlier when I suggested that Trumpism, and the Capitol Insurrection besides, developed under the cover of comedy. There is historical precedent for this sort of cover in politics. The political animal first conceived by Aristotle is one and the same as the laughing animal. Democratic politics can be deliberative. But they can be just as replete with the kinds of "animal, jesting, roguish, [and] foolish" antics that arouse a carnivalesque spirit.[109] This can make political work comic. It can also make it "corrosive."[110] The challenge is to figure out what to do with a comic mood that inspires a carnival mob.

This challenge is exacerbated by the fact that Trumpism provokes the "permanent carnival" that has led Lauren Berlant and Sianne Ngai to take issue with comedy.[111] Of course, their issue remains caught up in the trap of wondering whether something is or is not comedy, and whether comedy is as such when it is repurposed for tyrannical or undemocratic or oppressive comic effects. Comedy is as comedy does. This means we should be concerned about whether it does the work of the carnivalesque, for instance, or the work of democracy—or both, together. Or neither! What happens to our view of comedy when we imagine it *as* free expression or *as* the enactment of egalitarianism or the shared pursuit of life, liberty, and happiness? H. L. Mencken observed that when democracy becomes a carnival, and when comedy becomes an "egotistical trade" for the "obscene clownings" of political actors aiming to please people as "creatures of bitterness and *ressentiment*,"[112] all the laughter in the world cannot overcome the bunkum of comic debasement. Here comedy is not so much ambivalent as it is based on conflicting senses of who fits in and who does not, who should make fun and who should be made fun of, who plays the fool and who gets to be king.

Democracy can become anarchical, and comedy despotic. A madcap of the carnival can become the "distinguishing mark" of a democracy that is comically perfected, with morons in the seats of power and clownish underlings the "living exponent[s] of cruelty, dishonesty, and injustice."[113] Spectators of a spectacle like Trumpism can enjoy it so much that they cannot help but participate in democracy's tragic demise. There is no question that a comic egoism was central to the Capitol Insurrection, contributing to a way of doing cultural politics—of enacting democratic being—by denying the sort of reciprocity and shared foolishness necessary for democratic relationships. The death of some carnival spirit might therefore double as the death knell for democratic citizenship. Trumpism might represent a "carnivalesque hell."[114] Comedy is dead. Long live comedy.

CONCLUSION

The gallows is quite literally a matter of life and death. In the carnival, though, this matter is tied not only to who lives or dies but also to *what* is executed in the generative act of a killing "joke." At the Capitol Insurrection, the construction of a makeshift gallows for hanging so-called Trump turncoats was fodder for a mob of followers and would-be revolutionaries to threaten political violence in the name of fair play. For better or worse, it was an expression of a comic imagination that operated on a simple albeit complicated wonderment when it comes to clowning around in and with US democracy: Wouldn't it be funny if . . .?

The point is not that the Capitol Insurrection was particularly undemocratic or even antidemocratic. It is that it laid bare just how much the "for all" portion of liberty and justice *for all* is the hang up for so many who are motivated by nostalgia, rage, and resentment. In this sense, a complex psychology of groupthink and authoritarian populism can be boiled down to a plain truth, which is that most of us have fragile egos and seek ways to safeguard them. Comedy is such a compelling framework here because of how much it celebrates fragility and guards against the potentially dire effects of praise and blame. In this case, comedy oriented a carnival of cultural politics that, in a notably dark moment, made matters of saving America into means of living out delusions of self-grandeur not as a personality trait but rather as a basis for collective identity and action. In-groups and out-groups are coveted outcomes of cultural politicking (and, yes, of making and taking jokes too). This is reason enough to recognize that comedy is now as ever a resource for pushing the limits of democratic life to the end of its line. Once upon a time, carnival cleansed body and soul, let people gather and ward off evil spirits and make good on pursuits of human goodness. The carnival spirit placed virtue in an enactment of the ambiguities between good and evil. Shared laughter rendered us all fools. It was not supposed to convert those fools into fanatics. This conversion, though, is precisely what has emerged from a democratic carnival at the Capitol. Was it a rally gone wrong? Was it some form of wrongful comedy put to bad use? Was it a coup attempt that devolved into a feast of fools? Whatever it was, the Capitol Insurrection should prompt us to reconsider our comic pretexts for getting along together (or not) and then again our sense for how, when, why, and for whom comedy is doing the work of democracy (or not).

The carnival spirit stands out as a way to confront the evil human beings tend to do to each other. As Bradbury says of death, it is a thing best conceived as "strangely alive and greedy" even as it is nothing more than "a stopped watch, a loss, and, a darkness."[115] Bakhtin sought recourse to the gravity and graveness of this notion and, in the carnival, found good comic reasons for encouraging renewal, rejuvenation, and rebirth. Death "is life's rejuvenation."[116] As with death, so with carnival. That's the generative ambiguity of comedy. In Bradbury's tale of the dark carnival, the father figure of Charles Halloway embodies this ambiguity and, at one point, expresses it to one of his young sons. That comic clock "minute by minute, hour by hour, a lifetime, it never ends, never stops," and so "you got the choice this second, now this next, and the next after that, be good, be bad, that's what the clock ticks, that's what it says in the ticks."[117] Simplistic dichotomies aside, it is Halloway's sentiment that bespeaks a spirit of the carnivalesque that lets us all recognize that the only fools are those who do not realize—or, better, accept—that they are fools. There is folly in the Capitol Insurrection. But it is in the foolishness of predicating a life-and-death carnival on the permanence of certain cultural setups, certain social orders, certain political axioms about who and what should live. Comedy goes wrong in carnival when it exploits an end-all-be-all ethic of democratic conduct and, with it, a principle for unfettered freedom to act with cruelty, malice, and spite.

In the next chapter, a different kind of exploit is explored through the cultural, political, and economic institutionalization of wars of comedy against comedy. Therein, democracy is at once rightfully and wrongfully recast as the just desert of some of us, not all of us. What we call *our* brands of humor are therefore comprehensible when compared to *their* tastes for jokes. To take sides is to do one's work for the comedy of democracy. To do this is to make an excuse for folly that turns carnival actors into the hobgoblins of comedy. That folly is the stuff of lex talionis, the law of retaliation. Eyes for eyes. Teeth for teeth. It betrays a retaliatory approach to the world. Numerous insurrectionists acted in the name of self-defense when they chanted "Stop the Steal" and when they overtook the Senate Chambers. One insurrectionist among many, many others got violent, calling Capitol officers who were trying to keep people back from metal barricades "fucking pieces of shit" and "commie fucks" and eventually swinging a flagpole at one officer before gouging out his eye.[118] If the business end of the pole was a bludgeon, the leisure end was a flag that bore the insignia of the United States Marine Corps. That flag stood out in the crowd among many other flags, some bearing the iconography of attitudes like "Liberty or Death," of Trump-as-Rambo, of "shitposters" who comically espouse the Republic of Kekistan. The gallows makes perfect (truly comic) sense here, as do calls for summary executions. The thing is that comedy has conventionally been thought of as a resource for mitigating the felt need for revenge. It is what animates the carnival wherein Dante's "foul goads" can be rendered foolish. To be made fun of in a carnival spirit is to be subjected to the laws of comic justice. But, wouldn't it be funny if . . .?

NOTES

1. Michael Sean Comerford, "A Dark Carnival Comes to Life," *Los Angeles Review of Books*, March 27, 2021, https://lareviewofbooks.org/article/a-dark -carnival-comes-to-life/.

2. Nancy Isenberg, "Democracy's Thorn: The Mob and the Voice of the People," *Hedgehog Review* (Summer 2021), https://hedgehogreview.com/issues /distinctions-that-define-and-divide/articles/democracys-thorn.

3. Alec MacGillis, "Inside the Capitol Riot: What the Parler Videos Reveal," ProPublica, January 17, 2021, https://www.propublica.org/article/inside-the -capitol-riot-what-the-parler-videos-reveal.

4. Matt Taibbi, *Insane Clown President: Dispatches from the 2016 Circus* (New York: Random House, 2017).

5. Adam Serwer, *The Cruelty Is the Point: The Past, Present, and Future of Trump's America* (New York: One World, 2021), xiv.

6. Emily Nussbaum, "How Jokes Won the Election," *New Yorker*, January 15, 2017, https://www.newyorker.com/magazine/2017/01/23/how-jokes-won-the-election.

7. James Wolcott, "How Donald Trump Became America's Insult Comic in Chief," *Vanity Fair*, November 6, 2015, https://www.vanityfair.com/culture/2015/11/wolcott-trump-insult-comic.

8. See Elizaveta Gaufman and Bharath Ganesh, *The Trump Carnival: Populism, Transgression and the Far Right* (Berlin: De Gruyter, 2024).

9. Greg Grandin, "The Death Cult of Trumpism," *The Nation*, January 11, 2018, https://www.thenation.com/article/archive/the-death-cult-of-trumpism/.

10. Anne Applebaum, "History Will Judge the Complicit," *Atlantic*, August 2020, https://www.theatlantic.com/magazine/archive/2020/07/trumps-collaborators/612250/.

11. Mikhail Bakhtin, *Rabelais and His World*, trans. Hélène Iswolsky (Bloomington: Indiana University Press, 1984), 168, 174. Additionally, for more on "humor and hatred" as a "matter of enjoyment," see Michael Billig, "Humor and Hatred: The Racist Jokes of the Ku Klux Klan," *Discourse and Society* 12 (2001): 267–89.

12. Bakhtin, *Rabelais and His World*, 40.

13. Alfred F. Young, *Liberty Tree: Ordinary People and the American Revolution* (New York: New York University Press, 2006), 617.

14. Young, *Liberty Tree*, 559.

15. Brent Staples, "So the South's White Terror Will Never Be Forgotten," *New York Times*, April 25, 2018, https://www.nytimes.com/2018/04/25/opinion/american-lynchings-memorial.html. See also John Hammond Moore, *Carnival of Blood: Dueling, Lynching, and Murder in South Carolina, 1880–1920* (Columbia: University of South Carolina Press, 2006); Terry Anne Scott, *Lynching and Leisure: Race and the Transformation of Mob Violence in Texas* (Fayetteville: University of Arkansas Press, 2022); Amy Louise Wood, *Lynching and Spectacle: Witnessing Racial Violence in America, 1890–1940* (Chapel Hill: University of North Carolina Press, 2009); and "History of Lynching in America," National Association for the Advancement of Colored People, https://naacp.org/find-resources/history-explained/history-lynching-america.

16. Bakhtin, *Rabelais and His World*, 285.

17. Tweet by @nycsouthpaw, "Some of the Trump fanatics constructed a gallows near the Capitol reflecting pool and another group of them fashioned a crude noose from stolen AP camera cables and hung it from a tree," Twitter, January 8, 2021, https://twitter.com/nycsouthpaw/status/1347563271352676354?lang=en.

18. Elaine Godfrey, "It Was Supposed to Be So Much Worse," *Atlantic*, January 9, 2021, https://www.theatlantic.com/politics/archive/2021/01/trump -rioters-wanted-more-violence-worse/617614/.

19. Catie Edmondson, "'So the Traitors Know the Stakes': The Meaning of the Jan. 6 Gallows," *New York Times*, June 16, 2022, https://www.nytimes.com/2022 /06/16/us/politics/jan-6-gallows.html.

20. Jeff Sharlet, "'Executing Politicians? Lulz.' For Trump's Zombies, 'Funny' Cosplay Is the Language of Deadly Fascism," *Vanity Fair*, January 8, 2021, https:// www.vanityfair.com/news/2021/01/for-trumps-zombies-funny-cosplay-is-the -language-of-deadly-fascism.

21. Marilyn Ivy, "This Is (Not) a Gallows," Society for Cultural Anthropology, April 15, 2021, https://culanth.org/fieldsights/this-is-not-a-gallows.

22. Ivy, "This Is (Not) a Gallows."

23. Luke Mogelson, "Among the Insurrectionists at the Capitol," *New Yorker*, January 15, 2021, https://www.newyorker.com/magazine/2021/01/25/among-the -insurrectionists.

24. Alison Olson, "Political Humor, Deference, and the American Revolution," *Early American Studies* 3 (2005): 364.

25. MacGillis, "Inside the Capitol Riot."

26. Jesse David Fox, "When Jokes Fail," *Vulture*, January 8, 2021, https://www .vulture.com/2021/01/capitol-riot-trump-comedy.html.

27. Bakhtin, *Rabelais and His World*, 387, 120–21.

28. Bakhtin, *Rabelais and His World*, 7.

29. Krystyna Pomorska, foreword to *Rabelais and His World*, viii–xii.

30. Bakhtin, *Rabelais and His World*, 195.

31. Ivy, "This Is (Not) a Gallows."

32. Godfrey, "It Was Supposed to Be So Much Worse."

33. Bakhtin, *Rabelais and His World*, 197.

34. MacGillis, "Inside the Capitol Riot."

35. "Giuliani: 'Let's Have Trial by Combat,'" Politico, February 8, 2021, https://www.politico.com/video/2021/02/08/giuliani-lets-have-trial-by-combat -122543.

36. *United States of America v. Jacob Anthony Chansley*, Government's Memorandum in Aid of Sentencing, United States District Court for the District of Columbia, CR. NO. 21-CR-003 (RCL).

37. Dylan Stableford, "New Video Shows Alleged Jan 6. Capitol Rioters Threatening Pence," *Yahoo!News*, February 7, 2022, https://news.yahoo.com/new -video-jan-6-capitol-riot-pence-threat-drag-through-streets-195249884.html.

38. See Elena Sheppard, "Pro-Trump Capitol Rioters Like the 'QAnon Shaman' Looked Ridiculous—By Design," *Think*, January 13, 2021, https://www .nbcnews.com/think/opinion/pro-trump-capitol-rioters-qanon-shaman-looked

-ridiculous-design-ncna1254010. See also Kenneth Ladenburg, "Strange Costumes of Capitol Rioters Echo the Early Days of the Ku Klux Klan—Before the White Sheets," *Conversation*, January 25, 2021, https://theconversation.com /strange-costumes-of-capitol-rioters-echo-the-early-days-of-the-ku-klux-klan -before-the-white-sheets-153376.

39. Sheppard, "Pro-Trump Capitol Rioters."

40. Kim Kelly, "Is the 'QAnon Shaman' from the MAGA Capitol Riot Covered in Neo-Nazi Imagery?," *Rolling Stone*, January 8, 2021, https://www .rollingstone.com/culture/culture-features/qanon-shaman-maga-capitol-riot -rune-pagan-imagery-tattoo-1111344/.

41. Sheppard, "Pro-Trump Capitol Rioters."

42. Bakhtin, *Rabelais and His World*, 129.

43. Luke Winki, "What Those Animal Pelts Tell Us about the Future of the Far Right," *Atlantic*, January 12, 2021, https://www.theatlantic.com/culture /archive/2021/01/why-capitol-rioters-wore-animal-pelts/617639/.

44. Elaine Frantz Parsons, "Klan Skepticism and Denial in Reconstruction-Era Public Discourse," *Journal of Southern History* 77 (2011): 53.

45. Lorraine Ali, "Drunk Rudy. Loser Trump. How the Jan. 6 Hearings' Wild Comedy Weakens the Big Lie," *Los Angeles Times*, June 13, 2022, https:// www.latimes.com/entertainment-arts/tv/story/2022-06-13/jan-6-committee -hearings-stepien-barr-giuliani-trump-monday-day-2.

46. From Andrew L. Whitehead and Samuel L. Perry, *Taking America Back for God: Christian Nationalism in the United States*, quoted in Thomas B. Edsall, "'The Capitol Insurrection Was as Christian Nationalist as It Gets,'" *New York Times*, January 28, 2021, https://www.nytimes.com/2021/01/28/opinion /christian-nationalists-capitol-attack.html.

47. Brian L. Ott and Greg Dickinson, *The Twitter Presidency: Donald J. Trump and the Politics of White Rage* (New York: Routledge, 2019).

48. Doyle McManus, "Another Day, Another Vulgar Trump Tweet. The President Clearly Isn't Learning on the Job," *Los Angeles Times*, June 29, 2017, https://www.latimes.com/opinion/op-ed/la-oe-mcmanus-trump-tweet-mike -20170629-story.html.

49. Bakhtin, *Rabelais and His World*, 187.

50. MacGillis, "Inside the Capitol Riot."

51. David Freelander, "The Bonnie and Clyde of MAGA World," Politico, November 19, 2021, https://www.politico.com/news/magazine/2021/11/19 /dustin-stockton-jen-lawrence-trump-profile-522823.

52. See "Identifying Far-Right Symbols That Appeared at the U.S. Capitol Riot," *Washington Post*, January 15, 2021, https://www.washingtonpost.com /nation/interactive/2021/far-right-symbols-capitol-riot/.

53. Joe Kukura, "Feds Charge Capitol Insurrection Rioter Who Said of Pelosi, 'We Want to Hang That F**ing B*tch,'" *SFist*, May 19, 2021, https://sfist .com/2021/05/19/fbi-charges-capitol-insurrection-rioter-who-said-of-pelosi-we -want-to-hang-that-f-ing-b-tch/.

54. Mogelson, "Among the Insurrectionists."

55. Kerry Howley, "Gina. Rosanne. Guy. What Do You Do the Day after You Storm the Capitol?," *New York Magazine*, December 21, 2021, https://nymag .com/intelligencer/2021/12/january-6-insurrection-us-capitol-riots.html.

56. Matthew Rosenberg, "He Looted Speaker Pelosi's Office, and Then Bragged about It," *New York Times*, January 6, 2021, https://www.nytimes.com /2021/01/06/us/politics/richard-barnett-pelosi.html.

57. Monica Hesse, "A Capitol Invader Left a Note Calling Nancy Pelosi a B-Word. His Attempt to Walk It Back Has Been . . . Really Something," *Washington Post*, April 27, 2021, https://www.washingtonpost.com/lifestyle/style /nancy-pelosi-capitol-riot-note-richard-barnett/2021/04/27/727ef956-a6bc-11eb -8d25-7b30e74923ea_story.html.

58. Timothy Snyder, "The American Abyss," *New York Times*, December 28, 2021, https://www.nytimes.com/2021/01/09/magazine/trump-coup.html.

59. Bakhtin, *Rabelais and His World*, 240.

60. David Remnick, "The Inciter-in-Chief," *New Yorker*, January 9, 2021, https://www.newyorker.com/magazine/2021/01/18/the-inciter-in-chief.

61. Megan Garber, "When Hatred Is a Joke," *Atlantic*, July 3, 2017, https:// www.theatlantic.com/entertainment/archive/2017/07/when-hatred-is-a-joke /532509/.

62. Eric Lutz, "The Latest Batch Of Jan 6-Related Text Messages Are Even Dumber (And More Sinister) Than You Could Imagine," *Vanity Fair*, April 26, 2022, https://www.vanityfair.com/news/2022/04/mark-meadows-january -6-texts-marjorie-taylor-greene-marshall-law.

63. Olson, "Political Humor," 373.

64. Mogelson, "Among the Insurrectionists." See also Wilborn P. Nobles III, "Trump Calls Baltimore 'Disgusting . . . Rodent Infested Mess,' Rips Rep. Elijah Cummings over Border Criticism," *Baltimore Sun*, July 27, 2019, https:// www.baltimoresun.com/politics/bs-md-pol-cummings-trump-20190727 -chty2yovtvfzfcjkeaui7wm5zi-story.html.

65. Katie McDonough, "Die Laughing at the Capitol," *New Republic*, January 11, 2021, https://newrepublic.com/article/160846/die-laughing-capitol.

66. See Jonathan Chait, "A White House Aide Just Warned Us That Donald Trump Is a Sociopath," *Intelligencer*, September 18, 2020, https:// nymag.com/intelligencer/2020/09/pence-aide-trump-disregard-human-life -coronavirus-olivia-troye.html. See also Jonathan V. Last, "The President Is a

Sociopath. And 60 Million Americans Like It," *Bulwark*, September 30, 2020, https://www.thebulwark.com/the-president-is-a-sociopath-and-60-million-americans-like-it/.

67. MSNBC, "'Sociopath': Trump on Track to Win 2024 & Be a 'Dictator' Warns His Coauthor from 'Art of the Deal,'" YouTube, December 8, 2023, https://www.youtube.com/watch?v=lDhSgYVGqPk.

68. James Hamblin, "Donald Trump: Sociopath?," *Atlantic*, July 20, 2016, https://www.theatlantic.com/health/archive/2016/07/trump-and-sociopathy/491966/.

69. Mary L. Trump, *Too Much and Never Enough: How My Family Created the World's Most Dangerous Man* (New York: Simon and Schuster, 2020).

70. *The Daily Show*, "Welcome to President Trump's Reality," YouTube, January 27, 2017, https://www.youtube.com/watch?v=x2YLS80Nmls.

71. Ryan Lattanzio, "Trump Reportedly Screened 'Joker' at the White House and Liked It," *IndieWire*, November 17, 2019, https://www.indiewire.com/features/general/joker-donald-trump-1202190182/.

72. Paul Stocker, "Joker, the Far Right and Popular Culture," *Open Democracy*, November 1, 2019, https://www.opendemocracy.net/en/countering-radical-right/joker-far-right-and-popular-culture/.

73. Andy Borowitz, "Trump Named Person of the Year by Popular Sociopath Magazine," *New Yorker*, December 12, 2019, https://www.newyorker.com/humor/borowitz-report/trump-named-person-of-the-year-by-popular-sociopath-magazine.

74. Hunter Walker, "The 'JusticeForJ6' Rally Wasn't a Joke—It Was a Warning," *Rolling Stone*, September 18, 2021, https://www.rollingstone.com/politics/politics-features/justiceforj6-rally-insurrection-capitol-trump-1228690/.

75. Liam Kennedy, "American Carnival: The Aesthetic Politics of Trumpist Insurrection," UCD Clinton Institute, January 16, 2021, https://www.ucdclinton.ie/commentary-content/american-carnival-the-aesthetic-politics-of-trumpist-insurrection.

76. *The Daily Show*, "Jordan Klepper Sees It All at the Capitol Insurrection," YouTube, January 12, 2021, https://www.youtube.com/watch?v=YVDJqipoohc.

77. Roger Cohen, "Trump's Last Stand for White America," *New York Times*, October 16, 2020, https://www.nytimes.com/2020/10/16/opinion/trump-2020.html.

78. Arlie Russell Hochschild, *Strangers in Our Own Land: Anger and Mourning on the American Right* (New York: New Press, 2016).

79. Serwer, *Cruelty Is the Point*, 97.

80. Adam Serwer, "The Cruelty Is the Point," *Atlantic*, October 3, 2018, https://www.theatlantic.com/ideas/archive/2018/10/the-cruelty-is-the-point/572104/.

81. Bakhtin, *Rabelais and His World*, 246.

82. David Neiwert, "What the Kek: Explaining the Alt-Right 'Deity' behind Their 'Meme Magic,'" *Southern Poverty Law Center*, May 9, 2017, https://www.splcenter.org/hatewatch/2017/05/08/what-kek-explaining-alt-right-deity-behind-their-meme-magic.

83. John Wagner, "Trump Says It Was 'Common Sense' for Jan. 6 Rioters to Chant 'Hang Mike Pence!'" *Washington Post*, November 12, 2021, https://www.washingtonpost.com/politics/trump-hang-mike-pence/2021/11/12/64a17142-43b0-11ec-a88e-2aa4632af69b_story.html.

84. Ray Bradbury, *Something Wicked This Way Comes* (New York: Simon and Schuster, 1962), 127.

85. Robert Zaretsky, "With Huckster Trump in Charge, the Carnival Goes On—And On and On," *Forward*, December 23, 2020, https://forward.com/culture/460850/with-huckster-trump-in-charge-the-carnival-goes-on-and-on-and-on/.

86. Jon Skolnki, "'AmericaFest': Right-Wing Youth Just Held a Wild Carnival of Fun-Filled Fascism," *Salon*, December 21, 2021, https://www.salon.com/2021/12/21/americafest-right-wing-youth-just-held-a-wild-carnival-of-fun-filled-fascism/.

87. Mogelson, "Among the Insurrectionists."

88. Michael Kruse, "In on the Joke: The Comedic Trick Trump Uses to Normalize His Behavior," Politico, March 17, 2024, https://www.politico.com/news/magazine/2024/03/17/how-donald-trump-uses-humor-to-make-the-outrageous-sound-normal-00146119.

89. Jill Lepore, "The Last Time Democracy Almost Died," *New Yorker*, January 27, 2020, https://www.newyorker.com/magazine/2020/02/03/the-last-time-democracy-almost-died.

90. Henry Carlisle, "The Comic Tradition," *American Scholar* 28 (1958/59): 108.

91. Bakhtin, *Rabelais and His World*, 22.

92. Thomas Meaney, "Trumpism after Trump," *Harper's Magazine*, February 2020, https://harpers.org/archive/2020/02/trumpism-after-trump/.

93. Paul G. Casey, dir., "Dr. Phil McGraw; Tim Ryan; Batya Ungar-Sargon," *Real Time with Bill Maher*, season 22, episode 6, aired March 1, 2024, on HBO.

94. Pomorska, foreword, xviii.

95. Paul Buhle, "Horror in American Literature," in *Popular Culture in America*, ed. Paul Buhle (Minneapolis: University of Minnesota Press, 1987), 24.

96. Saidiya V. Hartman, *Scenes of Subjection: Terror, Slavery, and Self-Making in Nineteenth-Century America* (New York: Oxford University Press, 1997), 37.

97. Henry Fairlie, "The People, No," *Baffler* 18 (January 2010), https://thebaffler.com/salvos/the-people-no.

98. *The Late Show with Stephen Colbert*, "Abhor-Rent: 525,600 Minutes since the Insurrection," YouTube, January 6, 2022, https://www.youtube.com/watch?v=H_IxT2ei9gU.

99. Bakhtin, *Rabelais and His World*, 207, 122.

100. Dannagal Goldthwaite Young, *Irony and Outrage: The Polarized Landscape of Rage, Fear, and Laughter in the United States* (New York: Oxford University Press, 2020), 137.

101. James E. Caron, *Satire as the Comic Public Sphere: Postmodern "Truthiness" and Civic Engagement* (University Park: Pennsylvania State University Press, 2021).

102. Cynthia Willett, *Irony in the Age of Empire: Comic Perspectives on Democracy and Freedom* (Bloomington: Indiana University Press, 2008), 125.

103. Willett, *Irony in the Age of Empire*, 9.

104. Bakhtin, *Rabelais and His World*, 201.

105. Willett, *Irony in the Age of Empire*, 128. Emphasis added. See also Joshua Gunn, *Political Perversion: Rhetorical Aberration in the Time of Trumpeteering* (Chicago: University of Chicago Press, 2020).

106. Lawrence Grossberg, *Under the Cover of Chaos: Trump and the Battle for the American Right* (London: Pluto Press, 2018), 70, ix.

107. Grossberg, *Under the Cover of Chaos*, 12, 98.

108. Henry A. Giroux, "Anti-Politics and the Plague of Disorientation: Welcome to the Age of Trump," Truthout, June 7, 2016, https://truthout.org/articles/anti-politics-and-the-plague-of-disorientation-welcome-to-the-age-of-trump/.

109. Bakhtin, *Rabelais and His World*, 15.

110. Pomorska, foreword, xxii.

111. Lauren Berlant and Sianne Ngai, "Comedy Has Issues," *Critical Inquiry* 43 (2017), https://www.journals.uchicago.edu/doi/full/10.1086/689666.

112. H. L. Mencken, "The Clowns in the Ring," in *H. L. Mencken on Politics: A Carnival of Buncombe*, ed. Malcolm Moos (Baltimore: Johns Hopkins University Press, 1996), 14; and H. L. Mencken, "The Struggle Ahead," in *H. L. Mencken on Politics*, 152.

113. H. L. Mencken, "The Last Round," in *H. L. Mencken on Politics*, 25.

114. Bakhtin, *Rabelais and His World*, 395.

115. Bradbury, *Something Wicked This Way Comes*, 308.

116. Bakhtin, *Rabelais and His World*, 405.

117. Bradbury, *Something Wicked This Way Comes*, 125.

118. Mia Jankowicz, "DOJ Seeks the Longest Capitol Riot Prison Term Yet—17 Years for 'Eye Gouging' Ex-NYPD Officer Who Swung a Flagpole at Police," *Business Insider*, August 28, 2022, https://www.businessinsider.com/capitol-riot-17-years-sentence-sought-eye-gouger-ex-officer-2022-8.

FIVE

COMEDY IS DEAD, AND LIVING AS RAGE IN THE COMIC LANGUAGE OF THE ALT-RIGHT MACHINE

THERE IS A THIN LINE between *The Devil's Dictionary* and *Keywords: A Vocabulary of Culture and Society*. The one constitutes a comic lexicon and was compiled in the latter part of the nineteenth century by notorious journalist of sardonicism and wit Ambrose Bierce. The other is a glossary of terms by noted literary critic and cultural theorist Raymond Williams that was written in the mid-1970s and focuses on how certain ways of speaking take shape in reality and, in turn, make reality take shape. Bierce had a general "contempt for politics, religion, society, and conventional human values."[1] With that, the real meanings of words and phrases are best expressed in definitions that make a mockery by capturing, well, what they *really* mean. For Williams, such meanings are complicated because we all "have different immediate values or different kinds of valuation, or that we are aware, often intangibly, of different formations and distributions of energy and interest."[2] Yet whereas Bierce might say that politics is, to wit, nothing more than the "strife of interests masquerading as a contest of principles," Williams might suggest more succinctly that it is one of many realms wherein we get by—or not—by "speaking the same language."[3] A fine line, indeed.

This chapter deals with the rhetorical force of comic language. Comedy influences vocabularies of culture and society. Vocabularies of culture and society influence comedy. So, let us acknowledge some realities. First, proclamations that comedy is dead exist alongside pronouncements that comedy, in the era of wokeism and cancel culture, is alive and well. Second, conventional language of comedy is probably inapt for really understanding how certain forms of absurdity, transgression, cruelty, and rage have made it from some of the darker corners of the internet to the mainstream. Third, whether or not something is funny, there has been in comic discourse what Bierce might call a shift from some sense of humor to the primacy of humorous sentiment. Fourth, and finally, the alt-right has changed the language game.

Once upon a time, right-wing comedy was exemplified by the likes of Tim Allen, the blue-collar comedians, and Dennis Miller, with his iconic performances as an anchor on the *Saturday Night Live* segment "Weekend Update," not to mention his activities as a talk radio host. Right-wing comedy today tends to be typified by various podcasters, political commentators, and conspiracy theorists like Owen Benjamin and Shane Gillis, who carry on the legacy of Rush Limbaugh; stand-up comedians in the Legion of Skanks; pranksters and trolls like those in the troupe Million Dollar Extreme; and hard-liners like Gavin McInnes, who traverses the spaces of culture and politics with everything from his own stand-up comedy, a sardonic television series, and podcast *Get Off My Lawn* to on-the-ground activism with the Proud Boys, an extremist group he founded to promote Western chauvinism. Moreover, right-wing comedy thrives in top-rated shows like *Gutfeld!* on Fox News, which is hosted by Greg Gutfeld and positioned as the counterpoint to left-oriented comperes like Stephen Colbert and John Oliver. The purpose here is not to identify devils in the details of these exemplars, tempting as it might be to demonstrate how alt-right comedy has made a killing by ruining the comic spirit once seen as so resident in dominant political humor by mocking its ritual practice of tilting at windmills and, concomitantly, fiddling while Rome burns. Rather, the purpose here is to tease out some of the ways that the alt-right represents a comic spirit unto itself, transposing ironic political attitudes and mockingly sentimental moods into a vocabulary of culture and society. The problems this transposition poses are not so much for a comedy industry or even a democratic polity per se as much as they are for what we define *as* comedy and, thereby, how we keep in a comic spirit of speaking the same language.

This chapter begins with some observations about the significance of alt-right vernaculars that filter through catchphrases and visual imagery and emerge on social media platforms as well as ordinary speech, turning fun and games into political and cultural warfare. These observations are followed by considerations of alt-right comedy in action (i.e., in bromides, manifestos, and mainstream pabulum), which help form the basis for my key claim: the alt-right has instituted a peculiar kind of comedy that operates on a language of rage, on one hand, with the funny-not-funny frenzy of its so-called Hate Machine and, on the other, with the all too serious sentiment that if a joke doesn't kill, then they—the jokesters in the machine—will.

COMICALLY SPEAKING

The comic language of alt-right comedy has contributed to the mainstreaming of Far Right ideas. There is, no doubt, a good deal of wordplay and a cache of sight gags to be found in any number of examples worthy of attention. There are also resources for considering "the language of humor" that defines comedy.[4] Of interest here is how comic appeals and a supposed spirit of comedy relate, in Williams's terms, to "the created and creative meanings" of keywords (not to mention symbols and visual representations, which is to say what W. J. T. Mitchell has long portrayed as the deep relationship between words and images).[5] Of interest is the impact of comic language on this mainstreaming.

It is important to recognize from the outset, though, that comic language is hardly new. The slogan, "Join, or Die," was originally a political cartoon sketched by Benjamin Franklin, just as the donkey that now symbolizes the Democratic Party was popularized in political cartoons by Thomas Nast. But from the late 1980s through the early twenty-first century, the language of comedy became particularly tied up with the comedy of language. For example, in the nineteenth century, the term "truthiness" connoted a condition of truth. When Colbert coined it on the first episode of his satirical television show, he codified its contemporary meaning as truth more connected to feeling than facticity.[6] Some years prior, Limbaugh brought the portmanteau word "feminazi" into vogue as a trademark slur for vilifying advocates of women's rights and characterizing feminism as a joke. In a brief preface to his compendium, Bierce noted in 1911 that many of the "definitions, anecdotes, phrases and so forth" that he established in his sardonic dictionary "had become more or less current in popular speech."[7] Limbaugh made a career of what now counts as the source material for so much patter in right-wing rhetoric, like "owning the Libs." In 2006, the neologism to which Colbert laid claim was *Merriam-Webster*'s Word of the Year. This is the point. Comic language matters.

The comic language of the alt-right is perhaps even more significant than these other touchstones because it sets the tone for a grand narrative about white nationalism that promotes good fun in bad faith. In other words, the catchphrases and slogans and iconography of the alt-right derive a meaning of the comic from the understanding that dominance in political culture and cultural politics resides "*within* language."[8] The New World Order. The Clown World Order. A Trump World Order. These and any other emergent realities are possible only in and through the rhetorical order of things. In this regard, a sketch by Funny or Die from September 2016 simultaneously

138   WHEN COMEDY GOES WRONG

hits and misses the mark. The sketch was put up on YouTube less than two months before the presidential election of Donald J. Trump—a campaigner who, like a stand-up comic known for insult comedy in his own right, rallied support by borrowing the tenor of 4chan and the time-tested tactic of boiling down viewpoints to mottos and nicknames to crack jokes that appealed to "Intellectual" as well as "Natural" conservatives, the "men's-rights types, earnest white supremacists and anti-Semites" who might otherwise be pooh-poohed "as a humorless minority," not to mention ordinary Americans bothered by divisions of race, gender, and education.[9] It captures a certain proximity of revelry to revilement and the ways that mortification gets folded into humiliation and jest.

The sketch, dubbed "The Kings of Alt Right Comedy," features stereotypical white men at home on their computers being meme makers, message boarders, and trolls.[10] One man is a Pop-Tarts–eating, heavily bearded, and balding fatard who goes by the avatar @cuckslayer83. Another sports a black T-shirt with the hashtag #MENINIST (a tongue-in-cheek reference to those who oppose feminism and pay flippant tribute to men's rights), sits on a couch, types away on his computer, and laughs at the jokes he is making on some social media platform. The sketch portrays these men as mock comic heroes. They are fools who pretend to be prizefighters for the alt-right comedy cause, which is predicated on a sense of humor that privileges the harassment of women and minorities online. "Here's an actually FUNNY joke," one of the foolish kings says out loud as he composes a tweet directed at comedian Amy Schumer, "I want 2 rape and kill u." A laugh track plays as we get a glimpse of his screen. This spoof of a profile in comic courage concludes with the men variously looking at the camera and spouting some of their "favorite Alt-Right catchphrases." "You fucking cunt." "You fucking gay-ass fag." "You fucking Jew." As the video cuts from kingly fool to kingly fool, images of Twitter responses pop up in the frame (fig. 5.1). Followers and "friends" reinforce the sportive slights with "likes" heart symbols, and remarks such as "ROFL" (rolling on the floor laughing), "fucking funny," and "your hilarious." In the end, the men are seen with their eyes rolling back in their heads, and it is unclear whether they are getting off on the comic feeling held in common or simply falling asleep in the dreamscape of incels.

It is not hard to complete the logic of "The Kings of Alt-Right Comedy" and contend that the stuff is just not funny. In fact, in Jacqui Shine's words, the video betrays a "humorless, self-righteous, right-on social media sentimentality" made from "an anti-feminist, anti-mainstream-culture sensibility that is based on a mixture of punk's subcultural hypermasculinity and alternative

Fig. 5.1. Screenshot of pretend homegrown fool with Far Right sensibilities being showcased as a King of Alt-Right Comedy.

culture erudition married to pride in Western Cultural traditions."[11] This is why there is so much documentation of the alt-right as a cultural institution with, by and large, men who speak their own language in memes and symbols and various outlets that amount to what the Southern Poverty Law Center describes as a collection of "propaganda machines."[12] That signals of alt-right sentimentality are now mainstream, though, means that the diabolical comedy it inspires represents more than a sort of Devil's Bargain. When Bierce concocted his dictionary, he caricatured the vocabulary of culture and society by exposing the dark underbellies of discourse that nevertheless dwell on the surface of everyday speech and experience. Democracy is a carnival of self-interest, not a contest of principles. Such a sentiment is funny because it feels true. In alt-right comedy, a comic spirit is applied to a vocabulary for supporting, not satirizing, what amounts to "the establishment of a white ethno-state," underwritten by the "hipster irony" of Poe's Law and the cynicism of "separatist dreams."[13] The comic language here leverages "dark humor and love of transgression for its own sake."[14] It is ironic. It is sincere. It is about free expression with impunity and the comic appeal of telling it like it is. If these notions seem banal, it is because they are—except that they are the very fountainheads for a lingua franca that pervades the regular speech of everyone from "shitposters" to online trolls to celebrated chauvinists to political officials. We begin, then, with a keyword or two that exemplify how hateful language can be a foil for making fun in violating norms of discourse.

WHEN COMEDY GOES WRONG

AS "CUCK" WOULD HAVE IT

In 2015, there was a "cuckservative panic."[15] What does this mean?

At the time, cultural politics had become brazenly ill humored. Official politics had accepted, however unwittingly, a no-holds-barred, rude, and offensive quality, animated in part by the rhetorical style of Trump's presidential campaign. "Cuckservative," the "vulgar little portmanteau," was the appellation of choice for pilgarlics, signifying what Amber A'Lee Frost terms an "insufficiently masculine RINO [Republican in name only] who is unable and/or unwilling to vanquish the corrosive forces of Marxism, feminization, and reverse racism that threaten to destroy the very fabric of our once-beautiful country."[16] People seemed panic-stricken for a number of reasons. One is that the term established a Rorschach test for supporting Trump, a man whom Limbaugh once described as not "your average, ordinary, cuckolded Republican," and those who were sellouts, "traitors to their people" because they granted even the slightest bit of legitimacy to "certain liberal ideas."[17] Another is that "cuck" first gained prominence as an "ironic slur" that liberals used to mock conservatives on social media, namely, on sites like Something Awful.[18] In the age of Trumpism, the slur was reappropriated in right-wing discourse as a "gloriously effective insult," on one hand as a descriptor for emasculated conservatives—that is, *cuck*servatives—and, on the other, as a "political epithet du jour for liberals" and "PC liberalism run amok."[19] Generally speaking, if people do what they say, then many among us did the deeds of vulgarians, left, right, and center. Still, it is worth recognizing that things like "cuck" panics occur when someone is laughing out of the other side of their mouth.

At the height of presidential campaign season in 2016, there was another panic—a "clown panic."[20] Sightings of weird, vile-looking, sometimes apparently armed clowns were reported across the country. "Clowns in vans. Clowns in the woods. Clowns lurking in the shadows. Clowns chasing people or doing crimes."[21] Some were said to lure children. Some simply lingered in plain view to creep people out. The panic sparked fear in the populace, and at the same time provoked a Clown Lives Matter movement among some who made their livelihoods as comic entertainers. There is a history to this panic that dates back to at least the 1980s, and it has resonances with everything from fears of child kidnappings and satanic rituals to generalized social anxieties and primal fears. More pertinent in this case is that it does some of what the "cuckservative panic" did in its combination, and confusion, of buffoonery and bedevilment. Was the clown panic ultimately "a hoax, a marketing ploy, or simply child's play?"[22] It is unclear. What is clear, though, is that there is a comic element to the same rhetorical activity that is meant to torment others. So, we might do

COMEDY IS DEAD

141

better to ask not what the "cuckservative panic" means but rather what can be gleaned from its comic appeal.

A *cuck* is a *clown*. A cuckservative is a menace to society, even more so than any antiglobalist, racist, misogynist, shitposter, or troll. Anyone in the Clown World Order, be they coastal elites or members of Conservative Inc., are the real buffoons. Those who spout the insult online and elsewhere set the terms for insiders and outsiders, not unlike communities trying to distinguish between who is and who is not in on a joke. This is true for "conspiracy theorists, anti-feminists, white nationalists, Donald Trump supporters, and other disgruntled right-wingers" that exclaim the term as "a verbal badge of allegiance."[23] It is true as well for so-called cuck fetishists associated with Gamergate, and then again for mischief-makers like Sam Hyde who regularly use terms like "butt-hurt"— an expression used to make fun of anyone deemed to be foolishly, idiotically, unjustifiably, or excessively offended by something. Yes, a cuck is a clown according to that old Limbaughesque spirit of being absurd, or saying absurd (if not absurdly insulting) things, to demonstrate perceived absurdities.

In this comic spirit, the terms "cuck" and "cuckservative" are bromides loaded with banal identitarian content. Revisit "The Kings of Alt-Right Comedy." Look at the online handle used by the first man, which situates him as one who slays cucks. Look at the handles for the other two: @White_America69 and @pepeismyhomeboy. Funny or Die is a staple of the mainstream, cofounded by the likes of Will Ferrell and Judd Apatow, eventually backed by corporate stakeholders such as AMC Networks, and acquired in 2021 by business leader and finance chair of the Democratic National Committee Henry R. Muñoz III. That Funny or Die produced "The Kings of Alt-Right Comedy" is an indication of how central terms like "cuck" and references to white America and Pepe the Frog are to popular discourse. The same goes for the fact that comedian Tim Heidecker of Tim & Eric fame took it upon himself to channel the songwriting energies he shares with, dare we say, Paul Shanklin and compose the song "I Am a Cuck" to the tune of "I Am a Rock" by iconic folk duo Simon & Garfunkel—with all of its insinuations of walling oneself off from others and being isolated in particular worldviews. As the chorus goes,

> I am a cuck (*I am a rock*)
> I am a libtard (*I am an island*)

Tellingly, Heidecker has been dubbed the "Bard of the Anti-Trump Movement"[24] and has positioned himself as one who is intent to make opportunities from the limitations of "liberal comedy" that is ill-equipped for dealing with the realities of everyday life and ordinary people.[25] His satirical songs, of which there are many beyond "I Am a Cuck,"[26] are meant to urge naysayers and those who might be on the other extremes of politics to make fun in good faith instead of doing so to be, at base, "a piece of shit."[27] No surprise that Heidecker, who broke into the mainstream with comedy shows on Adult Swim and films like *Tim and Eric's Billion Dollar Movie* (2012), typifies "absurdist comedy" that comes at US public culture "from an unabashedly left-wing perspective."[28] So it goes that "I Am a Cuck" imagines a "shill" for the Democratic establishment and a "pussy who gets fucked right up the ass," a "gay" man and a "fag" who wants to live among Black people and share American rights and privileges with Arabs, and who is really a "douchebag" in comparison to Trump, the savior of white America. The lyrics cut both ways when it comes to how "cuck" applies to both the Left and Right. A "cuckservative" is essentially a man who should be ashamed of himself for countenancing anything that undermines his manhood.[29] A "cuck," more broadly yet better applied to a libtard, is any man who harbors white guilt or the attitudes of woke culture. Even more telling, though, is the song's conclusion: that cucks have no fun.

This conclusion brings us full circle to the roots of "cuck" in comic language. As described by the Southern Poverty Law Center, the combination of "cuckold" and "conservative" recuperates "a racist undertone" by "implying that establishment conservatives are like white men who allow black men to sleep with their wives."[30] The term's racism has even greater reach, according to the Anti-Defamation League, when it "is used by white supremacists to describe a white conservative who putatively promotes the interests of Jews and nonwhites over those of whites."[31] It is a "pornographic trope" that recollects the "racial fetish" of coitus between a Black man and a white woman. The term has overtones of bigotry, too, with the implication that a "cuck" is essentially a "sad sack."[32] Then there is the sexism in the insinuation that *real* men, or alpha males, are those who are not "snowflakes," who are "masculinists," and who rebuff "crybabies."[33] Undergirding this aggregate of "an ideology that promotes what many consider to be white nationalism, racism, antisemitism, homophobia, transphobia and misogyny" is a claim to free expression that echoes the many comedians who maintain their comic license when they assert a "right to say whatever they want, whenever they want, in any way they want to say it."[34] Think of it this way: if "cuck" is part of a joke cycle that perpetuates a more pervasive rhetoric of insult comedy, then it epitomizes a vocabulary of culture and society constituted by a laughable stock of commonplaces and clichés that enables one to amplify outrage, fear, and loathing with the crucial caveat, LMFAO—Laughing My Fucking Ass Off.

As "cuck" would have it, then, comic language provides an important means of being earnest. The insult "cuckservative" has origins in the "absurdist humor" of Something Awful. Users like @glopdemon applied the term as something of a "throwaway joke." Nonetheless, it captured what could be deemed examples of Glopdemon's Law, a concept predating Trumpism and the mainstreaming of alt-right comedy and proving that "extreme right-wing hysteria will always eventually eclipse any attempt to parody it."[35] There is an instructive analogy in the outcry around 1970s television sitcom *All in the Family*, with its presentation of "the real outrage" in people "laughing at what they should have been denouncing" when "right-wing intolerance" was exposed to "mass ridicule."[36] What this analogy overlooks is not that the more *comically* problematic question has to do with tensions between "the brazen coarseness of bigotry" or "the bigotry itself."[37] It misses the idea that comic language is what empowers and emboldens bigotry in the first place.

We might therefore move toward a further development of this language by defining "cuck" as evidence for a strife of interests, to borrow a phrase from Bierce, masquerading as a contest of comic principles. Some of the fallout from "I Am a Cuck" supports this move, as does tangential fallout from the well-publicized cancellation of Hyde's controversial series on Adult Swim, *Million Dollar Extreme Presents: World Peace* (on account of its barefaced racism, sexism, and bigotry). As detailed in the second chapter, Hyde is an infamous online troll who has gained notoriety for the pranks he pulls on those with liberal sensibilities. Heidecker has been a vocal critic of Hyde. In fact, he ardently supported the cancellation of Hyde's show. At least this is a claim that Hyde confronted Heidecker with when he called into his weekly podcast, *Office Hours*. The episodes of *Office Hours* feature comedy sketches and bits where Heidecker goes off on "rants and riffs." Sometimes they take on an air of talk radio when people call in to offer their two cents. On one occasion in December 2016, within days of losing his show, Hyde called in to confront Heidecker and express his aggravation both with liberal comedy and with the efforts of leftist comedians to silence voices from the other side. "I have heard that you campaigned to get our show taken off the air," Hyde said to Heidecker during the heated exchange.[38] Heidecker responded by denying the accusation and calling it a fantasy circulated online by fans of Hyde's comedy troupe. Heidecker then challenged Hyde by adding that in tandem with that fantasy was a flurry of "coordinated, consistent, nasty, violent" rhetoric flung at *him*, including death threats. Hyde laughs at this notion. What is more, he blames Heidecker for getting what he deserved after putting out his singsong comic politics in "I Am a Cuck."

Never mind that Hyde wants the platform for doing his comedy. And never mind the sentiment that pushing back on liberal comedy is a way of speaking truth to cultural power. Most instructive in this exchange is the situation of cruel, if not hateful, language as the comic foil for having fun in violating societal norms. In the idea that comedy has an alt-right problem is a recognition that comic language is a burden when it makes sense of racism, white supremacy, fascistic thinking, and so on with terms that are "vulgar, irreverent, ironic, and goofy."[39] To be a cuck is akin to being one who cannot take a joke. To announce that you are a cuck, in jest, is to imagine how comic language can be ridiculous, and yet how it can be right on. In his definition of "ridicule," Bierce laughingly refers to words that are "graphic, mimetic or merely rident," and goes on to mock "the doctrine of Infant Respectability."[40] Words are not meaningful in isolation just as sticks and stones are less profound when disconnected from pillory and lapidation. The meaning of culture, like the meaning of the comic, comes from the process and results of words in associations, in the spaces "between patterns learned and created in the mind and patterns communicated and made active in relationships, conventions, and institutions." This is what makes comedy what Williams might refer to as "a curiosity of language."[41] Hence my curiosity about statements of principles that take on a comic spirit, to which I now turn.

FOOLISH CONSISTENCIES AND
THE HOBGOBLINS OF MINDS

The cultural politics of the alt-right are hidden in plain sight. This is partly because the alt-right is less "alternative" these days than it is an accumulation of New Right, Dissident Right, Far Right, and other categories for conservative orthodoxy that have been congealed into a mainstream right wing. Enthusiasts and votaries from Hyde to avowed white supremacist and progenitor of the alt-right movement Richard Spencer have been mainstreaming for years. In his 2017 manifesto, "What It Means to Be Alt-Right," which is taken up in more detail in the following paragraphs, Spencer lays the groundwork for engagement in "situational and ideological" warfare based on a conception of spirit as "the wellspring of culture" and politics as everything "downstream of that."[42] At a conference in Washington, DC, on the eve of the 2016 presidential election, Spencer yelled, "Hail, Trump!" in a crowd of compatriots, among whom some performed a Nazi salute. He later defended his exclamation as something done "in the spirit of irony and exuberance."[43] Hyde conveys as much in his promotion of what he dubs the Perfect Guy Life, his disgust with feminization, his gratitude for white people, and his mockery of the Clown World Order. In short, though the alt-right has its war mentalities and its weaponized language, it also has a particularly comic spirit.

It is no joke that what Spencer has established as an "Identitarian Revolution" reeks of "old school fascism, 19th-century nativism, slavery-produced white supremacy, Goldwater conservativism, and 1970s-style disillusionment."[44] Notwithstanding the comic appeal of a term like "cuck," there is a measure of fun that comes with "the seductive power of extremism" in the main.[45] Comedians like Matt Rife are not entirely out of step with this orientation, especially given his insistence on being comically offensive and even being unfunny so long as what he says is funny to him.[46] This is where Henri Bergson is not entirely accurate in his sense that something comic arouses the intellect. It is, after all, the sentimentality of seduction, especially comic seduction, that leads us to give ourselves over to what we might otherwise know to be racist, bigoted, chauvinistic, wrong—extreme. The rigidity and foolish consistency of ideologies and situations behind this kind of fun make it at once laughable and comic.

The alt-right makes trouble for comedy. One problem has to do with the infusion of extreme right-wing views into a comic tradition of transgression, offense, and what we now refer to as cringeworthy humor. This infusion is long standing. Its roots are in uses of comedy as the attire to "cloak very real beliefs" in an effort to "normalize hateful ideologies."[47] The outgrowth is an operation of comedy as a fiefdom, of sorts, that—in this case—emboldens those who peddle "racism, sexism, homophobia, and flirtation with the far right" in the mainstream along with those who carry the same orientations over to the kind of rally that led to the Capitol riot.[48] Another problem relates to the death-of-comedy attitudes that accompanied Trump's presidency. There is a time and place, the argument goes, and while there can be kings of comedy, comedy cannot be king. Trump not only made it possible to feign comicality "to defang satirists" but also demonstrated how to reappropriate comedy "by shifting the place where jokes happen."[49] By some accounts, the result has been that "traditional forms of humor" appear "quaint and futile."[50] So it is when comedy cannot be separated from real-world culture wars waged with violent rhetoric and language games that erupt into political unrest.

None of these problems is all that unfamiliar. Comedy always toes the line. It is very often difficult to discern where the "true" perspective of comic content begins and the "false" thoughts or feelings end. Anonymous online trolls and social media shitposters and even hard-line right-wing media personalities make this discernment more fraught, for sure. But it remains that the real problem is always how we accept comedy *as* comedy. This goes beyond the comic judgments of any satirist or comedian or, for that matter, online prankster or political figure or talking head. We should be concerned about our judgments of what counts as comedy and therefore what we make from the meaning of "the comic." We should be concerned about how comedy influences meaning-making activities too.

Foolish consistencies are one thing. Coherence is another, especially in "the wholesale manufacture of comic effects" that coincide with "a certain stream of facts and fancies which flows straight from the fountain-head."[51] Spencer is such a fountainhead, and his "meta-political manifesto" (subtitled "The Charlottesville Statement") is, in many ways, a watershed. In it Spencer appeals to white nationalism, men's rights, antifeminism, and more in a sweeping yet pithy document that hearkens to a "shared civilization" as the heart of an "ethno-state" for white America; turns Christian values toward heterosexuality and away from "the futile denial of biological reality"; and perhaps most vehemently identifies "Leftism" as "an ideology of death" promulgated by childish narcissists that "must be confronted and defeated."[52] This, of course, was the framework for Spencer's headlining role in a two-day Unite the Right rally in Charlottesville, Virginia, which amounted to an unlawful assembly and ended with a thirty-two-year-old woman getting killed when a rallygoer drove his car into a crowd of counterprotesters. The violence was problematic for Spencer, not, though, for the reason one might think. By all means, he affirmed, conflict is vital. But "violent clashes and pitched battles" undermine alt-right politicking when "they aren't fun."[53]

This is where a different manifesto—composed less with an almost civil tongue than with tongue in cheek—might do the trick by speaking the same language in a "mood of revelry and laughter." That manifesto is one that had "Trumpworld talking" in 2019 and the American right in seeming comic lockstep thereafter.[54] It is entitled *Bronze Age Mindset*, a self-published statement of beliefs by Bronze Age Pervert (BAP), the alias of an on-again, off-again social media troll doing the deeds of the Far Right with a comic facade.[55] The manifesto itself is sprawling, filled with slipshod prose and scattershot argumentation, with the rhetorical sentiment of an author parodying Zarathustra coming down from the mountaintop to deliver his Nietzschean good news. The aforementioned "mood" is BAP's avowed comic spirit. With it, he guides readers through a range of "references to poets, philosophers, historians, scientists, and their theories" so as to commingle "crude" insults and "scatological slang" with what senior fellow at the Claremont Institute and conservative thought leader of "the Flight 93 election" fame Michael Anton defended as legitimate grounds for praising the manifesto's folly: "that natural inequalities exist, that strength and courage are real virtues, and that certain men are naturally more fit to rule than others."[56] Sure, the content is an "ugly mélange" of serious claims

COMEDY IS DEAD

and witty japes all tied together in a screed that "is clearly supposed to be funny, supposed to be political, and supposed to feature vicious slanders aimed at women, racial minorities, Jews, and more."[57] As BAP attests, though, it is an honest attempt to imagine that world anew for a "brotherhood of the damned" by descending into comic madness.

This is not the place for a full-on book review or rhetorical critique of the manifesto. It is the place, however, to point out the bigger picture of its comic language—language that comes from the BAP who is really Costin Alamriu, a Romanian American, avowed misogynist and nudist, and former PhD student in political science at Yale University who wrote a dissertation, "The Problem of Tyranny and Philosophy in Plato and Nietzsche," modeled after the orientation of Leo Strauss in the intellectual guise of Alan Bloom.[58] Build up the natural animalism of your body! Open your mind! These are the general conceits, and they take shape in an exhortation that urges readers to exploit the machinery of government to systematically eliminate "all people of color, feminists, socialists, and, of course, Jews" to manufacture "a pure and enduring whites-only ethno-utopia."[59] This conceit is presented for the author's "frog friends" (an obvious allusion to Pepe the Frog), and it is supported by a mock hierarchy of values that doubles as what can be read as a set of Nietzschean first principles. There is something to Darwinian evolution, survival of the fittest, animal nature, and an inexorable life force that will forever prevent human beings from serving as uncomplicated machines of the state. So says the authorial pervert. Coupled with these sentiments are comic maneuverings across multiple chapters wherein he extols manliness as the antidote to any "quirks, doxies and faggotries" that might turn people into "spiritual lesbians." Women, in other words, should be meninists, too, and embrace the distinctions between superiority and inferiority that could prevent the men of today from turning into "buffoons" imprisoned in the "default civilization" derived from wokeism and cancel culture. "Only the warrior is a free man," we are told, and any pursuit in the realm of culture, politics, or even comedy should be seen as "leisure for preparation for *war*." A true American is only in the right if he indulges his "lust for power" to pursue "self-glorification," thereby standing against the "sheer nonsense" of a Clown World Order. A certain clownishness can only be a virtue if it is leveraged "to intensify vice, to stir up demonic passions, to sow total confusion in the heart of the beast," and to compel "chaos, confusion and pressure on the Leviathan." These are the ends that justify BAP's comic means.

It makes sense that the closing argument of the manifesto reads like the peroration of Hyde's Ted Talk, which is discussed in the previous chapter. The author inveighs against "the evils of suburbs," the "worn-out and pee-stained" words of "social justice," the need for a military that is not "so full of homofaggotry," the "true *samizdat*" of meme making, and the consummate "power of a good prank." All the profanities, proselytization, postulations, and name drops reveal that the crux of the case is deathly serious much in the way that Hyde's own tricksterism is meant to culminate in the killing joke, literally and figuratively. The American right should strive to "make the enemy look ridiculous." He should be exposed for "his authoritarianism, his stupidity, his slavishness, his corruption," and his allegiances to any and all "organs of the left." What is more, the words and phrases of liberal politics and cultural warfare should be harnessed "as a great weapon" unto itself, making the language of the Left— which is otherwise "used to clobber and deceive others into submission and domestication"—into a comic language that can be repurposed as a cudgel of dissidence and revelation. In the real-world activities of internet troll and slaphappy novelist and king of shitposting @Catturd2, memes are counterparts to larger works like *The Adventures of Cowfart* and its satirical portrayal of climate denialism through a left-leaning logic of bovine flatus and environmental degradation.[60] The meaning of the comic for the Far Right is not farce, according to BAP. Comedy is a rudiment for what it means to be alt-right.

The *Bronze Age Mindset*, like Spencer's own manifesto, conjures "old spirits." In the former, they are presented as comic spirits that are wildly eccentric but contain a logic that is "at once accepted and understood by the whole of a social group."[61] In the latter, even though there is no obvious comic spirit, there is a stubbornness akin to what Nietzsche describes as a virtue of laughter: "taking a mischievous delight in the discomfort of another person."[62] Violent clashes and pitched battles in the war for civilization are all fine and good, Spencer tells us, so long as they are fun. It is unsurprising that Nietzsche provides inspiration for deploying laughter as a form of sufferance instead of finding ways to laugh in common because we suffer. Still, one does learn from Nietzsche that laughter is a manifestation of "being *schadenfroh*, but with a good conscience."[63] In the comic language of the Alt-Right, a "good" conscience turns cruelty on others rather than the self. To be cruel to oneself is to harbor guilt. It subjects the self to vainglory. To laugh off guilt, and to reroute cruelty, is to reappropriate what could be a will to contain and repress one's desires, one's power. Is this a comic mindset? Maybe an Alt-Right conscience feels "good." But the comedy is done in bad faith, especially if we also remember that cruelty, for Nietzsche, is a sign of weakness, as is resentment. Maybe this gives new meaning to what Nietzsche called "machine-culture." Or maybe it means that comedy is, and long has been, a ghost in the machine.

THE MACHINELIKE PECULIARITIES
OF THE COMEDY MACHINE

A machine connotes rigidity and momentum. This is the central feature of Bergson's sense that the "deflection of life towards the mechanical" is "the real cause of laughter," which is to say that the "laughable effect" of comedy comes from the manipulation of human being per se into the workings of a machine.[64] The challenge is therefore to laugh at—to see as comic—any "comedy" that gives us the impression of *being* comedy despite its mockeries of a universal human vitality. Put differently, if comedy takes on machinelike qualities, then the meaning of the comic has been tampered with.

Alt-right comedy entails both rage *against* cultural and political machines made to maintain a liberal world order and rage *in* the machine of right-wing claims to culture and politics. The notion of a "right-wing media machine" has been around since the mid-1990s.[65] Since then, human beings have become brooms in the system made to act as "meme machines."[66] Take the machinations of trolls. Many of their memes are like weaponry in a war machine through which cultural warfare gets "accelerated and intensified because of the infrastructure and incentives of the internet, which trades outrage and extremity as currency and rewards speed and scale, and flattens the experience of the world into a never-ending scroll of images and words."[67] An aura of "Rage on the Right" has grown,[68] animated by memes as packages of insinuation, innuendo, and meaning all culled from the iconologies of mainstream culture. This aura represents a "dark and constant rage" that has been lurking in right-wing culture warism, political commentary, and official politicking since the late 1980s.[69] At times, the specter of right-wing rage can feel like a left-wing projection. Still, it seems right to say that a "right-wing rage machine" exists,[70] has long existed, and operates on complicated foundational beliefs and unfounded phobias that feed into, shall we say, telltale signs of schadenfreude.

Before concluding, a note of caution is in order. Beware all the rage. For all his criminal activities and indictments and conspiracies to defraud US citizens, Trump stands as a folk hero for the Far Right who "lives, eats, and breathes defiance in the face of leftism's overwhelming cultural dominance." Diffuse forms of outrage signify a return of repressed fury and frustration that gets networked and staged as a "mix of wit, flair, and," without doubt, "sheer defiance."[71] So diffuse are these forms that BAP, too, has become "a leading cultural figure on the fascist right—among both elites, who have cottoned to his political philosophy, and non-elites, who love his brio and aspire to his erudition."[72] While a glut of people proceed with blind rage to point out all the ways that Trumpism and

BAPism (which, yes, is lately a thing) do us all wrong, there are plenty of others who look on the core messages in these -isms "without being rage-blinded" but instead with the ability and willingness to take their leads and "bond, network, and plot."[73] Language begets culture. Culture begets ways of being. Comedy is a rhetorical and cultural feature, not a bug, in the "Age of Rage."[74] It appears in the wild, sometimes revelatory, sometimes riotous activities of political rallygoers. It appears in the sensational comic antics of pranksters and in the sentimentalities of what could be considered a Make America Great Again caucus. It has, at times, a flavor of bedlam and, at other times, a "veneer of respectability."[75] Moreover, it appears in the rigid, momentous, outrageous machinery of the mainstream as it has emerged out of the ordinary culture of the Far Right.

To understand alt-right comedy is to recognize that devotees of the Far Right and disciples of both Trumpism and BAPism have contributed to the fabrication of a comedy machine. As Nick Marx and Matt Sienkiewicz suggest, *Gutfeld!* in particular is "an object lesson in the growth of right-wing comedy."[76] The satirical news show is popular. It is palatable, if replete with the sorts of bad jokes and easy laughs that make for good television. And its host is an exemplar of how alternative comedy can be transformed from the convention into the rule by keeping the machines of a polarized political culture and a system of warmongering cultural politics running.

One moment stands out. At the end of 2022, Stanford University released a treatise on "Harmful Language." Why? To institutionalize the elimination of language that has any resonances of racism, violence, or bias. This is an academic initiative. But it is also a cultural initiative with political implications. Gutfeld argued as much when he used an opening segment of his show to crack wise about the folly of this beacon for the institution of liberalism.[77] He looks at the camera with his signature furrowed brow and knowing smirk and then goes through some highlights of what not to say and what to say instead, with the Stanford treatise as his guide. For example, instead of calling someone a "Karen," one should use the phrase "demanding or entitled white woman." To get past our own sense of self-importance and superiority complex as the best in the Americas, we should not refer to ourselves as "Americans." "Knock-knock," he says to set up his punch line. He eggs on his audience. "Who's there?" "Fuck you, Stanford," Gutfeld exclaims.

A rendition of George Carlin's famous diatribe on "soft language" this is not. Gutfeld laughs at his own jokes. In a roundtable after the segment, he and his guests make fun of and ridicule cultural grammarians, anyone on the "woke bandwagon," and the "PC police." They spout off talking points in turn about free expression and come to the agreement that Stanford is trying to dumb

COMEDY IS DEAD 151

down society. The Carlin reference might be inapt. Instead, we might recollect Limbaugh's "politically correct liberal lexicon," which he detailed in his book *See, I Told You So* (1993). Either way, Gutfeld's segment relies on "ready-made formulas and stereotyped phrases" that can render comedy itself laughable.[78] And yet like BAP, like Hyde, and so on down the line to the likes of Limbaugh, Gutfeld comes off as Zarathustra, a laughing prophet.

The difference is that Gutfeld, too, has a history of doing anticomedy. In *Red Eye*, a daily talk show that ran at three o'clock in the morning on Fox News from 2007 to 2015, Gutfeld earned a reputation as a funnyman who performed bizarre monologues with commentary on current affairs, devised strange sketches, and conducted conversations with panels of guests who talked politics and waxed comic about US culture. Episodes looked and felt a bit like "liberal satire shows" but were actually "more akin to Adult Swim's absurdist, experimental comedies *Tim and Eric Awesome Show, Great Job!* and *The Eric Andre Show*."[79] It is not that Gutfeld represents "a funhouse version" of mainstream comedy, then and now.[80] It is that he is the fun house brought into the mainstream. The *Bronze Age Mindset* was characterized as part of a Far Right "literary canon" at the same time as it was a bestseller on Amazon and relatively high in the rankings under the category of humor.[81] Similarly, *Gutfeld!* is a logical outcome of outrageous, rage-filled comedy. Someone else, though, might loom even larger.

In April 2021, stand-up comedian and social media influencer Chrissie Mayr had Far Right *fauteur* (or troublemaker) Gavin McInnes on her podcast to discuss, to some degree, how the alt-right does not pose a problem for comedy. Tellingly, McInnes often distances himself from the alt-right, citing important distinctions between his own beliefs about white culture and the racist beliefs of many white nationalists. In this instance, he rejects the idea that comedy fiefdoms are somehow ruinous to culture or politics or that the reverse could also be true. Mayr and McInnes talk about how our structure of comic feeling is a by-product of the "strange climate" in which it percolates. They lament the state of comedy as evidence for what McInnes calls the "humorless times" we are living in and the fact that people who get upset by *any* joke only invigorate agelasts. McInnes gets raunchy for the sake of enjoyment, he proclaims, and portrays the comic character as one who—like a worthy sex partner—suspends disbelief and adopts a persona that allows him to play around with "bad" ideas.[82] For McInnes, free expression is a comic freedom and has shaped the way he advocates political violence, defends his express racism, and celebrates hypermasculinity in a way that would earn BAP's approval.

None of this would be quite so problematic for comedy if McInnes did not have such deep and enduring connections to mainstream conservatism, specifically the strong media personalities of people like Sean Hannity, Tucker Carlson, and, most prominently, Greg Gutfeld. In his book *The Joy of Hate* (2012), Gutfeld made the case for expressing outrage comically in order to wage real contests, real wars against the "phony" outrage of liberals and their rhetorical acts of "backslapping approval."[83] He also identified McInnes as a kindred spirit.[84] This bore out on *Red Eye* given that McInnes was one of his "most popular guests." Together, they made jokes to make fun out of their own outrage. Eventually McInnes made his jokester persona and trickster attitude more passable in the mainstream with regular appearances on Fox News.[85] Jokes aside, the real comic spirit of McInnes can be gleaned from his description of the neofascist organization he founded in 2016: "We will kill you," he said on his online program *The Gavin McInnes Show*. "That's the Proud Boys in a nutshell."[86] Speaking out of the other side of his mouth, McInnes would also allege that the Proud Boys is just "an outlet for harmless fun: an *Animal House*–style drinking club for male buddies" that enabled *him* to reject "the difference between being a clown and inciting violence."[87] This rejection is what undergirds what one member called the organization's "pro-white sentiment" and the "comedic ways" with which McInnes exudes them.[88]

Comedic ways are part and parcel of McInnes's cultural politics and political activity. He is a Western chauvinist. He abhors political correctness. "Maybe the reason I'm sexist," he said on his show in June 2017, "is because women are dumb. No, I'm just kidding, ladies. But you do tend to not thrive in certain areas." A statement like this is in line with his generalized detestation of demasculinization, his disgust with "bitches," and his veneration for housewives. A month earlier, he published an article with online paleoconservative magazine *Takimag* entitled "10 Things I Like about White Guys," the subtitle for which could have been "or 10 Things I Hate about You." His Proud Boys wore these and other sentiments quite literally on their sleeves with T-shirts with slogans like "Pinochet did nothing wrong" and "Death to Liberals," artfully crafted with the same white text on black background aesthetics as Black Lives Matter iconography. A popular meme among Far Right groups, including the Proud Boys, showcases a Hoppean Snake. It is "a joking homage to Pinochet" that is aligned with the "Don't Tread on Me" serpent from the Gadsden flag and used to show seemingly mock support for a "putschist, tyrant, torturer, mass murderer, puppet of the CIA, and hater of all things socialist, who ruled Chile form 1973 to 1990."[89] The overlap of comedy and violence reinforces McInnes's first principle of committing to a joke if and only if "you're willing to die to make people laugh."[90] It is one thing to acknowledge that most of what McInnes "calls his 'jokes' involve racist, sexist, ableist, petty, puerile, and mean attacks

COMEDY IS DEAD

on entire groups, as well as individuals."[91] It is another thing to recognize that a trickster figure, a chauvinistic clown, a self-proclaimed "professional troll," a pervert in the age of outrage embodies mainstream comic character in word and deed—that his comedic ways are de rigueur in right-wing discourse.

The conundrum we are left with is how to reconcile rage in the machines of politics and culture with comedy gone right, or wrong, in the real world.

CONCLUSION: THE PECULIAR LANGUAGE OF COMEDY

Dig into the etymology of "fun" and you will find connections to terms like *fon*, *fonne*, and *fonnen*, and so to various iterations of fools and folly, humorous content, and amusing funnymen. Dig into "comedy" and you will find an ancient sense of revelry relative to whatever it is that is made amusing or humorous. What is more, there is an early-twentieth-century notion that supports what many apologists for comic spirits on the Right and the Left say comedy should be: entertainment based on a presentation of life that is farcical, or funny, enough to provoke laughter "by the outrageous absurdity of the situations or characters exhibited."[92] Outrage and absurdity. These are core elements in the comic act of making fun.

The rise of the Far Right in and through comedy bespeaks this fundamental risibility in what is "fun." Lest we forget, though, that "fun" can also come from *fume* and from *fomme*. The word *fomme* connotes a simpleton, namely, a stupid woman, a maiden. The word *fume* is more familiar, and not for its association with folly and fools. *Fume* is rage. It is excitement. It is the fulminating, intense feeling that can provoke the sort of diversion from, say, a comedy of good manners to the very amusement that comes with tricks and hoaxes, never mind with the violence that McInnes and others of his ilk have long tried to pass off as a joke. In his definition of "doctrinaire," Williams outlines an oddity in the conflict it implies between what is principled or not and, perhaps more critically, what is "undesirable or absurd"—and how this conflict formulates a basis for the attempt "to reconcile two extreme positions."[93] We have here such a conflict. It is not, however, simply about indoctrination and right-wing extremism. Rather, it is about that old saying that turns on a singular wonderment, which is whether something is "funny ha-ha" or "funny peculiar."

This chapter has been largely about not only the peculiarities of comic language but also the peculiar language of comedy itself. I will return to these matters in a moment. It is worth first considering a few observations about comedy to help us figure out our contemporary comic spirits and to keep in mind that whether something "comic" is also "funny" is, in some measure, beside the point. Many things can be funny. Some of those things are outrageous or absurd. Some of them are malicious or cruel. The point is to take care with how we bestow the very label "comedy" in the first place and then again in the last instance.

The rise of alt-right comedy is nothing if not a reaction to, and from, what is variously dubbed an "Exhausted Majority," the "Exhaustion of American Liberalism," and a "Blue Fatigue." People are tired. Some people are tired of polarization in media and politics. Others are tired of the same old, same old. A certain comic fervor can be a way to get reinvigorated by having fun and being irreverent. It can combat fatigue—even a fatigue around how comedy has tended to be done in the mainstream. According to Will Kaufman, comedians or humorists as diverse as Ben Franklin, Mark Twain, Lenny Bruce, Kurt Vonnegut, and Bill Hicks (and, I would add, Ambrose Bierce) exemplify how a "comic masquerade" can serve as a veritable pretext for unsettling the conventional wisdom, and thus the vocabulary, of culture and society.[94] Yet there is a risk to keeping up the charade so much that we lock ourselves into comedy as a way of being. This risk is not unlike the dangers of locking ourselves into the egoism of what is now termed identity politics or the collective ego that corresponds with something like an identitarian revolution or a mindset that is trapped in the Bronze Age. Comedy is meant to nurture survival in the shared folly of being human. When a comic masquerade becomes the way to despoil comedy, fatigue can fold into forms of fanaticism that prevent us from grasping the complex totalities of situations and the strange configurations in the order of things. The problem with alt-right comedy is therefore as much about the limits of a comic perspective in what might be characterized as its "deplorable" content as it is about degenerations in the meaning of the comic.[95] The conman can play the confidence man.

With that, a brief detour. In October 2018, McInnes gave a talk at the Metropolitan Republican Club in New York City. The crux of it was a "commemoration and celebration of the 1960 televised assassination" of Inejiro Asanuma, the head of the Japanese Socialist Party.[96] McInnes played the part of a cutthroat, pretending to be the ultranationalist Otoya Yamaguchi, who killed Asanuma. He wielded a katana and performed a crude reenactment before taking the podium, opening a can of beer, and delivering "a rambling, stream-of-consciousness stand-up set that had McInnes ranting about everything from the evils of socialism to 'politically incorrect' style offensive jokes."[97] The "comedy routine" was met with revelry from fans and acolytes.[98] It was met with protest from detractors. The club was vandalized and defaced. A note was left on the door accusing the club members of inviting "a hipster-fascist clown to dance

COMEDY IS DEAD

155

for them, content to revel in their treachery against humanity."[99] Protesters clashed with Proud Boys. Fights broke out. People were injured. People were arrested. Ultimately, McInnes resigned his leadership post.

The comic masquerade continued. A black-and-white image of Asanuma's assassination is the picture of provocation in a popular meme among Far Right communities. Moreover, almost exactly four years after this routine, McInnes was invited by a student group, Uncensored America, to be part of a comedy event entitled "Stand Back & Stand By" at Pennsylvania State University.[100] The group claims to promote "honest and fun conversations with controversial figures to fight censorship and cancel culture." In other words, provocation is the point. University administrators initially defended against pushback by appealing to rights of free expression guaranteed by the Constitution, even when that expression is borne out as hatred and vitriol. Funny as he may be, McInnes takes pride in inciting political violence. The event was canceled because of threats to public safety, sparked before the event by attacks on students and journalists. The cancellation came while McInnes was in the middle of "The Cognitive Dissidents Tour," a series of shows featuring McInnes; white supremacist and "disgraced shock-jock" for radio show *Opie and Anthony* Anthony Cumia; and self-proclaimed "canceled" comedian Josh Denny, who once likened the term "straight white male" to the N-word by saying that both are "used to offend and diminish the recipient based on assumption and bias."[101] With all due respect for wordplay, the cognitive dissonance is most apparent in how all of this and more indicates comedy gone to the extremes. McInnes once praised the pejorative "cuckservative" as a designation for people who should be made fun of for being on the wrong sides of the right wing. Then he worried when its use had become intractable.[102] One is left to wonder when the comic mask is dropped or what will end the masquerade.

This wonderment might presage a fool's errand. After all, we use vocabulary to manage "the difficult relations between words and concepts; or the general processes of sense and reference; and beyond these the more general rules, in social norms and in the system of language itself, which both enable sense and reference to be generated and in some large degree to control them."[103] However, any vocabulary of culture and society is, in some large degree, out of our control. So, it is not just that some cultural or political vocabulary gets converted into comic language. It is also that the language of comedy gets folded into those vocabularies, and fortifies them in machineries of judgment. Human beings are, in Bergson's words, "judging machines." We might go so far as to say that we are *joking* machines that make fun from "the juxtaposition of a control against that which is controlled."[104] The plain truth is that we are rhetorical beings that use the mechanics of language to translate our thoughts into ways of living. Bergson was concerned with the tensions between "the comic *expressed* and the comic *created* by language," and how those tensions reveal how and when it is "language itself that becomes comic."[105] This chapter has established the grounds for grappling with comedy that becomes language—more precisely, the language of culture and society.

From terminology like "cuckservative" through the tutelage of talking heads like Gutfeld, a varied brand of alt-right comedy has facilitated the creation of a comic way of being. With it, comedy is not just absurd, not merely cruel, not only ridiculous but also peculiar. There are two reference points for this designation. One is the original sense of the word, which signifies something that is exclusive to an individual, private, owned. Something is peculiar in this regard insofar as it makes a position or point of view seem more or less special in society. The second reference point is more specific to the United States, and it bears the rhetorical weight of that pesky euphemism for slavery, the peculiar institution. Slavery, of course, entails all the horror and debauchery of keeping human chattel. But it also represents a more inveterate investment in and stubborn commitment to cultural realities that are, in the end, as weird as they are wretched. This is not to say that dittoheads or shitposters or frog friends occupy the heritage of a Lost Cause. It is to say, however, that peculiarity is a cornerstone for establishing what the vice president for the Confederacy once called "the proper status" of people in accordance with a certain "form of civilization."[106] There is likewise much more to the peculiarity of comedy in a US tradition that counteracts the language of trickster slaves and Black humorists (in both senses of the term) who harnessed a comic spirit to deal with the pathologies of plantation mentalities, which bear disturbing resemblances to Bronze Age mindsets.

The "peculiarities of language," says Bergson, reveal "peculiarities of character," and these are "peculiarities that are held in common."[107] These peculiarities lay bare the meaning of the comic when comedy "conveys the impression of pure mechanism, of automatism, of movement without life."[108] In a similar spirit, Derek Attridge identifies these peculiarities in the fact that something like a comic ruse relies on what both "is and is not the same language we use to think, to prove, to govern, to mourn, to dream."[109] A joke at once exploits and violates "ordinary diction" just as a comedian exploits the cultural or political significance of taking "aspects of a society's or a language community's ideology" and "turning them into comedy."[110] This does not mean that the devil is in the details of our dictionaries or our delineations of this or that bad actor. It means that comedy, when pushed to extremes, can constitute the first principles of a devil's advocate.

NOTES

1. "Ambrose Bierce," Poetry Foundation, accessed August 5, 2023, https://www.poetryfoundation.org/poets/ambrose-bierce.

2. Raymond Williams, introduction to *Keywords: A Vocabulary of Culture and Society* (New York: Oxford University Press, 1976), xxiii.

3. Ambrose Bierce, *The Devil's Dictionary* (Cleveland: World Publishing, 1911), 258. See also Williams, introduction, xxiii.

4. See, for instance, Alleen Pace Nilsen and Don L. F. Nilsen, *The Language of Humor: An introduction* (New York: Cambridge University Press, 2019).

5. Raymond Williams, *The Long Revolution* (1961; Ontario: Broadview Press, 2001), 319. See also W. J. T. Mitchell, *Picture Theory* (Chicago: University of Chicago Press, 1994).

6. "The Word—Truthiness," *The Colbert Report*, October 17, 2005, https://www.cc.com/video/63ite2/the-colbert-report-the-word-truthiness.

7. Bierce, preface to *The Devil's Dictionary*, 8.

8. Williams, introduction, xxxiii.

9. Emily Nussbaum, "How Jokes Won the Election," *New Yorker*, January 15, 2017, https://www.newyorker.com/magazine/2017/01/23/how-jokes-won-the-election.

10. Funny or Die, "Kings of Alt Right Comedy," YouTube, September 13, 2016, https://www.youtube.com/watch?v=TNGhCQ9tyH4.

11. Jacqui Shine, "Not with a Bang, but a Retweet: The Rise of the Alt-Right," *Los Angeles Review of Books*, July 30, 2017, https://lareviewofbooks.org/article/not-with-a-bang-but-a-retweet-the-rise-of-the-alt-right/.

12. "Identity Unmasked: Meet the Proprietors of the Internet's Largest Neo-Confederate Propaganda Machine," *Intelligence Report*, September 10, 2019, https://www.splcenter.org/fighting-hate/intelligence-report/2019/identity-unmasked-meet-proprietors-internets-largest-neo-confederate-propaganda-machine.

13. Catherine Liu, "Dialectic of Dark Enlightenments: The Alt-Right's Place in the Culture Industry," *Los Angeles Review of Books*, July 30, 2017, https://lareviewofbooks.org/article/dialectic-of-dark-enlightenments-the-alt-rights-place-in-the-culture-industry/.

14. Angela Nagle, *Kill All Normies: Online Culture Wars from 4Chan and Tumblr to Trump and the Alt-Right* (Alresford, UK: Zero Books, 2017).

15. Amber A'Lee Frost, "No Such Cuck," *Baffler* 29 (October 2015), https://thebaffler.com/salvos/no-such-cuck-frost.

16. Frost, "No Such Cuck."

17. Jeet Heer, "Conservatives Are Holding a Conversation about Race," *New Republic*, July 26, 2015, https://newrepublic.com/article/122372/conservatives-are-holding-conversation-about-race. See also "Alt-Right," Southern Poverty

Law Center, accessed March 11, 2020, https://www.splcenter.org/fighting-hate
/extremist-files/ideology/alt-right.

18. Frost, "No Such Cuck."

19. MILO, "'Cuckservative' Is a Gloriously Effective Insult That Should Not
Be Slurred, Demonised, or Ridiculed," *Breitbart*, July 28, 2015, https://www
.breitbart.com/politics/2015/07/28/cuckservative-is-a-gloriously-effective-insult
-that-should-not-be-slurred-demonised-or-ridiculed/. See also John McDermott,
"How the Alt-Right Made 'Cuck' the Word of the Year," *Medium*, November
28, 2016, https://medium.com/mel-magazine/how-the-alt-right-made-cuck-the
-word-of-the-year-2164daco1e66.

20. Matt Taibbi, *Insane Clown President: Dispatches from the 2016 Circus* (New
York: Spiegel and Grau, 2017).

21. Christopher Mele, "Creepy Clown Hoaxes Lead to 12 Arrests in Multiple
States," *New York Times*, September 29, 2016, https://www.nytimes.com/2016/09
/30/us/creepy-clown-hoaxes-arrests.html.

22. Suzanne Zuppello, "'Killer Clowns': Inside the Terrifying Hoax Sweeping
America," *Rolling Stone*, September 29, 2016, https://www.rollingstone.com
/culture/culture-news/killer-clowns-inside-the-terrifying-hoax-sweeping
-america-129505/.

23. Nikhil Sonnad and Tim Squirrell, "The Alt-Right Is Creating Its Own
Dialect. Here's the Dictionary," *Quartz*, October 30, 2017, https://qz.com
/1092037/the-alt-right-is-creating-its-own-dialect-heres-a-complete-guide.

24. Reggie Ugwu, "Tim Heidecker, Bard of the Anti-Trump Movement,"
Buzzfeed News, April 4, 2017, https://www.buzzfeednews.com/article
/reggieugwu/tim-heidecker-trump-songs.

25. Will Sloan, "The Limits of Liberal Comedy," *Current Affairs*, December 10,
2020, https://www.currentaffairs.org/2020/12/the-limits-of-liberal-comedy.

26. See his parody album, *Too Dumb for Suicide: Tim Heidecker's Trump Songs*
(2017).

27. Ugwu, "Tim Heidecker."

28. Sloan, "Limits of Liberal Comedy."

29. Damon Young, "The Racist Roots of 'Cuck' (the White Supremacist's
Favorite Insult), Explained," *Root*, August 15, 2017, https://www.theroot.com/the
-racist-roots-of-cuck-the-white-supremacists-favo-1797868917.

30. "Alt-Right."

31. "Alt Right: A Primer on the New White Supremacy," Anti-Defamation
League, June 18, 2020, https://www.adl.org/resources/backgrounder/alt-right
-primer-new-white-supremacy.

32. Note that this is the core idea in the flop of a film *Cuck* (2019), about men
who turn their political and cultural emasculation into overt forms of resentment.

COMEDY IS DEAD

33. Jessica Roy, "Analysis: 'Cuck,' 'Snowflake,' 'Masculinist': A Guide to the Language of the 'Alt-Right,'" *Los Angeles Times*, November 15, 2016, https://www.latimes.com/nation/la-na-pol-alt-right-terminology-20161115-story.html.

34. Roy, "Analysis."

35. Frost, "No Such Cuck."

36. Frost, "No Such Cuck."

37. Frost, "No Such Cuck."

38. Megh Wright, "Sam Hyde Lashed Out at Tim Heidecker Over 'Million Dollar Extreme's Cancellation," *Vulture*, December 8, 2016, https://www.vulture.com/2016/12/sam-hyde-lashed-out-at-tim-heidecker-over-million-dollar-extremes-cancellation.html.

39. George Hawley, *Making Sense of the Alt-Right* (New York: Columbia University Press, 2017), 3. See also Raúl Pérez, *The Souls of White Jokes: How Racist Humor Fuels White Supremacy* (Stanford, CA: Stanford University Press, 2022).

40. Bierce, *Devil's Dictionary*, 295.

41. Williams, *Long Revolution*, 89.

42. Richard Spencer, "What It Means to Be Alt-Right," ALTRIGHT.com, August 11, 2017, https://altright.com/2017/08/11/what-it-means-to-be-alt-right/.

43. Juju Chang and Victoria Thompson, "White Nationalist Richard Spencer on Being Confronted by Protestors at Texas A&M Appearance," ABC News, December 8, 2016, https://abcnews.go.com/US/white-nationalist-richard-spencer-confronted-protestors-texas-appearance/story?id=44061233#:~:text=Spencer%20said%20he%20yelled%20out%20"Hail%20Trump%2C"%20"in,said%20if%20felt%20like%20a%20kind%20of%20"miracle.

44. Daniel Lombroso, "Four Years Embedded with the Alt-Right," *Atlantic*, June 11, 2020, https://www.theatlantic.com/politics/archive/2020/06/white-noise-documentary-alt-right/612898/. See also Ryan Bohl, "The Global History of the Alt-Right," *Salon*, March 19, 2017, https://www.salon.com/2017/03/19/the-global-history-of-the-alt-right/.

45. Lombroso, "Four Years."

46. Aja Romano, "What Matt Rife's Baffling Netflix Special Tells Us about Comedy," *Vox*, November 29, 2023, https://www.vox.com/culture/23980945/who-is-matt-rife-netflix-special-natural-selection-backlash-controversy-tiktok.

47. Ashwin Rodrigues, "The Far-Right Has Deep Roots in New York Comedy," *Vice*, February 12, 2021, https://www.vice.com/en/article/dy8j4k/alt-right-new-york-comedy-new-republic.

48. Seth Simons, "The Comedy Industry Has a Big Alt-Right Problem," *New Republic*, February 9, 2021, https://newrepublic.com/article/161200/alt-right-comedy-gavin-mcinnes-problem.

49. Dan Brooks, "How President Trump Ruined Political Comedy," *New York Times Magazine*, October 8, 2020, https://www.nytimes.com/2020/10/07/magazine/trump-liberal-comedy-tv.html.

50. Justin E. H. Smith, "The End of Satire," *New York Times*, April 8, 2019, https://www.nytimes.com/2019/04/08/opinion/the-end-of-satire.html.

51. Henri Bergson, *Laughter: An Essay on the Meaning of the Comic*, trans. Cloudesley Brereton and Fred Rothwell (New York: MacMillan, 1911), 12.

52. Spencer, "What It Means."

53. Natasha Lennard, "Is ANTIFA Counterproductive? White Nationalist Richard Spencer Would Beg to Differ," *Intercept*, March 17, 2018, https://theintercept.com/2018/03/17/richard-spencer-college-tour-antifa-alt-right/.

54. Ben Schreckinger, "The Alt-Right Manifesto That Has Trumpworld Talking," Politico, August 23, 2019, https://www.politico.eu/article/right-wing-manifesto-that-has-trumpworld-talking-military-rule-bap-bapism-cult-book-bronze-age-mindset/.

55. Bronze Age Pervert, *Bronze Age Mindset: An Exhortation* (self-pub., June 2018).

56. Michael Anton, "Are the Kids Al(t)right?," *Claremont Review of Books* (Summer 2019), https://claremontreviewofbooks.com/are-the-kids-altright/.

57. Matt Sienkiewicz and Nick Marx, *That's Not Funny: How the Right Makes Comedy Work for Them* (Oakland: University of California Press, 2022), 156.

58. See Blake Smith, "Bronze Age Pervert's Dissertation on Leo Strauss," *Tablet Magazine*, February 14, 2023, https://www.tabletmag.com/sections/arts-letters/articles/bronze-age-pervert-dissertation-leo-strauss.

59. Ian Allen, "The Far Right's Apocalyptic Literary Canon," *New Republic*, October 1, 2019, https://newrepublic.com/article/155217/far-rights-apocalyptic-literary-canon.

60. Miles Klee, "Who Is @Catturd2, the Sh-tposting King of MAGA Twitter?," *Rolling Stone*, February 9, 2023, https://www.rollingstone.com/culture/culture-features/catturd2-maga-twitter-shitposting-king-1234674671/.

61. Bergson, *Laughter*, 2.

62. Friedrich Nietzsche, *The Gay Science*, trans. Walter Kaufmann (New York: Vintage Books, 1974), 207.

63. Nietzsche, *Gay Science*, 207.

64. Bergson, *Laughter*, 34.

65. Robert Parry, "The Rise of the Right-Wing Media Machine," Fairness & Accuracy in Reporting, March 1, 1995, https://fair.org/home/the-rise-of-the-right-wing-media-machine/.

66. Susan Blackmore, *The Meme Machine* (Oxford: Oxford University Press, 1999).

67. Joan Donovan, Emily Dreyfuss, and Brian Friedberg, *Meme Wars: The Untold Story of the Online battles Upending Democracy in America* (New York: Bloomsbury, 2022), 9–10.

68. "Rage on the Right," *Intelligence Report*, March 2, 2010, https://www
.splcenter.org/fighting-hate/intelligence-report/2010/rage-right.

69. "A Dark and Constant Rage: 25 Years of Right-Wing Terrorism in the United States," Anti-Defamation League, May 17, 2017, https://www.adl.org/resources
/report/dark-and-constant-rage-25-years-right-wing-terrorism-united-states.

70. "The Power of the Right-Wing Rage Machine," CNN, April 14, 2019, https://www.cnn.com/videos/business/2019/04/14/the-power-of-the-right
-wing-rage-machine.cnn.

71. David French, "The Rage against the Machine—Understanding the Milo Phenomenon," *National Review*, February 21, 2017, https://www.nationalreview
.com/2017/02/milo-phenomenon-understanding-right-wing-rage/. See also Joshua Gunn, *Political Perversion: Rhetorical Aberration in the Time of Trumpeteering* (Chicago: University of Chicago Press, 2020), 50, 64, 99; and Bob Woodward, *Rage* (New York: Simon and Schuster, 2020).

72. Graeme Wood, "How Bronze Age Pervert Charmed the Far Right," *Atlantic*, August 3, 2023, https://www.theatlantic.com/magazine/archive/2023
/09/bronze-age-pervert-costin-alamariu/674762/.

73. Wood, "How Bronze Age Pervert Charmed the Far Right."

74. Adi Robertson, "Alt-Right: Age of Rage Is a Snapshot of One of 2017's Darkest Moments," *Verge*, March 14, 2018, https://www.theverge.com/2018/3/14
/17113514/alt-right-age-of-rage-antifa-film-review-sxsw-2018.

75. Robertson, "Alt-Right."

76. Nick Marx and Matt Sienkiewicz, "A Fox News Host's Strange Backstory Shows How Liberals Lost Comedy," *Slate*, June 13, 2022, https://slate.com
/culture/2022/06/greg-gutfeld-fox-news-show-conservative-comedy.html.

77. Amy Nelson, "'Gutfeld!' Roasts Stanford's List of Harmful Words Like 'American': 'The Idiots Are Running the Show,'" Fox News, December 22, 2022, https://www.foxnews.com/media/gutfeld-roasts-stanford-list-harmful-words
-american-idiots-running-show.

78. Bergson, *Laughter*, 112.

79. Sienkiewicz and Marx, *That's Not Funny*, 36.

80. Sienkiewicz and Marx, *That's Not Funny*, 36.

81. Allen, "Far Right's Apocalyptic Literary Canon."

82. Chrissie Mayr, "Comedy Does NOT Have an Alt-Right Comedy Problem ft. Gavin McInnes," YouTube, April 27, 2021, https://www.youtube.com/watch
?app=desktop&v=Ww1QtqmZD_s.

83. Greg Gutfeld, *The Joy of Hate: How to Triumph Over Whiners in the Age of Phony Outrage* (New York: Crown Forum, 2012), 47.

84. Gutfeld, *Joy of Hate*, 193.

85. Parker Molloy, "How Fox News Helped Turn Proud Boys Founder Gavin McInnes into a Right-Wing Media Star," Media Matters for America, October

2, 2020, https://www.mediamatters.org/gavin-mcinnes/how-fox-news-helped -turn-proud-boys-founder-gavin-mcinnes-right-wing-media-star.

86. "Proud Boys," Anti-Defamation League, November 2, 2018, https://www .adl.org/resources/backgrounder/proud-boys-0.

87. Adam Leith Gollner, "The Secret History of Gavin McInnes," *Vanity Fair*, June 29, 2021, https://www.vanityfair.com/news/2021/06/the-secret-history-of -gavin-mcinnes. See also "White Haze," *This American Life*, September 22, 2017, https://www.thisamericanlife.org/626/transcript.

88. "Proud Boys," Southern Poverty Law Center, accessed April 11, 2020, https://www.splcenter.org/fighting-hate/extremist-files/group/proud-boys.

89. Christopher Ketcham, "What the Far-Right Fascination with Pinochet's Death Squads Should Tell Us," *Intercept*, February 4, 2021, https://theintercept .com/2021/02/04/pinochet-far-right-hoppean-snake/.

90. Gollner, "Secret History."

91. Sharona Coutts, "How Hate Goes 'Mainstream': Gavin McInnes and the Proud Boys," Rewire News Group, August 28, 2017, https://rewirenewsgroup .com/2017/08/28/hate-goes-mainstream-gavin-mcinnes-proud-boys/.

92. H. W. Fowler, *A Dictionary of Modern English Usage* (Oxford: Clarendon Press, 1927), 84.

93. Williams, introduction, 68.

94. Will Kaufman, *The Comedian as Confidence Man: Studies in Irony Fatigue* (Detroit: Wayne State University Press, 1997).

95. Viveca S. Greene, "'Deplorable' Satire: Alt-Right Memes, White Genocide Tweets, and Redpilling Normies," *Studies in American Humor* 5, no. 1 (2019): 31–69.

96. Cassie Miller, "Why Are the Proud Boys So Violent? Ask Gavin McInnes," Southern Poverty Law Center, October 18, 2018, https://www.splcenter.org /hatewatch/2018/10/18/why-are-proud-boys-so-violent-ask-gavin-mcinnes.

97. Carol Schaeffer, "Inside the Proud Boys Event That Sparked Violence Outside of Uptown GOP Club," *Bedford + Bowery*, October 13, 2018, https:// bedfordandbowery.com/2018/10/inside-the-proud-boy-event-that-sparked -violence-outside-of-uptown-gop-club/.

98. Miller, "Why Are the Proud Boys So Violent?"

99. Shane Goldmacher, "Fight Breaks Out Near Republican Club after Visit by Gavin McInnes," *New York Times*, October 18, 2012, https://www.nytimes .com/2018/10/12/nyregion/gavin-mcinnes-republican-club-vandalized.html.

100. The title is a reference to the recommendation made to the Proud Boys by President Trump during a presidential debate in 2020 after being urged to condemn white supremacists.

101. See Tina Moore and Emily Saul, "Disgraced Shock Jock's Girlfriend Live-Streams Alleged Abuse," *New York Post*, December 20, 2015, https://nypost

.com/2015/12/20/disgraced-shock-jock-arrested-for-beating-his-girlfriend/. See also Tara Mahadevan, "Comedian Josh Denny Gets Roasted for Comparing 'N-Word' to 'Straight White Male,'" *Complex*, May 19, 2018, https://www.complex.com/pop-culture/2018/05/comedian-josh-denny-gets-roasted-for-comparing-n-word-to-straight-white-male#:~:text=On%20Friday%2C%20comedian%20Josh%20Denny%20was%20dragged%20by,diminish%20the%20recipient%20based%20on%20assumption%20and%20bias.

102. BlazeTV, "Gavin McInnes Describes the Signs of Being a 'Cuckservative,'" YouTube, February 4, 2016, https://www.youtube.com/watch?v=YnYr-DX7dy0.

103. Williams, introduction, xxxii.

104. Mary Douglas, "Jokes," in *Implicit Meanings: Essays in Anthropology* (London: Routledge, 1978), 150.

105. Bergson, *Laughter*, 103.

106. Alexander H. Stephens, "Cornerstone Speech," Savannah, Georgia, March 21, 1861, https://teachingamericanhistory.org/document/the-corner-stone-speech/.

107. Bergson, *Laughter*, 129.

108. Bergson, *Laughter*, 87.

109. Derek Attridge, *Peculiar Language: Literature as Difference from the Renaissance to James Joyce* (New York: Routledge, 1988), 2.

110. Attridge, *Peculiar Language*, 184–85.

CONCLUSION

Comedy on the Low Road

COMEDY IS AN INDEX OF culture.

If culture constitutes particular (if not *peculiar*) ways of life, then we are wise to take stock of the comic way when it appears to be so utterly caught up in our experiences of ordinary reality.

At the risk of sounding nostalgic, comedy used to be for demonstrating "true" meanings by saying or doing something laughingly or mockingly or ridiculously contrary to what was meant. This is still the case. However, comedy is now as much about making fun to showcase who we truly are, with some familiar baggage. On one hand is that old hat of us-them ideations. On the other is the nagging fantasy that a joke can ever be just a joke. Ours is an era of trolls out to get perceived enemies, amassing followers and fellow shitposters with cruel humor that doubles as a pledge of allegiance to some system of beliefs. Comedians target minority groups on principle, in the name of creative freedom. Killing jokes extend from laugh riots to actual instances of festive, joyful violence. These tendencies extend from bombasts like Rush Limbaugh to comedy troupes like Million Dollar Extreme. A defining feature is that one can get away with murder so long as what is said and done betrays a comic spirit. Within our current setup for identity politicking and cultural warfare is a legacy of comedy on the low road.

Numerous instances of low-road comedy have cropped up in recent years. Besides the topics of the preceding chapters in this book, such instances animate a great deal of what should concern us about comedy gone wrong, not least because of what seems to be a prevailing assumption that the comic license is a crucible for free expression. These instances, and those concerns, are taken up more specifically in what follows. But first, some full disclosure.

I like to make jokes. Surprise, surprise. Much of my scholarship centers on comedy. At any rate, on occasion, I make jokes that are too soon, or in poor taste, or simply devised to rub someone the wrong way. Rarely do I do so in public. Now and again, in the classroom. Instead, I make jokes at home or in the company of friends. So, one can imagine that my wife and kids have unique insight into my sense of humor—indeed, my comic spirit. Once upon a time, and every so often, I made jokes that amused me but bothered or even offended or simply did not amuse my wife. "What?" I would say, smiling wryly while feigning disbelief, upon seeing that I ruffled her feathers. "That was funny!" "Maybe to you," she'd reply. Precisely.

This sense of humor, or comic spirit, can easily carry over into more public interactions. People regularly laugh at the expense of others. People frequently get a rise out of stuff that is offensive because it is, on the surface, in jest. My wife is anything but an agelast. She has an enchanting, distinctive laugh and an even more catching knack for identifying comical moments in the daily routines of our lives. In these moments there usually emerges a laughter that we can share. It is therefore unsurprising that my wife sometimes reminds me that, joke or not, a comic gesture has less to do with intentions than impacts. She is not wrong. I realized this perhaps more than ever when my elementary school–aged son used to crack wise, say, about how his mom parks the car or how I do the lion's share of things like cooking and shopping for groceries. I realize, too, that matters relating to who and what comedy is for situate us squarely in the realm of what Henri Bergson calls the "manufacture of comic effects."[1] What do we expect from comedy? To what ends are we putting it? How is it making or breaking our relationships with others? I think my wife would agree that it is not so much that my "bad" jokes are unscrupulous or even wrongful as it is that they can be lazy, unthinking, simplistic, ill-considered—foolish. In the suggestion that there is something wrong with comedy these days, then, is the insinuation that a comic license is not entirely unlike a license to drive a car or own a gun. We can all laugh at jokes. We can all take joy in making fun. If we are not careful, though, we might forget that embedded in comedy is a license to kill.

The lines between killing jokes and jokes that kill, literally and figuratively, can be disturbingly blurry.

In 2014, long after Limbaugh cemented his reputation as the Dittohead Doctor of Democracy and Most Dangerous Man in America, he joked that he could breathe because he was capable of following the law. The joke was on Eric Garner, a Black man who uttered "I can't breathe" eleven times before he died at the hands of a New York City Police officer during an arrest for selling single cigarettes on the street. The officer put him in a chokehold after Garner tried to explain that he was minding his own business. At a campaign rally in January 2016, presidential candidate Donald Trump joked that he could "stand in the middle of Fifth Avenue and shoot somebody" without fear of losing voters.[2] Memes characterizing Sam Hyde as the shooter after nearly every mass shooting since 2012 are among the most popular on 4chan and other online platforms. As one user puts it, the meme is "really funny actually," evolving from an internet hoax into something that became an allegation that mainstream news outlets had to fact-check and debunk.[3] This was no less the case when Hyde was falsely, foolishly, identified as the local Pennsylvanian who attempted to assassinate Donald Trump at a campaign rally in July 2024. These examples almost herald more recent events.

One involves self-proclaimed GOAT (greatest of all time) comedian Dave Chapelle. *The Closer* (2021), Chapelle's third of three Netflix comedy specials—after *Equanimity* (2017) and *Sticks & Stones* (2019)—is awash with jokes about the trans community. In it, Chappelle amplified a running theme in his routines, which is that LGBTQIA+ people are useful dupes for dwelling on categories of racial, ethnic, and gender identity. Without getting into all the elements of the controversy, suffice it to say that *The Closer* stands out because the old hat of Chappelle's transphobic, if not anti-trans, jokes were taken to new heights of offensiveness. Specifically, he used a fellow comedian and member of the trans community who died by suicide as a lodestar in his effort to defend the idea that any joke, and a joke about anyone or anything, is fair game. Period. *The Closer* was met with much public outcry. Members of the LGBTQIA+ community reiterated their fear that Chappelle's comic normalization of hate speech put them in danger, whether through a justification for aversion to difference or through an implied warrant for violence. There were employee walkouts at Netflix. Chappelle himself received death threats. In a video he posted to Instagram, Chappelle called the controversy "nonsense," and said it was about "corporate interests" and attempts to police what he can and cannot say.[4] The following year, Netflix released the speech he delivered at Duke Ellington School of the Arts in Washington, DC, his alma mater. It was billed as a special unto itself, and titled *What's in a Name?* The school had plans to name its performing arts theater after Chappelle. The comedian refused to lend his name and instead offered up the signifiers of "freedom" and "expression." He did so as a statement of protest and as a reminder that controversies over comedic content should never be allowed to overshadow the artistry—*his* artistry—as a comedian.

CONCLUSION

Another example. This one involves the moment when nominee for best actor Will Smith got into it with comedian Chris Rock on stage during the Oscars in March 2022. Rock was set to announce the winner for best documentary film. During some banter before his announcement, Rock cracked a joke about Smith's wife, Jada Pinkett, who had recently disclosed her struggles with alopecia. The comedian looked at her in the front row, observed her bald head, and proclaimed that he could not wait to see the sequel to *G.I. Jane*, a film from the 1990s in which Demi Moore plays a woman who makes it as a Navy SEAL. An iconic scene in the film depicts Moore shaving her head. Smith laughed at the joke. His wife laughed at first and then rolled her eyes. Smith saw the eye roll, stood up, walked onstage, and slapped Rock across the face. "Keep my wife's name out your *fucking* mouth!" yelled Smith after retaking his seat. Rock kept his cool and, though shaken, moved on with his presentation. Critics of Rock were quick to recount the comedian's history of making fun of Black women. Critics of Smith saw in the famed actor an uncharacteristic personification of the Angry Black Man. Some said Rock deserved to get hit. Some said he was a victim. The next day, we had "Slapgate" on our hands.

These and other examples are enough to merit not only a newfangled treatise on laughter and the meaning of the comic but also a consideration of truth and lies in a comedic sense. To put it in slightly different terms, there is reason to take stock of the true comic spirits that lie in the ways that low-road comedy has escaped the basement and become established on the ground floor of what it means to fight for position in culture and politics.

From the absurdities of Limbaugh to the nonsense of Chappelle and then again to the skulduggery of shitposters, there is a sentiment that comedy is in a class of its own—the outcome of a competitive drive to make fun so as to be free. The problem is that in this drive is an in-built demand that people take a joke at the same time as they allow a talk radio gascon or legendary stand-up comic or stock-in-trade troll to abandon the privilege and responsibility that goes along with making jokes that can be consequential and doing comedy that can have real consequences. To assert a right of free expression only to write off contentious content as just a joke is to affirm the egotism of a "comedian" as reason enough to be judged as just a comedian. As David Frum put it, when we admit that a jokester is not kidding we own up to the notion that "*the content still matters.*"[5] Similarly, when we realize that "wokeness," when made fun of, is as much an object lesson in Freudian inhibitions and the cathartic releases that follow from them as it is a plea for accountability, we can fathom a spirit of comedy embodied by those who really just do not want to be bothered even as they want to bother others. It is therefore not only about the conditions of comedy. It is also the conditions that comedy conditions. These days, the comic spirit is volatile. The "Spirit of 1776" represents an insurgent mood of the American Revolution as much as the festive intemperance of the Capitol Insurrection. Comedy exists in and as a spirit of the times. What passes as a politically correct joke then and now is not the measure of consequence. The measure of consequence is what happens when comedy is brought under, or let out of, control.

—∭—

One last digression.

A favorite musician of mine is Stephen Kellogg. For some time now, he has identified himself as "Raffi for Adults," with his catalog of honest, heartfelt songs about family, and friends, and life's many trials and tribulations. Tellingly, just as he claims to be one who chases songs and tells stories, Kellogg also stakes a claim in comedy by regularly cracking jokes in between tunes during his shows and, now, dabbling in some stand-up. What is more, in a short essay entitled "The Conflict" that appears in his collection *Objects in the Mirror: Thoughts on a Perfect Life From an Imperfect Person* (2020), he offers a way to think of the kind of parsing that can take place in response to a joke. Kellogg recounts a moment when his wife says to him, "You're such a dick." Bothered, he presses his wife to clarify the comment by making clear if she thinks Kellogg *is* a dick or, in that moment, was "just acting like a dick." In the difference is everything. To be a dick is terrible. To act like a dick and get called on it, well, that is to keep open the possibility for resolution, if not amusement.[6] Consequently, Kellogg offers something of a framework for the rhetorical ontology of jokers, butts of jokes, and jokes themselves.

So what?

On March 28, 2022, the day after "Slapgate," Kellogg said this on Twitter: "I've been Will Smith and I've been Chris Rock and I will probably be both again at some point." At the end of his tweet is the yellow emoji of a hand forming the peace sign. I read this tweet and thought it could be a lyric to one of Kellogg's songs. I read it and was immediately reminded of my own comic missteps. I read it and thought about the consequences of jokes and their content, of making and taking jokes as different versions of the comic license to be a dick, of the sense and nonsense in acting out, and of making jokes to turn words into sticks and stones. I read it and thought of how much is simmering under the surface of so much comedy. Not two months later Chappelle was charged by a man who leaped on stage and tried to tackle him while he was doing stand-up at the Hollywood Bowl. The man had a fake handgun with a knife blade attached

CONCLUSION 169

to it. It came out later that he self-identified as bisexual and was "triggered by the comedian's jokes."[7] In the month between these occurrences, Bill Maher used a "New Rules" segment on his show *Real Time with Bill Maher* to count the ways (with continual reference to Slapgate) that we should end the "war on jokes."[8] As the saying goes, freedom is forgiveness. Make jokes, not war. It is one thing to reflect on the potential cross-purposes of a comic way by considering the tensions between *la comédie pour la comédie*, comedy for its own sake, and the various interpretations of forgiving by getting sweet revenge. Even Arthur Fleck's actions in the film *Joker* are somewhat impulsive at first before they are choreographed. It is another thing, though, to recognize that no freedom can be guaranteed, not even a comic freedom, which is most apparent when we are confronted with the overlap of free expression, violence, and art.

Comedy is not just comedy. It is the rule through which societal control is affected and expressed. According to Mary Douglas, jokes only really work as jokes when they give rise to "the juxtaposition of a control against that which is controlled." If jokes are to be perceived as jokes (or not), there needs to be a "pattern of control" revealed in the repetition of some "truth" that is subjected to comic difference.[9] The artfulness of a comedian or any other comic figure lies in the ability to expose the butt of a joke as "a set-up mechanism," in Bergson's terms. To make a joke is to take control. Following the fallout of Chappelle's comedy specials, Joe Rogan was at the forefront of commentary about jokes being "just jokes" and about the need to designate comedians as a "protected class." It is "wrong," said Rogan, to equate a joke with any real sentiment or sensibility, hateful or otherwise. "Look, it's fun," he said of Chappelle's comedy. "It's just making jokes."[10] But what about the combination of strength and weakness in laughter? There is strength in laughing *at*. There is solidarity in laughing *with*. There is vulnerability in being a *laughingstock*. And what about the risk and reward of being the one who provokes the laughter with the will to kill or be killed?

Jokes are just jokes. It is a fanciful conviction that even the most successful comedians do not really believe is true. Consider how habitually comic character is defended in egoistic terms. Beyond the corporate disclaimers and expressions of solidarity from people like Maher who professed to be on "Team Dave" are the defense mechanisms of comic characters themselves. In his speech at Duke Ellington, Chappelle dubbed *The Closer* a "masterpiece," lauded himself as a "once-in-a-lifetime talent," and goaded anyone listening to "beat" him by communicating their ideas better than he communicates his. In his own comedy special on Netflix, one year after Slapgate, Rock refused to accept the victim status even as he touted his own superiority over Smith and those who might continue to support him. Notwithstanding his use of the descriptor "bitch" in the closing argument of his set, Rock went so far as to characterize Smith as a cuck—a man who took out his frustration on Rock because he was clearly still reeling from the well-publicized "entanglements" with his wife after she cheated on him with their son's friend. Like Chappelle, Rock made the case that comedy can be the scene of a fight, but only among those who are willing to make and take jokes with the veritable death drive of a comic spirit that is also guided by a principle of delight in the sufferance of others. Live and let laugh is just another way to say live and let die.

There are two issues that emerge from these examples. One is that claims to free expression tend to complicate the rhetorical violence of comedy. Another is the relative humorlessness that is so rife in the performance of comic egoism.

When Umberto Eco stated that comic freedom prevails when "fools are crowned," and therefore when comedians and jokesters and the like are at liberty to be villainous, violate rules, and even commit crimes, he did not mean that comedy is free of consequence.[11] There is a certain "nuance of art and activism," Chappelle told his audience at Duke Ellington, and comedy above all cannot become an "instrument of oppression" if "artistic freedom and expression" are to be preserved.[12] Such an appeal to the high road is not unlike Rock's defense for why he didn't strike back against Smith, physically. "I have parents," he announced, which means that he was taught above all else that he should not fight "in front of white people."[13] Before this, though, Rock confessed that he watched *Emancipation* (2022)—a film in which Smith plays a runaway slave in the Civil War era—for the joy in siding with Ole Massa and seeing Smith's character "get whooped." And do not forget Chappelle's challenge to fight back against him with yet more fighting words. It is like a struggle with what Shakespeare dubbed the folly of truth in King Lear. Take heed, fools; the whip!

Surely, comedy is good when it is permitted to evade repressive norms in society, put forth new perspectives on the order of things, and foster the vitality of fellow feeling that comes with being in on a joke. If we also acknowledge that the spirit of comedy is very often pragmatic, which is to say that it is used in the spirit of embracing specific values and particular preferences for this viewpoint over that one, then we need to take pause when it presents people with the "tools, strategies, and tactics for reinforcing social patterns of domination and exclusion."[14] The comic freedom yearned for by Chappelle, Rock, Rogan, and so many others is based on the belief that we live in "a world dominated by diabolical powers," leaving comedy as the key resource for sustaining "a world of everlasting transgression."[15] Carnivals do not come to town in this world. The world *is* a carnival.

CONCLUSION 171

Comedy therefore goes wrong when transgression is passed off as a form of liberation that enables groups of free selves to remain happy and at one with worldviews that foreclose anything that threatens to disorder them. When we pit the "freedom to enjoy" against the will to "evaluate our enjoyment,"[16] comedy risks becoming beyond judgment at best and, at worst, beyond reproach. This is probably why comedians like Chappelle and Rock and Rogan and Maher sound so much like the erstwhile Titular Head of the Remains of the Republican Party as well as the rabble-rousing, rightist diehard of a prankster Sam Hyde when they stand on principle in doing and saying what they want. "Too many Americans can't laugh at themselves anymore," that titular head, Limbaugh, forewarned in the second iteration of his "undeniable truths of life."[17] Maher echoes these sentiments in his recurring lamentation about people being unable to take a joke. In Chappelle's logic that nothing should be off-limits in comedy are resonances of Hyde's claim that his comic freedom demands that he make fun as a matter of life and death. Rock worries about "selective outrage," as he says in his Netflix special, muddling together a confused argument that boils down to freedom for me and not freedom for thee.

Herein lies the sticking point: there is an authoritarian impulse in comedy, and it cuts both ways. There are those who want to "punish" comedians for having fun at somebody else's expense. There are those who want to exert a comic license with impunity, mocking anyone who is upset or offended or ostensibly harmed by activities that range from the rhetorically vile to the materially violent. All the while jokes are laid out as the line for determining what we decide we are free to express and what kinds of expression, never mind people, should be forbidden, expunged. There is no such thing as being merely offended when jokes are harmful. There is likewise no such thing as doing comedy without the risk of doing damage. Wokeness, goes one argument, is the death knell for it all.[18] Hence why, for many, making a mockery of woke culture and political correctness is "the new norm in comedy."[19] But the dangers faced by members of the trans community are real. Shills for right-wing extremism are doing comedy to blaspheme devotees in the Church of Woke. Stand-up comics have been assaulted. The US Capitol has been sieged by rioters in free assembly who assailed police officers and acted out cultural and political fantasies. We, the people, are free to "behave like the animal-like characters of comedy" in an "upside-down world" wherein "even kings act like the populace" of democracy's children who are innocent in laughter.[20] Yet the propensity from all sides is to make things personal, to expose who is to blame, and to prop up a politico-cultural complex that thrives on the sort of hype created around how someone like Rock—a famous comedian with a microphone and a rapier wit—will hit back, comically, despite his thinly veiled contention in *Selective Outrage* that words cannot do the hurt that hands can do.

All of this presents something particularly troublesome for comedy, especially with regard to that authoritarian impulse. It's the ego, stupid. I do not mean this as an affront to anyone's sense of humor or sensibilities. Rather, I mean it to be a point of reference for figuring out when and where comedy might truly go wrong.

It is silly to think that cancel culture is the culprit. The line between identity politics and egoism, after all, is quite thin. As one critic writes, comedians across the board are "smug, narcissistic, self-righteous, petty."[21] We know this when we see it in the selective outrage that makes an ad hominem attack part and parcel of an overarching joke pattern. Preferences and principles. Passions and prejudices. What people stand for and what they represent. These are the footings for our shared delight in rhetorical violence acted out on others in public. Accordingly, whether some bad actor is a comedian or the butt of a joke, the scapegoat is the comic *objet petit a*, the object of desire, always just out of reach. This is true for comic figures cum free expression purists who want to say and do what they want, everyone else be damned. It is true, too, for targets of comedy that get set up as what Kenneth Burke might call "sacrificial receptacles" for making fun so that a select community can, through humor, unburden itself.[22] That teams and tribes and opposing sides are so much the order of the day suggests that the egotism of comic character lines up with the collective egoism of those who revile and those who revere the "comic scapegoat."[23] To cancel. To cross lines. Comically speaking, both are mechanisms for taking control of how reality can and should be experienced (and why). Rogan, for example, has taken control by opening the Comedy Mothership, his own antiwoke, anti–cancel culture stand-up club. It caters to "his usual edgelord posse."[24] One message this sends is that there is no need to get beyond the joke.

We simply cannot remain caught in old notions about comedy, like the notion that laughter is "no longer comic" when it "passes into derision, mockery, and the grotesque."[25] In mainstream institutions, online, on the fringes of society, there is a comic spirit to be found in laughter that holds others in contempt. There is a sense of humor in depriving someone else of their way of being. For some, a crisis in comedy doubles as a crisis in freedom. If freedom is struggle, comedy therefore invites the toil needed to deal with the problems of acting as if anything at all can be made into something that is *just* a joke and at the same time to stoke resentment in those who do not want to explain jokes let alone apologize for whatever it is that enlivens their joy. For some, too, the issues with comedy bring us back to ancient tensions between "comedic pleasure" and

CONCLUSION   173

anyone or anything that functions "as an interference" with that "core freedom" to humor whatever it is that amuses.[26] When these amusements amount to "recognitions and similarities" they represent the "ego-boosting pleasures" of comedy.[27] However, when conventional ideas of pleasure are linked with things like clickbait and faux controversies, we are left in the lurch when it comes to comedy that relies on automatic, indeed mechanical, responses to bad objects. It is high time we come to terms with comedy. Doing so has less to do with matters of malice, aggression, and evil on this side, or of the inanities, confusions, and vices of fragile egos on that one, than with what happens when comic judgment does not "get the better of vanity."[28] A few last words, then, on self-righteousness in comedy that becomes self-flattery, and in so doing alienates selves and others in truly anticomedic fashion.

—〰—

It is a bad omen when a two-faced proselytizer like Tucker Carlson pronounces the death of comedy.

In a February 2023 episode for his Fox News series *Tucker Carlson Originals*, the talking head used many of the aforementioned examples to concoct a narrative about how comedy is the battleground for cultural warfare and homegrown realpolitik.[29] An opening montage of Chappelle getting attacked on stage, Smith slapping Rock, and Maher lambasting soldiers of social justice in the joke wars leads Carlson to regard comedy as "the hallmark of a free society." If true, the prevalence of comic *un*freedom should trouble us. Mainstream comedians like Stephen Colbert are nothing but cynical power players championing a liberal narrative for the woke establishment and playing into the posturing and capitulation that goes along with the partisanship of virtue signaling. *They* are the enemies in our "civilizational battle." *They* are the dyed-in-the-wool authoritarians of cancel culture. *They* are the real scandalmongers and monitors in the control society. We need a newfangled culture industry for "real" comedy, says Carlson.

To waken this comic spirit, he highlights a handful of comedians as "canaries in the coal mine" of free expression. Self-proclaimed "Amazing Racist" Ari Shaffir, who argues that all is fair in a war of jokes if people laugh. Former host of television series *The Man Show* on Comedy Central and lately of an eponymous podcast, Adam Carolla, who calls himself a "divining rod" for comedy in society. Luis J. Gomez, creator of "the Most Offensive Podcast on Earth," *Legion of Skanks*. Toward the end of the episode, Carlson features Lou Perez, writer for satirical online news outlet the *Babylon Bee*, who maintains that the shtick of "fake news you can trust" is really about "fact-checking" the mainstream.

174   WHEN COMEDY GOES WRONG

There is more in the half-hour installment, but the gist is that comedy is dead and we, as a society, have killed it.

On the surface, "The Death of Comedy?" comes off as somewhat reasonable in its presentation of woke mobs and killjoys and in its promotion of comic characters who are trying to breathe new life into the dying spirit of comedy by being cheeky, confrontational, and at times offensive. When Maher chatted with right-leaning comedian Greg Gutfeld during an episode of his podcast, *Club Random*, in February 2023, the two agreed to disagree about their political views while drawing some of the same conclusions that Carlson did about the cultural authority that must be given to comedy. Comic freedom should be unfettered. People need to get over themselves in order to make and take jokes as part of getting by. The kind of tribalism made possible by comedy is the best kind since it facilitates survival through "shared struggle" in the cultural production of "comic bonding."[30] It is a show of making a play at being tied together.

Across the chapters of *When Comedy Goes Wrong*, jokes and laughter and senses of humor have revealed how a comic spirit can give rise to ties that bind. But to what effect? The singsong satire of Paul Shanklin revels in a way of doing humor politically, and doing politics humorously, through the outrageous enjoyment gotten from entertaining outrage. Songs, for example, like "Walking in a Welfare Wonderland," chaunt along with conservative talking points about tarnished Americanism and actually apply *enjoyment* as a watchword for "the hobos and clowns" who embody liberal democracy in a manner "that offends the Right." Such a song unites people by bringing what is familiar into strange relation with what is contemptuous. This goes for Hyde, too, and his penchant for pulling pranks and using jokes for targeted rhetorical killings. Liberal outrage is collateral damage, and Hyde's comic license to be vicious by being virtuous in his conceit is grease to the skids of moving from a Clown World Order to yet another New Order in America. Likewise, the notion that fun is made in a comic spirit but not in jest in *Joker* makes sense in light of appeals to comedy as a means of cultural and political and, to be sure, personal liberation. There is comic freedom in the literalization of killer clowns. There is comic freedom in the provocation to consider when, or if, a joke goes too far. What to do with the comic spirit when there is a mainstream and there is everyone else and the trouble is who gets to be center stage? On January 6, 2022, the Capitol Insurrection provided an answer. That answer was to perform a strange rebirth of freedom, with Poe's Law as the law of retaliatory justice. There is cultural authority and political power to be exploited in the exhibition of gallows humor. There is reason to believe

CONCLUSION

that one can take back control not through the folly of fanaticism but rather through the act of acting as if seditious fanaticism makes good comic sense. Do not change minds. Do not change the subject. These are dicta as much for the peculiar institutionalization of comedy as for the fanatic who aims to remake the Capital of the Free World into a Fool's Paradise. The transposition of Far Right comedy from the fringes to the mainstream demonstrates just how far jokes can be taken when the new rule is to tolerate sufferance by suffering fools, gladly.

When presented this way, coming to terms with comedy almost feels like conceding the limits of carnival and, in them, the limitations of what Mikhail Bakhtin celebrated as a "comic, carnivalesque spirit."[31] Laughing in public is a prototypical democratic act. It is an essential human activity, too, which is why comedy is so crucial for our relief from human folly and a capacity to relieve ourselves in and of being foolish. The "carnival attitude" is precisely what was seen in the carnival of the Capitol Insurrection, not to mention the historical arc from talk radio to online trolls. In that attitude is a mingling of both fellow feeling and the kind of communal fury that can lead to violence. Infernal comedy, says Caryl Emerson, "is populated with rogues, tricksters, deceivers, cynical minds in tough vigorous bodies."[32] Purgatorial comedy moves these public menaces from the depths of evil to the interstices of foolish pride and genuine idiocy. Paradisal comedy is magical, inspired, artful, divine. The trick is to figure out how to harness a comic spirit for human flourishing and earthly survival with energies of procreation instead of destruction, and a collective will to help the jester serve at once as artist and sage.

It is tempting to look at the mixture of bad faith and banality that permeates comedy today and recommend the greater comic effect of ridding ourselves of the bad to make good on those jokes that move the soul as much as the sun and the stars. Except—yikes. The specters of wrath and pride and excommunications are everywhere in this setup. To root out perceived evil is to tap the root of all evil, perhaps never more so than when such rooting out is done with a laugh. Keep in mind the larger-than-life character of figures from Limbaugh to Trump. Keep in mind the struggles of clowns and kings, and the assumptions about who or what should exist that come up when comedy exemplifies cultural politics pushed to the extreme. Keep in mind the frog trying to make itself as large as an ox. Upon our souls. . . .

An alternative way to wrap up might begin with a metaphor for comedy that I borrow from Bergson. In a sense, "any arrangement of acts and events is comic which gives us, in a single combination, the illusion of life and the distinct impression of a mechanical arrangement."[33] The metaphor Bergson uses to substantiate this claim is that of a child playing with a jack-in-the-box. The comic effect of this childish plaything is given to us from the very act of a child pushing this clown, this jester, this *diable en boîte* (devil in a box) down only to delight in seeing him pop up again. In the "struggle between two stubborn elements," says Bergson, there is comedy in the triumph of the child over the thing that is "simply mechanical." It provides "the same kind of amusement" that a cat gets from "playing with a mouse." The conclusion? That thing is comedic, and thereby laughable, that is revealed to be machinelike even though it appears to be full of life. If we push this metaphor toward the end of its line, we can imagine the comic character messing with members of a jack-in-the-box society. We can also imagine the cultural politics in a society that puts comic characters in the box and then hands it over to audiences of comedy. Either way, we can get to Bergson's point about how the pattern of pushing the jack lower and seeing it shoot up higher, as it is repeated, becomes less and less amusing—that is, it becomes less and less comic.

Comedy is an index of culture.

What we *deem* to be comedy leaves us with indications of just how vital a joke can be to who we are and what we do.

As I write, the precise content and underlying plot of the sequel to *Joker* is unclear. What is clear is that it is a musical and so will call forth the deep feelings and depths of being that can be used to call a tune, however foolish. What is clearer is that its comic spirit will establish the conditions of laughter in terms of folie à deux, or the folly of two. The simple conceit is one of split personalities. The bigger picture alludes to a certain madness that connects a self and an other, the delusions that move us from spaces of one to many, and those figments of our collective imagination that give us our identities. In addition to his work on laughter and the meaning of the comic, Bergson mulled over issues with freedom, with the ego, and with dreams. In dreamworlds, we give ourselves over to the madness of detaching from reality by using the very materials of that reality. There is freedom in that detachment. There is freedom, too, in "the relation of the concrete self to the act which it performs" in real life. When we transform this freedom into something like comedy, we mess up material reality so that we do not have to simply live with it. As with this spiritedness of comedy, so with the liveliness of a comic character. Following Bergson, comedy done right *as comedy* gives way to comic characters who pull back "the cleverly woven curtain of our conventional ego" to reveal a "fundamental absurdity."[34] That fundamental absurdity is our tendency to get stuck in "ego states" that double as self-deceptions. Comedy is a means of breaking free from "the impulsive zeal with which we take sides."[35] It is a means

CONCLUSION

of recalibrating those fantasies and dreamworlds that have taken shape as egotistical projections of friends and enemies, those who are dupes and those who are in on the joke. Comic freedom is only freedom "if it admits of degrees."[36] As with comic freedom, so with comedy.

Comedy goes wrong when all is vanity, when battles of wits are merely battles of egos. Comedy goes wrong when the motivation to correct or remake undesirable situations no longer entails the demand of us to have any earthly idea how to make fun *with* others. Comedy goes wrong when egotism is the principal conceit. None of this is to say that there is some particular measure for making comedy this way or that way again. It is to say, though, that we would do well to get comedy back on a strong footing. The world might be cold. The putrid "trail of Ego," as George Meredith calls it, is probably a cold trail. But comedy does not need to rely on what Bakhtin calls "a cold humor," driven by "a reduced form of laughter" and "deprived of positive regenerating power."[37] Laughter might have come to earth by the luck of the devil. But it does not need to be the end all be all of a devil-may-care attitude. We are not laughing machines. That might be the good news for anyone hoping to leave the low road for higher ground in a reinvigoration of the comic spirit.

NOTES

1. Henri Bergson, *Laughter: An Essay on the Meaning of the Comic*, trans. Cloudesley Brereton and Fred Rothwell (New York: MacMillan, 1911), 11.

2. Colin Dwyer, "Donald Trump: 'I Could . . . Shoot Somebody, and I Wouldn't Lose Any Voters,'" January 23, 2016, https://www.npr.org/sections /thetwo-way/2016/01/23/464129029/donald-trump-i-could-shoot-somebody -and-i-wouldnt-lose-any-voters.

3. "Who's Samuel Hyde and Why Are There Memes around Him and Shootings/Terrorist Attacks?," r/NoStupidQuestions, Reddit, https://www .reddit.com/r/NoStupidQuestions/comments/xzkr5f/whos_samuel_hyde _and_why_are_there_memes_around/.

4. Adam Barnes, "Dave Chappelle Says Distributors Canceling His Documentary," *The Hill*, October 26, 2021, https://thehill.com/changing -america/enrichment/arts-culture/578559-dave-chappelle-says-distributors -cancelling-his/.

5. Davd Frum, "Dave Chappelle's Not Kidding," *Atlantic*, June 21, 2022, https://www.theatlantic.com/ideas/archive/2022/06/dave-chappelle-high -school-theater-name/661339/. Emphasis in original.

6. Stephen Kellogg, *Objects in the Mirror: Thoughts on a Perfect Life from an Imperfect Person* (Herndon, VA: Mascot Books, 2020), 14.

7. Sheila McClear, "David Chapelle Attacker Says Comedian's Jokes 'Triggered' Him," *Los Angeles Magazine*, May 23, 2022, https://lamag.com/news-and-politics/david-chapelle-attacker-says-comedians-jokes-triggered-him.

8. *Real Time with Bill Maher*, "Explaining Jokes to Idiots: Oscars Edition Real Time with Bill Maher (HBO)," YouTube, April 8, 2022, https://www.youtube.com/watch?v=p-c2eUltH58.

9. Mary Douglas, "Jokes," in *Implicit Meanings: Essays in Anthropology* (London: Routledge, 1975), 150.

10. PowerfulJRE, "Joe on the Outrage around Dave Chappelle's New Special," YouTube, October 19, 2021, https://www.youtube.com/watch?v=cqcslpX1hGo. See also Daniel Kreps, "Surprising No One, Joe Rogan Defends Dave Chappelle: 'His Jokes Are Just That: Jokes,'" *Rolling Stone*, October 20, 2021, https://www.rollingstone.com/tv-movies/tv-movie-news/joe-rogan-defends-dave-chappelle-the-closer-1244854/.

11. Umberto Eco, "The Frames of Comic Freedom," in *Umberto Eco, V. V. Ivanov, and Monica Rector: CARNIVAL!*, ed. Thomas A. Sebeok (Berlin: Mouton, 1984), 2.

12. Dave Chappelle, *What's in a Name?*, dir. Rikki Hughes, Netflix Special, 2022, https://www.netflix.com/title/81625055. See also Conor Friedersdorf, "When the Punishment Doesn't Fit the Joke," *Atlantic*, June 22, 2022, https://www.theatlantic.com/newsletters/archive/2022/06/when-the-punishment-doesnt-fit-the-joke/661362/.

13. Chris Rock, *Selective Outrage*, dir. Joel Gallen, Netflix Special, 2023, https://www.netflix.com/title/80167499.

14. Cynthia Willett, *Irony in the Age of Empire: Comic Perspectives on Democracy & Freedom* (Bloomington: Indiana University Press, 2008), 116.

15. Eco, "Frames of Comic Freedom," 7.

16. Umberto Eco, *The Open Work*, trans. Anna Cancogni (Cambridge, MA: Harvard University Press, 1989), 100.

17. "Rush's Second 35 Undeniable Truths of Life," *The Rush Limbaugh Show*, https://www.rushlimbaugh.com/second35undeniabletruthsoflife/.

18. Cindy Adams, "Wokeness Is Killing Everything, Including Comedy," *New York Post*, May 16, 2022, https://nypost.com/2022/05/16/wokeness-is-killing-everything-including-comedy/.

19. Christian Toto, "Mocking Woke May Be the New Norm in Comedy, Thanks to Sebastian Maniscalco," Fox News, December 13, 2022, https://www.foxnews.com/media/mocking-woke-new-norm-comedy-thanks-sebastian-maniscalco.

20. Eco, "Frames of Comic Freedom," 3.

21. Judy Berman, "Comedians' Obsession with Their Haters Is Ruining Comedy," *TIME*, April 14, 2022, https://time.com/6166982/bill-maher-adulting-comedians-obsessed-with-haters/.

CONCLUSION   179

22. Kenneth Burke, *Permanence and Change: An Anatomy of Purpose* (Berkeley: University of California Press, 1954), 16.

23. See Hugh Dalziel Duncan, "The Comic Scapegoat," in *Communication and Social Order* (New York: Oxford University Press, 1968), 393–405.

24. James Hibberd, "Joe Rogan Opens His Anti-Cancel Culture Club in Austin," *Hollywood Reporter*, March 7, 2023, https://www.hollywoodreporter.com/news/general-news/joe-rogan-comedy-mothership-review-austin-club-1235343105/.

25. Duncan, "Comic Scapegoat," 404.

26. Lauren Berlant and Sianne Ngai, "Comedy Has Issues," *Critical Inquiry* 43 (Winter 2017), https://www.journals.uchicago.edu/doi/full/10.1086/689666.

27. R. D. V. Glasgow, *Madness, Masks, and Laughter: An Essay on Comedy* (Madison, NJ: Fairleigh Dickinson University Press, 1995), 80.

28. Bergson, *Laughter*, 173.

29. "The Death of Comedy," *Tucker Carlson Originals*, July 2023, https://nation.foxnews.com/tucker-carlson-originals-death-of-comedy-nation/.

30. Kenneth Lincoln, *Indi'n Humor: Bicultural Play in Native America* (New York: Oxford University Press, 1993), 63.

31. Caryl Emerson, "Coming to Terms with Bakhtin's Carnival: Ancient, Modern, *sub Specie Aeternitatis*," in *Bakhtin and the Classics*, ed. R. Bracht Branham (Evanston, IL: Northwestern University Press, 2002), 5–26. See also Mikhail Bakhtin, *Rabelais and His World*, trans. Hélène Iswolsky (Bloomington: Indiana University Press, 1984), 245.

32. Emerson, "Coming to Terms with Bakhtin's Carnival," 16.

33. Bergson, *Laughter*, 69.

34. Henri Bergson, *Time and Free Will: An Essay on the Immediate Data of Consciousness*, trans. F. L. Pogson (London: George Allen and Unwin, 1910), 133.

35. Bergson, *Time and Free Will*, 134.

36. Bergson, *Time and Free Will*, 166.

37. Bakhtin, *Rabelais and His World*, 42.

—Ⅲ—

EPILOGUE

There Is No Denying the Comedy
of Earthly Survival

IN 2014, JUST AS THE Joe Rogan Experience (JRE) *was becoming one of the most popular podcasts, animator Paul Trineer (aka @paulytoon) began creating JRE Toons as comic takes on Rogan's long-form content. They are archived on YouTube and linked to the glut of clips collected under the PowerfulJRE channel. Each toon captures a moment from an episode. "The Toilet Water Moment" with comedian Bert Kreischer, for example. "Snoop Dogg Whisperer Moment." "Theo Von's Mortality Moment." (There are lots of Theo Von moments.) And so on. These moments might be "funny." Or they might feature something that can be made funny, and so given new life when turned into an animated cartoon. According to Trineer himself, these cartoons begin with striking, punchy dialogue. From there, it is all a matter of making fun, and thereby serving as an extension of JRE as well as the élan vital for what Trineer characterizes as the creative evolution of comedy.[1] This evolution is coextensive with Rogan's own sense of freedom as a principle of letting "people do whatever the fuck they want to do" so they can "find ways to succeed and grow and thrive."[2] All is one in this amalgam, and it amounts to a comedy of survival. Or so it would seem.*

What follows is a JRE Toon entitled "A Comedy of Earthly Survival Moment." More accurately, it is the script for a JRE Toon in reverse, which is to say that it represents an animated cartoon that captures a moment in an episode from an undated time when Rogan happened to have Mother Nature herself as a guest on his podcast. It is not for sure that the episode actually took place. Nothing but the JRE Toon exists. Still, the dialogue is as the dialogue was, at least if we take Rogan's words seriously. Additional notations throughout the transcript indicate what a cartoon Rogan and a cartoon Mother Nature were doing during the conversation

180

and what was going on around them. Beyond these details, it is up to us to imagine what took place, with the knowledge that not a single thing was generated with the help of an AI chatbot.

The setting for Joe Rogan's conversation with Mother Nature is not his studio in Austin, Texas, equipped as it is with shiplap walls and microphones and the aesthetic of a roadhouse relic that differs from the "claustrophobic, blood-red space capsule" that was his original studio in the Woodland Hills of the City of Angels.[3] Instead, Rogan is sitting underneath a large chestnut tree in an undisclosed hardiness zone. Mother Nature is there with him. This is true in multiple senses, but for the purpose of the cartoon, she is a personification that resembles Miss Columbia as illustrated by Paul C. Stahr but with the aura of Mona Lisa. Rogan is sitting cross-legged. He is wearing jeans and a dark green hoodie. He is not smiling, but does have a sort of wry grin on his face, which shines below his bald head and through the gray tinge of a five o'clock shadow. Mother Nature is not smiling either. Nor is she frowning. Rather, her countenance is prepossessing without being obviously beautiful or subtly off-putting. The locks of hair on her head are like catkins blowing in the wind. She is also sitting, although as if she had been wrested from a piece of ancient pottery while handing over Erichthonius to Athena. The sun is glistening. There is not a cloud in the sky.

—⁓—

JR: Do you know the origins of the term "swan song"?
(*Zoom in on Mother Nature, who appears as if she is trying to conjure an answer that does not make it seem like she knows the origins of everything.*)
MN: I know that most ends are new beginnings.
(*Pan to Rogan.*)
JR: (*laughs*) That sounds like something I would say after a mushroom trip. But, really, I am wondering because you were just saying something about how these trees used to be prevalent in Swan Woods, in the Piedmont region, but they were blighted and so we have some restoration projects in arboretums and in spots that are away from forests where fungi thrive.
(*Zoom back out so that both are back in the frame.*)
MN: (*now smiling*) You probably want me to talk about Swan Maidens.
JR: (*laughs*) Well, I certainly wouldn't choose an ice bath over a swim with a Valkyrie.
MN: That's a fitting response. Swan songs have an ancient heritage as the last gestures of living things before they die.
JR: (*nodding*) Mmmm.
MN: Cold comfort, perhaps.
JR: (*still nodding*)

MN: Figures from Aesop to Odin fancied the dismal tunes sung by one of the world's finest balladeers. They were considered remarks on a life lived, aural portents for what things may come.

JR: Is that what inspired the Bee Gees song? (*laughs*)

(*Mother Nature sits still, almost expressionless, as if she is posing for a portrait in Montefeltro.*)

JR: You know. "Swan Song." By the Bee Gees. "Love, to build castles in the air. Love, to make the music of the world."

MN: I'm not familiar, but the sentiment seems right to me.

JR: You thought I was starting a joke. (*laughs*)

(*Mother Nature is motionless, except for her hair.*)

JR: It's a reference to another Bee Gees song. "I Started a Joke." In the song the singer dies and the whole world begins to live again.

(*Mother Nature remains motionless, except. . . .*)

JR: Oh, no.

MN: What?

JR: "That joke was on me."[4] (*laughs*)

(*All is quiet, except for a light wind.*)

MN: Not all one's swans are geese.

(*Rogan crosses his legs closer to his body.*)

JR: And now I have goose flesh when I thought the whole world would be laughing. (*laughs*) No? Nothing? Anyway, let's go back to that idea of a dying gesture. Didn't Socrates say something about swan songs being prophetic? Or about them having something to do with our relationship to the natural world?

MN: Sounds right. A gadfly like him would be as concerned about earth and sky as he was about what makes a good human. A swan song tends to be beautiful. But *to* swan is to seek pleasure without a care in the world. To sing that song is to sing of a flamboyant egotism defined by buffoonish, and sometimes laughable, folly. Pleasure tends to be good. Pain tends to be bad. I can see Socrates engaged in a line of questioning about the force of human nature on these tendencies.

JR: Yea. That's actually why I'm a comedian. Because it is the pinnacle of comedy not just to laugh at our own folly but to laugh at our own demise. (*laughs*)

MN: Some people wonder if Jesus ever laughed. Do you wonder if Socrates smiled as he took a swig from the goblet of hemlock?

JR: I wonder if comedy isn't at the heart of the Socratic method!

MN: The madness of civilization does require a comic spirit to answer that fundamental question once posed by the Absurdist with blackened feet about self-glorification as self-sacrifice.

JR: Uh, is that like another way of saying live free or die?

EPILOGUE 183

MN: It is a way of imagining a blissful freedom in singing songs of Happy Deaths.

JR: I don't know. These days I imagine shows like *Cunk on Earth* and various ways of documenting how we have lost ourselves, or given ourselves over, to human conceit. And I think we can just as well imagine a series like, I don't know, *Cuck on Earth*, with Tim Heidecker singing the soundtrack. (*laughs*)

MN: (*sighs*)

(*Rogan lifts a tumbler from the ground beside him, takes a drink, then takes a deep breath. Mother Nature smiles. Rogan clears his throat.*)

JR: You know, a few years ago, I had Cornell West on. Philosopher. Political activist. Presidential candidate. (*laughs*) Brother West. He had a lot to say about social justice and spirituality and nihilism as what he called "a natural consequence of a culture (or civilization)" that is "ruled and regulated" by an order of things that is predicated on the "mastery and domination of peoples and nature."[5]

MN: (*nodding*) Mmmm.

JR: And he talked about *self*-mastery and *self*-awareness, and he recommended that I read the plays and short stories of Anton Chekhov.

MN: The myth of Sisyphus is an unfinished symphony.[6]

(*Rogan clears his throat.*)

JR: Yea. . . . And Brother West urged me to read Chekhov alongside comic writers like Mark Twain.

MN: Enemies conquered. Love triumphant. There is no cure for the blues.[7]

JR: Yea. . . . I never got around to reading Chekhov. But I know his stuff has to do with an appreciation for the absurd, and how the same, uh, disillusionments and disappointments that inspire so many of us to take up comedy relate to the struggles of being. . . . What does he call it? Uh, of being a suffering agent, or maybe an agent of suffering.

MN: And to think that Socrates was convinced he could learn nothing from trees.

JR: Yea. . . . (*clears his throat*)

MN: "Trees suffer, like races, down the long ages.
They wander and are exiled, they live in exile through long ages
Like drawn blades never sheathed, hacked and gone black,
The alien trees in alien lands: and yet
The heart of blossom,
The unquenchable heart of blossom!"[8]

JR: Exactly.

(*Mother Nature smiles. Rogan looks up and down at the chestnut tree. Zoom in on Mother Nature.*)

MN: Did you know that Chekhov wrote a one-act play called *Swan Song*?

(*Zoom in on Rogan.*)

JR: No. Really?

(*Zoom back out so that both are back in the frame.*)

MN: Yes. It is about an old comic actor and an even older theater prompter who listens to jazz and ruminates on what it means to be a public intellectual.

JR: Interesting.

MN: Do you get it?

JR: Get what? Is that supposed to be a joke?

MN: No.

JR: Hmmm. Hmmm. You know, a lot of times I just want to laugh. I just want to come up with stuff that makes people crease up. Isn't that part of the brute instinct of humanity? Not love supreme. *Laugh* supreme! Take your roots and branches. Give me a Big Stump!

MN: This sounds like the beginning of a joke about a zoologist and a deacon debating about a tree that is dead and yet still sways in the wind.[9]

JR: No. I'm serious. I'm talking about the basis for a comedy of survival in the very survival of comedy!

MN: If you are talking about the all too Human Comedy, you are gesturing to the "universal Wisdom" at play in the ecology of things, which is therefore also "in the rose bush that sends forth new rootlets toward any new source of food, no less than in the mother partridge that stages a comedy to attract your attention while her young are hiding; in the social impulse which draws the crow or the beaver to his kind for mutual pleasure and protection, and which has builded all the towns and institutions of men."[10]

JR: Yea.... That's what I'm saying. (*laughs*)

MN: Human beings are laughing animals.

JR: Laughter is a by-product of being human.

MN: I suppose. But there is more to it than that.

JR: Lord knows. (*laughs*) But isn't laughter an instinct? An impulse, uh, that follows from a response to some funny stimulus? Like pratfalls and stand-up shows, and even the violent flurries of activity like protests or even insurrections. The violence of comedy is stupid, but it is real. It matters.

MN: The kill of a chicken by a fox. The smile on the beak of a predatorial bird as it makes off with its prey.

JR: Exactly! Comedy can help us better ourselves. But we can't get beyond our animality! We have to feed into our visceral, even brutish, sensibilities. We have to be human. And we have to be *free* to be human. Comedy doesn't go wrong with this kind of comic freedom, as some people think. It's a problem for comic freedom when people are wrongheaded about how comedy coevolves with us.

EPILOGUE   185

MN: It is hard to deny that the meanings *in* life and the meanings *of* life
coincide with a natural order of things.

JR: Absolutely!

MN: So, what does it mean when humans are fond of laughing at others and
laughing off their own foibles?

JR: Laugh and the world laughs at you? (*laughs*)

(*Mother Nature smiles.*)

JR: Everyone can be made fun of. Anything can be made into a joke.

MN: Is it a joke when contempt feeds the punch line for anything deemed
ridiculous? Is it a joke when everyone finds pleasure in the virtue of their
own self-righteousness? What happens when tragedy is taken to comic
extremes? What happens when the farce of a me-against-the-world frame
becomes a comic way of being?

JR: Mmmm.

MN: These days, as you say, jokes seem to be the predeterminants for
crowning kings of comedy, for glorifying clown princes, for elevating
someone like a man I have heard referred to as Fuckface von Clownstick
to the American presidency, for scourges and stooges to disguise
themselves as shitposters and supervillains. I am trying meet you
where you are here, on a human level, so let me ask something by way of
analogy: Are you saying that the problem for comedy has less to do with
Gothamites than with Gotham?

JR: I guess I am saying that there is a vitalism to comedy that cannot be
suppressed. The natural order of comedy, I think, is predation: kill or be
killed. Does this mean that scapegoats are used as setups for laughter in
ridicule and disgust and renunciation? Yes. Does this mean that a morbid
fascination with owning others and killing off ideas (or even people) that
we don't like is everywhere in the tribalism of our politics? Yes. But I'll be
the first to say that political clowns or silly psychopaths or online trolls
that use comedy to fight *any* fight, good or bad, are insane! It is not the
Provence—provenance?—of comedy to keep up false impressions and
pledge allegiance to this or that ideology, idea, or inane conspiracy theory.
The provenance—Providence?—of comedy is survival of the *funniest*.
That's what we mean by "killing it." Period. Jokes are jokes.

MN: When maltreated clowns become killers, when internet hobgoblins
with Bronze Age mindsets draw from the dregs of the Dark Ages to darken
the doorstep of the Great Derangement, when a carnival becomes an
attempted coup d'état, survival of the fittest (or, if you will, the funniest) is
death by a thousand jokes. No?

(*A spiky green cupule, too unripe to bear fruit, falls to the ground as if the chestnut
tree was performing a mic drop.*)

JR: (*regarding the cupule, as if he might scoop it up, but he doesn't*) I don't think so. No. I think some people are just goofy. And some people are just fucking bonkers. Dave Chappelle. Chris Rock. Like George Carlin before them. Like Lenny Bruce. Pryor. They are geniuses. And I think they are just disenchanted with people who are not willing to suffer through the challenge of dark humor or provocative jokes. You have to suffer to survive. And you have to suffer to be funny. I mean *really* funny. That's how you learn and grow. Lash yourself to the mast. Kick down the ladder. Burn the boats! Life is a battle. Anyone who doesn't think so is a fool.

MN: More fool you, then?

JR: See!? That's what I'm talking about! I don't remember his name. Some dude recently published a sort of mock manifesto about people who are no longer willing to actually free their minds, and liberate their bodies, and escape states of weakness and powerlessness and impotence. I don't remember his name. I heard he is a pervert. Anyway. It doesn't matter. What matters is his argument against these "computer fools" who either keep themselves imprisoned in quiet lives of depravation or act out in public as if what happens online is what is going on in the real world, as if virtual conditions are real conditions. It's a ruse. So, he's upset with "the denuded state of the spirit and intellect," with people who "walk around 'demystified' and 'disenchanted.'"[11] That's the state of the comic spirit today.

MN: Pious idiots with Bronze Age mindsets. *Our* values represent the cradle of civilization. *Their* values are wicked and depraved. It is hard to see the intellect at work in the rationale that jokes should be the resources of better weapons, if not better tools, as if a comic figure with top billing on a show like *Gutfeld!* could be a modern-day Gilgamesh.

JR: Yea. I don't know. But I do know that many hunters are heroes.

MN: But the hunt is not what motivates the vitalism of comedy. The vitalism in comedy is a balance of humors, in the ancient sense. It is an art of living. You are no less a machine than a clock if you allow yourself to be stuck in a certain way, being wrong most of the time but right—more or less—a couple times a day. The life force of the comic spirit is based on an all too human ecology, but it can be alive yet not thriving. This is why some of the ancients reimagined the cosmic egg as a *comic* egg, and thereby figured a world mythology of "spiritual" vitality that gives birth to earthly things. What you are suggesting is not the provenance of comedy in predation. What you are suggesting is an ontology of the comic spirit in entropy. A self-regulating comic way is a balancing act that is not mechanistic. It allows for disorder in a spirit of giving life, not taking it.

EPILOGUE

JR: Yea. We definitely have too much confidence in our intellect, especially given our tendencies toward mechanical thinking. But isn't that the point of a comic license? Isn't the good of comedy in the capacity of human beings to mock the Big Lie and the Big Think and all the Big Data? It seems to me that comedy is what enables some of us to become Too Big to Cancel precisely because of the good sense in our dark humor.[12]

MN: A comic license . . .

(*Mother Nature picks up the cupule.*)

MN: . . . that's an old chestnut.

JR: Exactly.

MN: Perhaps it is time to pull it out of the fire. Perhaps it is time to recognize that good comedy comes from the reminders it gives about how human beings need to be saved from the dangers they create.

JR: That's what I'm saying! We need to nurture a comic license. We need to savor it.

MN: And yet so many today are simply salvaging it, which is to say making do with what remains after something is already dead or dying. Once upon a time, in the American colonies, the lumber from chestnut trees was used as foundations for log cabins and fence posts—and caskets. The tree was mostly wiped out in the US by *Cryphonectria parasitica*, a pathogen that kills every part of the tree aboveground but cannot kill its root system. Consequently, while the tree remains dead or dormant, it experiences moments of intense albeit fleeting regeneration. I wonder if this is not something of a metaphor for the blight of comedy.

JR: Mmmm.

MN: Did Jesus laugh? Did Socrates smile? Maybe you need to ask yourself if trees laugh. Listen to the leaves. The wind that moves them is no different than your punch line. Look at the sky.

(*Rogan looks up with the People's Eyebrow.*)

See the birds. Now imagine the avifauna mocking *you* for *your own delusions* about a bird's-eye view. Laugh, and the world laughs at you. . . .

JR: Mmmm.

MN: A natural philosopher once said that one is only "free" (*Mother Nature does air quotes*) when one performs a "strong recoil" on one's personality; embraces the complexities of a given present; resists the fixity that comes with constantly separating this and that, these and those, friends and enemies, kingdoms and Clown World Orders; and tries to be truly self-possessed.[13]

JR: Mmmm.

MN: Comedy can be such a means of self-possession—a self-possession, as the natural philosopher might say, that "admits of degrees."[14] That makes us free by empowering us to be aware of what is acting on us, of how and why we are acting.

(*Mother Nature rolls the cupule on the ground toward Rogan.*)

Comedy is what happens when something, like a human being, that should not be able to be mechanized ends up becoming a machine—a machine for doing politics, for making money, for cracking jokes. You say a joke is just a joke. Jokes, at their best, make sense of the world. They enliven a comic spirit for characterizing the order or disorder in ways of living. But jokes can be machines of turmoil and bedlam and unrest. Or they can be means of enrichment and enlivenment and self-effacement. This is why a joke can never be *just* a joke. To say that it can be is to turn comedy into the stuff of bare, barren animals with overrated intellects. Even that is not the real meaning of the Human Comedy.

JR: So what're you saying? That tricksters or pranksters or jokesters like, well, me and other comedians who have a primordial knack for survival are in the wrong by going the comic way as the way of survival?

MN: I am saying that you cannot be a trickster if you are preparing for doomsday. It is not cunning or clever to get by while others die. Tricksters survive so others, too, can live. They play their tricks to remind people how to keep their wits about them, together. Humans today worry about machine learning. You should worry about machine laughter. You can teach a cyborg to make jokes and cackle and guffaw. You can make an algorithmic sense of humor that coordinates comedy in and against the rage machines of your cultural politics and political cultures. You can revert back to the Bronze Age and proclaim that "AI" is the golem of those who hate life.[15] You can find folly in thinking that there is some technofix for the Anthropocene. You have imagined all of this and more on your podcast. But I wonder if you can do comedy that captures the joy in the living, not the joy of the kill.

JR: Uh, oh! (*laughs*) Party's over? Is that what you're saying? The comic spirit is too spasmodic in Amerika, with a "k," with the fatalism of the Kafkaesque, with the cultural arrogance and political extremism of the Far Right *and* the Far Left? I don't know. I'm tempted to act naturally and move on. Tomorrow will ultimately be the day after tomorrow and the party might still be over, but I'm just as eager to keep talking for my 15 million listeners and get back on the Comedy Mothership![16] (*laughs*)

MN: Mock heroism is tragedy, which in turn is comedy taken to the extreme. Laugh and the world laughs with you? Only if it is not canned laughter.

JR: Fuck canned laughter. (*laughs*) And, I'm no hero. I'm just a "fucking moron" who uses comedy to both connect to and disconnect from the moment.[17] (*laughs*)

MN: And therein lies the path to the low road.

JR: Another dead end! (*laughs*)

EPILOGUE

MN: I'm not saying comedy is dead. Comedy cannot be killed. War mentalities and manufactured conflicts and institutional confidence games—these conceits of human being—do little more than make life harder than it needs to be. Tragedy is maintaining a system that keeps you down. Comedy is laughing when you finally realize this act of keeping people down is what you are doing. Remember what Satan said through the mouthpiece of your Great Humorist: laughter is everything, so long as you do not squander it. The comic spirit is a life force. It is a life force inspired by Comus, from the Latin, *comoedia*, and the Greek, *kōmōidia*. A more recent poet with a Crooked Inheritance once wrote of low roads taken by tyrannical mobs doing wrong by individuals, individuals coming together to fight back, and organized groups with power and media and a cause taking back their country.[18] She had the right sentiment in the "we," in the collective nature, but her outcome was misguided. The high road she envisioned could be built on the bodies of those left behind, or shall we say left below.

JR: That's why I worry about the illusion of freedom! That's why I make fun of the charades *and* the parades! I don't want comedy itself to become a joke.

MN: Then remember that comedy is predicated on songs sung in revelry, in festivity, in jest, in the spirit of those who acknowledge the human penchant to take things too far. Comedy is nothing if all it does is compel you to chasten lionhearts and celebutantes, and call everyone a clown or a fool who gleans no sense of humor from the peculiarities in certain perspectives. Comedy is everything when we can laugh in communion with others who are as able and willing to laugh at themselves, like the wind and the trees. Tragic choruses are those whose laughter is consolatory. Comic carouses are for those whose laughter is cathartic. When comedy becomes the setup for scapegoats, the foolish pride of human beings emerges in a tendency to expurgate and punish.

JR: That's why I actually *do* appreciate the complexities in the fact that the setup for a joke, not unlike the cultural setup for comedy, can be a provocation to heroism or villainy. Comedy really is like the mask with a comic *and* a tragic face. One bleeds into the other.

MN: Especially in comedy provoked by a spirit of being out for blood.

JR: Mmmm.

MN: Whenever laughter sounds like a death rattle.

JR: Wait! Wait! Here's a good joke. (*smiles*)

MN: I think I already know the punch line.

JR: Well, that's just it! (*laughs*)

MN: Then, in the words of that old comic actor: O, farewell!

(*The interview did not end there, at least as it was presented on screen. Rogan set up his joke, standing up to do so. Mother Nature crossed her legs and settled into the grass. As he leaped to his feet, Rogan bumped his head on a branch of the chestnut tree. A cupule fell to the ground and rolled toward Mother Nature. They both laughed. Then, the screen faded to black as a soft wind could be heard in the background and Rogan's voice tailed off along with the closing seconds of the video clip. The final image is that familiar logo for JRE. A photorealistic tinted-red close-up illustration of Rogan's face, his eyes wide, eyebrows raised, big grin, and the locus of insight—an organ of percipience—on his forehead. "Audio by Joe Rogan and Mother Nature," reads yellow text across the screen as psychedelic sound effects seem to propel the logo, spasmodically, at the viewer. "Designed and Animated by PAULYTOON.")*

NOTES

1. A2 The Show, "Meet the Animator of Joe Rogan's Cartoons Paul Trineer of Paulytoons," YouTube, March 11, 2021, https://www.youtube.com /watch?v=InY5uPD_gzI.

2. PowerfulJRE, "Breakthrough Cases and Vaccine Passports," YouTube, August 6, 2021, https://www.youtube.com/watch?v=tiwsv51Il4k.

3. Tracey Minkin, "The Building of Joe Rogan's Austin Empire," *Austin Monthly*, June 2022, https://www.austinmonthly.com/the-building-of-joe -rogans-austin-empire/.

4. A line from "I Started A Joke" by the Bee Gees (1968).

5. Cornel West, "Nietzsche's Prefiguration of Postmodern American Philosophy," in *The Cornel West Reader* (New York: Basic Civitas Books, 1999), 208.

6. I borrow this terminology from Ivan Bunin, *About Chekhov: The Unfinished Symphony* (Evanston, IL: Northwestern University Press, 2007).

7. I borrow this terminology from Mark Twain's satirical takes on writings by Samuel Watson Royston.

8. D. H. Lawrence, "Almond Blossom," in *The Complete Poems of D. H. Lawrence* (Ware, UK: Wordsworth Editions, 1994), 241–42.

9. I borrow this language from Anton Chekhov's works "The Duel" and "Three Sisters."

10. William J. Long, *Mother Nature: A study of Animal Life and Death* (New York: Harper and Brothers, 1923), 283.

11. Bronze Age Pervert, *Bronze Age Mindset: An Exhortation* (self-pub., June 2018).

12. Matt Flegenheimer, "Joe Rogan Is Too Big to Cancel," *New York Times*, February 17, 2022, https://www.nytimes.com/2021/07/01/business/joe-rogan .html.

13. Henri Bergson, *Creative Evolution*, trans. Arthur Mitchell (New York: Henry Holt, 1913), 200.

14. Henri Bergson, *Time and Free Will: An Essay on the Immediate Data of Consciousness*, trans. F. L. Pogson (London: George Allen and Unwin, 1910), 166.

15. GRITCULT, "AI: An Uncanny Golem of Those Who Hate Life. Their Messiah and Their Vengeance," *Medium*, February 1, 2019, https://medium.com/meditations-observations/ai-an-uncanny-golem-of-those-who-hate-life-their-messiah-and-their-vengeance-408449790e0c.

16. The name of Rogan's comedy club in Austin, Texas.

17. PowerfulJRE, "Joe Rogan Clarifies His Vaccine Comments," YouTube, April 29, 2021, https://www.youtube.com/watch?v=PloZ-GB9tzA.

18. Marge Pierce, "The Low Road," *The Sun*, October 2017, https://www.thesunmagazine.org/issues/502/the-low-road.

BIBLIOGRAPHY

A2 The Show. "Meet the Animator of Joe Rogan's Cartoons | Paul Trineer of Paulytoons." YouTube, March 11, 2021. https://www.youtube.com/watch?v=InY5uPD_gzI.

Abad-Santos, Alex. "The Fight over Joker and the New Movie's 'Dangerous' Message, Explained." *Vox*, September 25, 2019. https://www.vox.com/culture/2019/9/18/20860890/joker-movie-controversy-incel-sjw.

Abramovitch, Seth. "Sam Hyde Speaks: Meet the Man behind Adult Swim's Canceled 'Alt-Right' Comedy Show (Exclusive)." *Hollywood Reporter*, December 8, 2016. https://www.hollywoodreporter.com/news/general-news/sam-hyde-speaks-meet-man-behind-adult-swims-canceled-alt-right-comedy-show-954487/.

Adams, Cindy. "Wokeness Is Killing Everything, Including Comedy." *New York Post*, May 16, 2022. https://nypost.com/2022/05/16/wokeness-is-killing-everything-including-comedy/.

Aesop. "The Ox and the Frog." In *The Fables of Aesop*. New York: Hurd and Houghton, 1865.

Alexander, Bryan. "How Accurate Is 'Joker's' Portrayal of Mental Illness? The Answer Is Complicated." *USA TODAY*, October 23, 2019. https://www.usatoday.com/story/entertainment/movies/2019/10/23/what-joker-movie-gets-right-wrong-about-mental-illness-violence/3978028002/.

Ali, Lorraine. "Drunk Rudy. Loser Trump. How the Jan. 6 Hearings' Wild Comedy Weakens the Big Lie." *Los Angeles Times*, June 13, 2022. https://www.latimes.com/entertainment-arts/tv/story/2022-06-13/jan-6-committee-hearings-stepien-barr-giuliani-trump-monday-day-2.

Allen, Ian. "The Far Right's Apocalyptic Literary Canon." *New Republic*, October 1, 2019. https://newrepublic.com/article/155217/far-rights-apocalyptic-literary-canon.

Amarasingam, Amarnath, ed. *The Stewart/Colbert Effect: Essays on the Real Impacts of Fake News.* Jefferson, NC: McFarland, 2011.

Anderson, Sam. "The Weirdly Enduring Appeal of Weird Al Yankovic." *New York Times,* April 9, 2020. https://www.nytimes.com/2020/04/09/magazine/weird-al-yankovic.html.

Anti-Defamation League. "Alt Right: A Primer on the New White Supremacy." June 18, 2020. https://www.adl.org/resources/backgrounder/alt-right-primer-new-white-supremacy.

Anti-Defamation League. "A Dark and Constant Rage: 25 Years of Right-Wing Terrorism in the United States." May 17, 2017. https://www.adl.org/resources/report/dark-and-constant-rage-25-years-right-wing-terrorism-united-states.

Anti-Defamation League. "Proud Boys." November 2, 2018. https://www.adl.org/resources/backgrounder/proud-boys-0.

Anton, Michael. "Are the Kids Al(t)right?" *Claremont Review of Books* (Summer 2019). https://claremontreviewofbooks.com/are-the-kids-altright/.

Applebaum, Anne. "History Will Judge the Complicit." *Atlantic,* August 2020. https://www.theatlantic.com/magazine/archive/2020/07/trumps-collaborators/612250/.

Archive.org. "*Million Dollar Extreme Presents: World Peace* (Uncut)." January 14, 2020. https://archive.org/details/worldpeaceuncut/World+Peace+Uncut.

Attridge, Derek. *Peculiar Language: Literature as Difference; From the Renaissance to James Joyce.* New York: Routledge, 1988.

Baker, Henry. "Comedian Delivers Prank Speech at TEDx Event." *Yahoo!News,* October 11, 2013.

Baker, Jackson. "Playing the Fool." *Memphis Flyer,* January 15, 2009. https://www.memphisflyer.com/playing-the-fool.

Bakhtin, Mikhail. *Rabelais and His World.* Translated by Hélène Iswolsky. Bloomington: Indiana University Press, 1984.

Ballif, Michelle. *Seduction, Sophistry, and the Woman with the Rhetorical Figure.* Carbondale: Southern Illinois University Press, 2001.

Barnes, Adam. "Dave Chappelle Says Distributors Canceling His Documentary." *The Hill,* October 26, 2021. https://thehill.com/changing-america/enrichment/arts-culture/578559-dave-chappelle-says-distributors-cancelling-his/.

Bergson, Henri. *Creative Evolution.* Translated by Arthur Mitchell. New York: Henry Holt, 1913.

Bergson, Henri. *Laughter: An Essay on the Meaning of the Comic.* Translated by Cloudesley Bremerton and Fred Rothwell. New York: Macmillan, 1914.

Bergson, Henri. *Time and Free Will: An Essay on the Immediate Data of Consciousness.* Translated by F. L. Pogson. London: George Allen and Unwin, 1910.

Berlant, Lauren, and Sianne Ngai. "Comedy Has Issues." *Critical Inquiry* 43 (2017). https://www.journals.uchicago.edu/doi/full/10.1086/689666.

BIBLIOGRAPHY

Berman, Judy. "Comedians' Obsession with Their Haters Is Ruining Comedy." *TIME*, April 14, 2022. https://time.com/6166982/bill-maher-adulting-comedians-obsessed-with-haters/.

Bernstein, Joseph. "The Underground Neo-Nazi Promo Campaign behind Adult Swim's Alt-Right Comedy Show." *BuzzFeed News*, September 13, 2016. https://www.buzzfeednews.com/article/josephbernstein/neo-nazi-promo-adult-swim-million-dollar-extreme.

Berry, Jeffrey M., and Sarah Sobieraj. "Understanding the Rise of Talk Radio." *PS: Political Science and Politics* 44 (2011): 762–67.

Bierce, Ambrose. *The Devil's Dictionary*. Cleveland: World Publishing, 1911.

Billig, Michael. "Humor and Hatred: The Racist Jokes of the Ku Klux Klan." *Discourse and Society* 12 (2001): 267–89.

Binswanger, Harry, ed. *The Ayn Rand Lexicon: Objectivism from A to Z*. New York: Meridian, 1986.

Blackmore, Susan. *The Meme Machine*. Oxford: Oxford University Press, 1999.

Blake, John. "Dave Chappelle Insulted Another Audience No One Mentions." *CNN*, October 21, 2021. https://www.cnn.com/2021/10/20/entertainment/dave-chappelle-controversy-netflix-black-comic-tradition/index.html.

BlazeTV. "Gavin McInnes Describes the Signs of Being a 'Cuckservative.'" YouTube, February 4, 2016. https://www.youtube.com/watch?v=YnYr-DX7dyo.

Blistein, Jon. "Adult Swim Cancels Controversial Show 'Million Dollar Extreme.'" *Rolling Stone*, December 6, 2016. https://www.rollingstone.com/tv-movies/tv-movie-news/adult-swim-cancels-controversial-show-million-dollar-extreme-118787/.

Blount, Roy, Jr. "Southern Humor." In *What's So Funny? Humor in American Culture*, edited by Nancy A. Walker, 153–68. Wilmington, DE: Scholarly Resources, 1998.

Blum, Alexander. "Pepe the Frog: The Roots of a Symbol." *Merion West*, November 5, 2017. https://merionwest.com/2017/11/05/pepe-the-frog-the-roots-of-a-symbol/.

BNO News (@BNOFeed). "Congressman Vicente Gonzalez just told CNN that the Texas shooter is Sam Hyde. This is false, it's an internet hoax." Twitter, November 5, 2017. https://twitter.com/BNOFeed/status/927300884417204228?lang=en.

Bohl, Ryan. "The Global History of the Alt-Right." *Salon*, March 19, 2017. https://www.salon.com/2017/03/19/the-global-history-of-the-alt-right/.

Borowitz, Andy. "Trump Named Person of the Year by Popular Sociopath Magazine." *New Yorker*, December 12, 2019. https://www.newyorker.com/humor/borowitz-report/trump-named-person-of-the-year-by-popular-sociopath-magazine.

Bradbury, Ray. *Something Wicked This Way Comes*. New York: Simon and Schuster, 1962.

BIBLIOGRAPHY

Bronze Age Pervert. *Bronze Age Mindset: An Exhortation*. Self-published, June 2018.

Brooks, Dan. "How President Trump Ruined Political Comedy." *New York Times Magazine*, October 8, 2020. https://www.nytimes.com/2020/10/07/magazine/trump-liberal-comedy-tv.html.

Buhle, Paul. "Horror in American Literature." In *Popular Culture in America*, edited by Paul Buhle, 21–25. Minneapolis: University of Minnesota Press, 1987.

Bump, Philip. "Rush Limbaugh Created the Politics That Trump Used to Win the White House." *Philadelphia Inquirer*, February 18, 2021. https://www.inquirer.com/opinion/commentary/rush-limbaugh-obituary-death-trump-20210218.html.

Bunin, Ivan. *About Chekhov: The Unfinished Symphony*. Evanston, IL: Northwestern University Press, 2007.

Burke, Kenneth. *Attitudes toward History*. 3rd ed. Berkeley: University of California Press, 1959.

Burke, Kenneth. *Permanence and Change: An Anatomy of Purpose*. Berkeley: University of California Press, 1954.

Burke, Kenneth. *The Philosophy of Literary Form: Studies in Symbolic Action*. Berkeley: University of California Press, 1967.

Carlisle, Henry. "The Comic Tradition." *American Scholar* 28 (1958–59): 96–107.

Carman, Ashley. "What You Learn after 350 Hours of Joe Rogan." *Verge*, December 7, 2021. https://www.theverge.com/2021/12/7/22821823/joe-rogan-media-matters-hot-pod-spotify-moderation.

Caron, James E. *Satire as the Comic Public Sphere: Postmodern 'Truthiness' and Civic Engagement*. University Park: Pennsylvania State University Press, 2021.

Casey, Paul, director, and Matt Wood, producer. "Dr. Phil McGraw, Tim Ryan, Batya Ungar-Sargon." *Real Time with Bill Maher*. Season 22, episode 6. Aired March 1, 2024, on HBO.

Chabon, Michael. Foreword to *Trickster Makes This World: Mischief, Myth, and Art*, by Lewis Hyde. New York: Farrar, Straus and Giroux, 1998.

Chafets, Ze'ev. *Rush Limbaugh: An Army of One*. New York: Sentinel, 2010.

Chait, Jonathan. "A White House Aide Just Warned Us That Donald Trump Is a Sociopath." *Intelligencer*, September 18, 2020. https://nymag.com/intelligencer/2020/09/pence-aide-trump-disregard-human-life-coronavirus-olivia-troye.html.

Chang, Juju, and Victoria Thompson. "White Nationalist Richard Spencer on Being Confronted by Protestors at Texas A&M Appearance." ABC News, December 8, 2016. https://abcnews.go.com/US/white-nationalist-richard-spencer-confronted-protestors-texas-appearance/story?id=44061233#:~:text=Spencer%20said%20he%20yelled%20out%20"Hail%20Trump%2C"%20"in,said%20if%20felt%20like%20a%20kind%20of%20"miracle.

BIBLIOGRAPHY

Chappelle, Dave. *What's in a Name?* Directed by Rikki Hughes, produced by Dave Chappelle (Pilot Boy Productions), performed and recorded at Duke Ellington School of the Arts, Washington, DC. Netflix Special, 2022.

Club Random Podcast. "'Weird Al' Yankovic." YouTube, November 13, 2022. https://www.youtube.com/watch?v=0TgoL5aT2cg.

CNN. "The Power of the Right-Wing Rage Machine." April 14, 2019. https://www.cnn.com/videos/business/2019/04/14/the-power-of-the-right-wing-rage-machine.cnn.

Cocksworth, Ashley. "*The Dark Knight* and the Evilness of Evil." *Expository Times* 120 no. 11 (2009): 541–43.

Coffman, Keith. "Landmark Theaters Bans Costumes at Screening of Upcoming 'Joker' Movie." Reuters, September 26, 2019. https://www.reuters.com/article/film-joker/landmark-theaters-bans-costumes-at-screening-of-upcoming-joker-movie-idUSL2N26I00L/.

Cohen, Roger. "Trump's Last Stand for White America." *New York Times*, October 16, 2020. https://www.nytimes.com/2020/10/16/opinion/trump-2020.html.

The Colbert Report. "The Word—Truthiness." October 17, 2005. https://www.cc.com/video/63ite2/the-colbert-report-the-word-truthiness.

Columbus Dispatch. "Limbaugh Colors Debate on Obama with a Song." May 10, 2007. https://www.dispatch.com/story/opinion/cartoons/2007/05/10/limbaugh-colors-debate-on-obama/23462989007/.

Comerford, Michael Sean. "A Dark Carnival Comes to Life." *Los Angeles Review of Books*, March 27, 2021. https://lareviewofbooks.org/article/a-dark-carnival-comes-to-life/.

Corliss, Richard. "Conservative Provocateur or BIG BLOWHARD." *TIME*, October 26, 1992. https://time.com/archive/6721514/conservative-provocateur-or-big-blowhard/.

Coutts, Sharona. "How Hate Goes 'Mainstream': Gavin McInnes and the Proud Boys." Rewire News Group, August 28, 2017. https://rewirenewsgroup.com/2017/08/28/hate-goes-mainstream-gavin-mcinnes-proud-boys/.

Critchley, Simon. *On Humour.* New York: Routledge, 2002.

Crosbie, Jack. "Joe Rogan and Jordan Peterson Wax Idiotic on Climate Change and What It Means to Be Black." *Rolling Stone*, January 26, 2022. https://www.rollingstone.com/culture/culture-news/jordan-peterson-joe-rogan-interview-climate-change-1290696/.

C-SPAN. "Presidential Radio Interview." June 24, 1994. https://www.c-span.org/video/?58239-1/presidental-radio-interview.

C-SPAN. "Resistant to Politically Incorrect Stories." September 24, 1994. https://www.c-span.org/video/?60430-1/resistance-politically-incorrect-stories.

The Daily Show. "Jordan Klepper Sees It All at the Capitol Insurrection." YouTube, January 12, 2021. https://www.youtube.com/watch?v=YVDJqipoohc.

BIBLIOGRAPHY

The Daily Show. "Welcome to President Trump's Reality." YouTube, January 27, 2017. https://www.youtube.com/watch?v=x2YLS8oNmls.

Dallek, Matthew. "The Conservative 1960s." *Atlantic*, December 1995. https://www.theatlantic.com/magazine/archive/1995/12/the-conservative-1960s/376506/.

Daro, Ishmael N. "Reddit Banned a Page That Trafficked in White Supremacist Content, but the Problem Is Much Bigger." *BuzzFeed News*, September 11, 2018. https://www.buzzfeednews.com/article/ishmaeldaro/reddit-sam-hyde-million-dollar-extreme-ban.

Davis, D. Diane. *Breaking Up (at) Totality: A Rhetoric of Laughter*. Carbondale: Southern Illinois University Press, 2000.

deez. "Sam Hyde's 2070 Paradigm Shift." YouTube, January 28, 2014. https://www.youtube.com/watch?v=KTJn_DBTnrY.

Dewey, Caitlin. "The Only Guide to Gamergate You Will Ever Need to Read." *Washington Post*, October 14, 2014. https://www.washingtonpost.com/news/the-intersect/wp/2014/10/14/the-only-guide-to-gamergate-you-will-ever-need-to-read/.

Docker, John. *Postmodernism and Popular Culture: A Cultural History*. New York: Cambridge University Press, 1994.

Donovan, Joan, Emily Dreyfuss, and Brian Friedberg. *Meme Wars: The Untold Story of the Online Battles Upending Democracy in America*. New York: Bloomsbury, 2022.

Douglas, Mary. *Implicit Meanings*. London: Routledge, 1978.

Driscoll, Annabel, and Mina Husain. "Why Joker's Depiction of Mental Illness Is Dangerously Misinformed." *The Guardian*, October 21, 2019. https://www.theguardian.com/film/2019/oct/21/joker-mental-illness-joaquin-phoenix-dangerous-misinformed.

Duncan, Hugh Dalziel. *Communication and Social Order*. New York: Oxford University Press, 1968.

Dwyer, Colin. "Donald Trump: 'I Could . . . Shoot Somebody, and I Wouldn't Lose Any Voters.'" January 23, 2016. https://www.npr.org/sections/thetwo-way/2016/01/23/464129029/donald-trump-i-could-shoot-somebody-and-i-wouldnt-lose-any-voters.

Eagleton, Terry. *Humour*. New Haven: Yale University Press, 2019.

Eco, Umberto. "The Frames of Comic Freedom." In *Umberto Eco, V. V. Ivanov, and Monica Rector: CARNIVAL!*, edited by Thomas A. Sebeok, 1–10. Berlin: Mouton, 1984.

Eco, Umberto. *The Open Work*. Translated by Anna Cancogni. Cambridge, MA: Harvard University Press, 1989.

Edmondson, Catie. "'So the Traitors Know the Stakes': The Meaning of the Jan. 6 Gallows." *New York Times*, June 16, 2022. https://www.nytimes.com/2022/06/16/us/politics/jan-6-gallows.html.

BIBLIOGRAPHY

Edsall, Thomas B. "'The Capitol Insurrection Was as Christian Nationalist as It Gets.'" *New York Times*, January 28, 2021. https://www.nytimes.com/2021/01/28 /opinion/christian-nationalists-capitol-attack.html.

Ellis, Emma Grey. "Can't Take a Joke? That's Just Poe's Law, 2017's Most Important Internet Phenomenon." *WIRED*, June 5, 2017. https://www.wired.com/2017/06 /poes-law-troll-cultures-central-rule/.

Emerson, Caryl. "Coming to Terms with Bakhtin's Carnival: Ancient, Modern, *sub Specie Aeternitatis*." In *Bakhtin and the Classics*, edited by R. Bracht Branham, 5–26. Evanston, IL: Northwestern University Press, 2002.

Eordogh, Fruzsina. "How 4chan Tricked the Internet into Believing This Comedian Is a Mass Shooter." Forbes, June 2, 2016. https://www.forbes.com /sites/fruzsinaeordogh/2016/06/02/explaining-the-sam-hyde-as-mass-shooter -meme/?sh=205c67211270.

Evans, Greg. "Alec Baldwin Still Hates Playing Trump on 'SNL' but Says Parody Helps Fans 'Manage Their Pain.'" *Deadline*, September 6, 2019. https://deadline .com/2019/09/alec-baldwin-snl-saturday-night-live-donald-trump-kevin-nealon -interview-1202713730/.

Evon, Dan. "Did Rush Limbaugh's 'AIDS Update' Mock the Deaths of Gay People?" *Snopes*, February 17, 2021. https://www.snopes.com/fact-check/rush -limbaugh-mock-aids-gays/.

Fairlie, Henry. "The People, No." *Baffler* 18 (January 2010). https://thebaffler.com /salvos/the-people-no.

Fairness & Accuracy in Reporting. "The Way Things Aren't: Rush Limbaugh Debates Reality." July 1, 1994. https://fair.org/home/the-way-things-arent/.

Fallows, James. "Talent on Loan from the GOP." *Atlantic*, May 1994. https://www .theatlantic.com/magazine/archive/1994/05/talent-on-loan-from-the-gop /303852/.

Farnsworth, Stephen J., S. Robert Lichter, and Farah Latif. *Late-Night in Washington: Political Humor and the American President*. New York: Routledge, 2024.

Flegenheimer, Matt. "Joe Rogan Is Too Big to Cancel." *New York Times*, July 1, 2021. https://www.nytimes.com/2021/07/01/business/joe-rogan.html.

Fowler, H. W. *A Dictionary of Modern English Usage*. Oxford: Clarendon Press, 1927.

Fox, Jesse David. *Comedy Book: How Comedy Conquered Culture—And the Magic That Makes It Work*. New York: Farrar, Straus and Giroux, 2023.

Fox, Jesse David. "When Jokes Fail." *Vulture*, January 8, 2021. https://www.vulture .com/2021/01/capitol-riot-trump-comedy.html.

Fox, Samantha Dale. "JOKER: A Plea for Empathy." *Medium*, December 26, 2019. https://medium.com/@samanthadalefox/joker-a-plea-for-empathy-c25b7 a70976f.

BIBLIOGRAPHY

Franken, Al. *Rush Limbaugh Is a Big Fat Idiot and Other Observations.* New York: Dell Trade Paperback, 1996.

Freelander, David. "The Bonnie and Clyde of MAGA World." Politico, November 19, 2021. https://www.politico.com/news/magazine/2021/11/19/dustin-stockton-jen-lawrence-trump-profile-522823.

French, David. "The Rage against the Machine—Understanding the Milo Phenomenon." *National Review,* February 21, 2017. https://www.nationalreview.com/2017/02/milo-phenomenon-understanding-right-wing-rage/.

Freud, Sigmund. *Wit and Its Relation to the Unconscious.* New York: Moffat, Yard, 1916.

Friedersdorf, Conor. "When the Punishment Doesn't Fit the Joke." *Atlantic,* June 22, 2022. https://www.theatlantic.com/newsletters/archive/2022/06/when-the-punishment-doesnt-fit-the-joke/661362/.

Frost, Amber A'Lee. "No Such Cuck." *Baffler* 29 (October 2015). https://thebaffler.com/salvos/no-such-cuck-frost.

Frum, David. "Dave Chappelle's Not Kidding." *Atlantic,* June 21, 2022. https://www.theatlantic.com/ideas/archive/2022/06/dave-chappelle-high-school-theater-name/661339/.

Fuller-Seeley, Kathryn. *Jack Benny and the Golden Age of American Radio Comedy.* Berkeley: University of California Press, 2017.

Funny or Die. "Kings of Alt Right Comedy." September 13, 2016. https://www.youtube.com/watch?v=TNGhCQ9tyH4.

Garber, Megan. "When Hatred Is a Joke." *Atlantic,* July 3, 2017. https://www.theatlantic.com/entertainment/archive/2017/07/when-hatred-is-a-joke/532509/.

Gaufman, Elizaveta, and Bharath Ganesh. *The Trump Carnival: Populism, Transgression and the Far Right.* Berlin: De Gruyter, 2024.

Gilbert, Sophie. "The New Anti-comedy of Jon Stewart." *Atlantic,* October 1, 2021. https://www.theatlantic.com/culture/archive/2021/10/problem-jon-stewart-apple-tv-plus/620277/.

Giroux, Henry A. "Anti-Politics and the Plague of Disorientation: Welcome to the Age of Trump." Truthout, June 7, 2016. https://truthout.org/articles/anti-politics-and-the-plague-of-disorientation-welcome-to-the-age-of-trump/.

Glasgow, R. D. V. *Madness, Masks, and Laughter: An Essay on Comedy.* Madison, NJ: Fairleigh Dickinson University Press, 1995.

Godfrey, Elaine. "It Was Supposed to Be So Much Worse." *Atlantic,* January 9, 2021. https://www.theatlantic.com/politics/archive/2021/01/trump-rioters-wanted-more-violence-worse/617614/.

Goldmacher, Shane. "Fight Breaks Out Near Republican Club after Visit by Gavin McInnes." *New York Times,* October 18, 2012. https://www.nytimes.com/2018/10/12/nyregion/gavin-mcinnes-republican-club-vandalized.html.

Gollner, Adam Leith. "The Secret History of Gavin McInnes." *Vanity Fair*, June 29, 2021. https://www.vanityfair.com/news/2021/06/the-secret-history-of-gavin-mcinnes.

Gordon, Devin. "Why Is Joe Rogan So Popular?" *Atlantic*, August 19, 2019. https://www.theatlantic.com/entertainment/archive/2019/08/my-joe-rogan-experience/594802/.

Grandin, Greg. "The Death Cult of Trumpism." *Nation*, January 11, 2018. https://www.thenation.com/article/archive/the-death-cult-of-trumpism/.

Greene, Viveca S. "'Deplorable' Satire: Alt-Right Memes, White Genocide Tweets, and Redpilling Normies." *Studies in American Humor* 5, no. 1 (2019): 31–69.

GRITCULT. "AI: An Uncanny Golem of Those Who Hate Life. Their Messiah and Their Vengeance." *Medium*, February 1, 2019. https://medium.com/meditations-observations/ai-an-uncanny-golem-of-those-who-hate-life-their-messiah-and-their-vengeance-408449790e0c.

Grossberg, Lawrence. *Under the Cover of Chaos: Trump and the Battle for the American Right*. London: Pluto Press, 2018.

Grynbaum, Michael M., Tiffany Hsu, Katie Robertson, and Keith Collins. "How Right-Wing Radio Stoked Anger before the Capitol Siege." *New York Times*, February 12, 2021. https://www.nytimes.com/2021/02/10/business/media/conservative-talk-radio-capitol-riots.html.

Gunn, Joshua. *Political Perversion: Rhetorical Aberration in the Time of Trumpeteering*. Chicago: University of Chicago Press, 2020.

Gutfeld, Greg. *The Joy of Hate: How to Triumph over Whiners in the Age of Phony Outrage*. New York: Crown Forum, 2012.

Hamblin, James. "Donald Trump: Sociopath?" *Atlantic*, July 20, 2016. https://www.theatlantic.com/health/archive/2016/07/trump-and-sociopathy/491966/.

Harris, Mary. "Rush Is Dead, but We're Still Living in the World He Created." *Slate*, February 18, 2021. https://slate.com/news-and-politics/2021/02/rush-limbaugh-republican-party-conservative-media.html.

Hartman, Saidiya V. *Scenes of Subjection: Terror, Slavery, and Self-Making in Nineteenth-Century America*. New York: Oxford University Press, 1997.

Hawley, George. *Making Sense of the Alt-Right*. New York: Columbia University Press, 2017.

Heer, Jeet. "Conservatives Are Holding a Conversation about Race." *New Republic*, July 26, 2015. https://newrepublic.com/article/122372/conservatives-are-holding-conversation-about-race.

Heffernan, Virginia. "Trump Dittoes Limbaugh's Bigotry with a Presidential Medal of Freedom." *Los Angeles Times*, February 7, 2020. https://www.latimes.com/opinion/story/2020-02-07/rush-limbaugh-presidential-medal-of-freedom-donald-trump.

Hemmer, Nicole. *Messengers of the Right: Conservative Media and the Transformation of American Politics*. Philadelphia: University of Pennsylvania Press, 2018.

Hényel, Gábor. "Joe Rogan—Devolution of Stupid People (Stand-up)." YouTube video, 10:55, September 24, 2014. https://www.youtube.com/watch?v=6YhKZTdqnco.

Hesse, Monica. "A Capitol Invader Left a Note Calling Nancy Pelosi a B-Word. His Attempt to Walk It Back Has Been . . . Really Something." *Washington Post*, April 27, 2021. https://www.washingtonpost.com/lifestyle/style/nancy-pelosi-capitol-riot-note-richard-barnett/2021/04/27/727ef956-a6bc-11eb-8d25-7b30e74923ea_story.html.

Hibberd, James. "Joe Rogan Opens His Anti-Cancel Culture Club in Austin." *Hollywood Reporter*, March 7, 2023. https://www.hollywoodreporter.com/news/general-news/joe-rogan-comedy-mothership-review-austin-club-1235343105/.

Higgins, Abigail. "Men Who Joined in Violently Storming the US Capitol Describe a Carnival Atmosphere Inside." *Insider*, January 7, 2021. https://www.insider.com/men-who-broke-into-the-capitol-describe-a-carnival-atmosphere-2021-1.

Hochschild, Arlie Russell. *Strangers in Our Own Land: Anger and Mourning on the American Right*. New York: New Press, 2016.

Horne, Mark. "Rush Limbaugh: An Ego on Loan from God." *Christianity Today*, July 18, 1994. https://www.christianitytoday.com/ct/1994/july18/4t8062.html.

Howley, Kerry. "Gina. Rosanne. Guy. What Do You Do the Day after You Storm the Capitol?" *New York Magazine*, December 21, 2021. https://nymag.com/intelligencer/2021/12/january-6-insurrection-us-capitol-riots.html.

Hutcheon, Linda. *A Theory of Parody: The Teachings of Twentieth-Century Art Forms*. Urbana: University of Illinois Press, 1985.

Hyde, Lewis. *Trickster Makes This World: Mischief, Myth, and Art*. New York: Farrar, Straus and Giroux, 1998.

Hyde, Sam, Nick Rochefort, and Charls "Coors" Carroll. *How to BOMB the U.S. Gov't: The OFFICIAL Primo™ Strategy Guide to the Collapse of Western Civilization*. Self-published, 2016.

Hyers, Conrad. *The Laughing Buddha: Zen and the Comic Spirit*. Eugene, OR: Wipf and Stock, 1989.

Hyers, Conrad. *The Spirituality of Comedy: Comic Heroism in a Tragic World*. New Brunswick, NJ: Transaction, 1996.

Illing, Sean. "The Fantasy-Industrial Complex Gave Us the Capitol Hill Insurrection." *Vox*, January 8, 2021. https://www.vox.com/policy-and-politics/22217822/us-capitol-attack-trump-right-wing-media-misinformation.

Intelligence Report. "Identity Unmasked: Meet the Proprietors of the Internet's Largest Neo-Confederate Propaganda Machine." September 10, 2019. https://www.splcenter.org/fighting-hate/intelligence-report/2019/identity

-unmasked-meet-proprietors-internets-largest-neo-confederate-propaganda
-machine.

Intelligence Report. "Rage on the Right." March 2, 2010. https://www.splcenter.org
/fighting-hate/intelligence-report/2010/rage-right.

Isenberg, Nancy. "Democracy's Thorn: The Mob and the Voice of the People."
Hedgehog Review (Summer 2021). https://hedgehogreview.com/issues
/distinctions-that-define-and-divide/articles/democracys-thorn.

Ivins, Molly. "Lyin' Bully." *Mother Jones*, May/June 1995. https://www.motherjones
.com/politics/1995/05/lyin-bully/.

Ivy, Marilyn. "This Is (Not) a Gallows." Society for Cultural Anthropology, April
15, 2021. https://culanth.org/fieldsights/this-is-not-a-gallows.

Jamieson, Kathleen Hall, and Joseph N. Cappella. *Echo Chamber: Rush Limbaugh
and the Conservative Media Establishment*. New York: Oxford University Press,
2008.

Jankowicz, Mia. "DOJ Seeks the Longest Capitol Riot Prison Term Yet—17 Years
for 'Eye Gouging' Ex-NYPD Officer Who Swung a Flagpole at Police." *Business
Insider*, August 28, 2022. https://www.businessinsider.com/capitol-riot-17-years
-sentence-sought-eye-gouger-ex-officer-2022-8.

Jenkins, Henry. "'Fifi Was My Mother's Name!': Anarchistic Comedy, the
Vaudeville Aesthetic and *Diplomaniacs*." *Velvet Light Trap* 26 (1990): 3–27.

JRE Clips. "Kevin Hart: Dave Chappelle Is the GOAT!" YouTube video, 11:53,
May 25, 2020. https://www.youtube.com/watch?v=8kJacGNg_9w.

Katz, Tony. "Rush Limbaugh Was Conservative Radio's 'Happy Warrior.'
That's What Liberals Don't Understand." *THINK*, February 18, 2021. https://
www.nbcnews.com/think/opinion/rush-limbaugh-was-conservative-radio
-s-happy-warrior-s-what-ncna1258193.

Kaufman, Will. *The Comedian as Confidence Man: Studies in Irony Fatigue*. Detroit:
Wayne State University Press, 1997.

Kellogg, Stephen. *Objects in the Mirror: Thoughts on a Perfect Life from an Imperfect
Person*. Herndon, VA: Mascot Books, 2020.

Kelly, Kim. "Is the 'QAnon Shaman' from the MAGA Capitol Riot Covered in
Neo-Nazi Imagery?" *Rolling Stone*, January 8, 2021,.https://www.rollingstone
.com/culture/culture-features/qanon-shaman-maga-capitol-riot-rune-pagan
-imagery-tattoo-1111344/.

Kendi, Ibram X. "The Violent Defense of White Male Supremacy." *Atlantic*,
September 9, 2020. https://www.theatlantic.com/ideas/archive/2020/09/armed
-defenders-white-male-supremacy/616192/.

Kennedy, Liam. "American Carnival: The Aesthetic Politics of Trumpist
Insurrection." UCD Clinton Institute, January 16, 2021. https://www.ucdclinton
.ie/commentary-content/american-carnival-the-aesthetic-politics-of-trumpist
-insurrection.

Ketcham, Christopher. "What the Far-Right Fascination with Pinochet's Death Squads Should Tell Us." *Intercept*, February 4, 2021. https://theintercept.com/2021/02/04/pinochet-far-right-hoppean-snake/.

Klee, Miles. "Who Is @Catturd2, the Sh—tposting King of MAGA Twitter?" *Rolling Stone*, February 9, 2023. https://www.rollingstone.com/culture/culture-features/catturd2-maga-twitter-shitposting-king-1234674671/.

Kramer, Staci D. "The Gospel according to Rush." *Chicago Tribune*, November 30, 1992. https://www.chicagotribune.com/news/ct-xpm-1992-11-30-9204190360-story.html.

Kreps, Daniel. "Surprising No One, Joe Rogan Defends Chappelle: 'His Jokes Are Just That: Jokes.'" *Rolling Stone*, October 20, 2021. https://www.rollingstone.com/tv/tv-news/joe-rogan-defends-dave-chappelle-the-closer-1244854/.

Kruse, Michael. "In on the Joke: The Comedic Trick Trump Uses to Normalize His Behavior." Politico, March 17, 2024. https://www.politico.com/news/magazine/2024/03/17/how-donald-trump-uses-humor-to-make-the-outrageous-sound-normal-00146119.

Kukura, Joe. "Feds Charge Capitol Insurrection Rioter Who Said of Pelosi, 'We Want to Hang That F**ing B*tch.'" *SFist*, May 19, 2021. https://sfist.com/2021/05/19/fbi-charges-capitol-insurrection-rioter-who-said-of-pelosi-we-want-to-hang-that-f-ing-b-tch/.

Ladenburg, Kenneth. "Strange Costumes of Capitol Rioters Echo the Early Days of the Ku Klux Klan—Before the White Sheets." *Conversation*, January 25, 2021. https://theconversation.com/strange-costumes-of-capitol-rioters-echo-the-early-days-of-the-ku-klux-klan-before-the-white-sheets-153376.

Lane, Anthony. "Todd Phillips's 'Joker' Is No Laughing Matter." *New Yorker*, October 7, 2019. https://www.newyorker.com/magazine/2019/10/07/todd-phillips-joker-is-no-laughing-matter.

Larson, Mary Strom. "Rush Limbaugh—Broadcast Demagogue." *Journal of Radio Studies* 4 (1997): 189–202.

Last, Jonathan V. "The President Is a Sociopath. And 60 Million Americans Like It." *Bulwark*, September 30, 2020. https://www.thebulwark.com/the-president-is-a-sociopath-and-60-million-americans-like-it/.

Late Show with Stephen Colbert. "Abhor-Rent: 525,600 Minutes since the Insurrection." YouTube, January 6, 2022. https://www.youtube.com/watch?v=H_IxT2ei9gU.

Lattanzio, Ryan. "Trump Reportedly Screened 'Joker' at the White House and Liked It." *IndieWire*, November 17, 2019. https://www.indiewire.com/features/general/joker-donald-trump-1202190182/.

Laufer, Peter. *Inside Talk Radio: America's Voice or Just Hot Air?* New York: Birch Lane Press, 1995.

BIBLIOGRAPHY

Laurie, Penny. "Laurie Penny on Rush Limbaugh: A Vicious Clown." *New Statesman*, March 9, 2012. https://www.newstatesman.com/world/2012/03/limbaugh-women-sex-real-attack.

Lawrence, D. H. "Almond Blossom." In *The Complete Poems of D. H. Lawrence*, 241–43. Ware, UK: Wordsworth Editions, 1994.

Lee, Judith Yaross. *Twain's Brand: Humor in Contemporary American Culture*. Jackson: University Press of Mississippi, 2012.

Lennard, Natasha. "Is ANTIFA Counterproductive? White Nationalist Richard Spencer Would Beg to Differ." *Intercept*, March 17, 2018. https://theintercept.com/2018/03/17/richard-spencer-college-tour-antifa-alt-right/.

Lepore, Jill. "The Last Time Democracy Almost Died." *New Yorker*, January 27, 2020. https://www.newyorker.com/magazine/2020/02/03/the-last-time-democracy-almost-died.

Levy, Piet. "Joe Rogan Addresses Controversial Vaccine Comments, Rips Cancel Culture, at Unapologetically Tasteless Milwaukee Show." *Milwaukee Journal Sentinel*, August 8, 2021. https://www.jsonline.com/story/entertainment/2021/08/08/joe-rogan-addresses-vaccine-comments-tasteless-milwaukee-show-cancel-culture/5478667001/.

Lewis, Helen. "Dave Chappelle's Rorschach Test." *Atlantic*, October 13, 2021. https://www.theatlantic.com/ideas/archive/2021/10/dave-chappelle-the-closer/620364/.

Lewis, Helen. "The Joke's On Us." *Atlantic*, September 30, 2020. https://www.theatlantic.com/international/archive/2020/09/how-memes-lulz-and-ironic-bigotry-won-internet/616427/.

Lewis, Paul. *Cracking Up: American Humor in a Time of Conflict*. Chicago: University of Chicago Press, 2006.

Limbaugh, Rush. "Are Americans Stupid?" *Limbaugh Letter* 3, no. 4 (April 1994): 13.

Limbaugh, Rush. "Message to My Fans." Google Groups Conversations. https://groups.google.com/g/alt.fan.rush-limbaugh/c/p3FeoDbdvwE/m/FolMfx1-QoAJ.

Limbaugh, Rush. *See, I Told You So*. New York: Pocket, 1994.

Limbaugh, Rush. "Why Liberals Fear Me." Heritage Foundation, February 18, 2021. https://www.heritage.org/conservatism/commentary/why-liberals-fear-me.

Lincoln, Kenneth. *Indi'n Humor: Bicultural Play in Native America*. New York: Oxford University Press, 1993.

Lipsky, David. *Although of Course You End Up Becoming Yourself: A Road Trip with David Foster Wallace*. New York: Broadway Books, 2010.

Liu, Catherine. "Dialectic of Dark Enlightenments: The Alt-Right's Place in the Culture Industry." *Los Angeles Review of Books*, July 30, 2017. https://

lareviewofbooks.org/article/dialectic-of-dark-enlightenments-the-alt-rights-place-in-the-culture-industry/.

Lombroso, Daniel. "Four Years Embedded with the Alt-Right." *Atlantic*, June 11, 2020. https://www.theatlantic.com/politics/archive/2020/06/white-noise-documentary-alt-right/612898/.

Long, William J. *Mother Nature: A Study of Animal Life and Death*. New York: Harper and Brothers, 1923.

Luippold, Ross. "Comedian Sam Hyde Pranks TED Talks with Nonsense Buzzword Speech." *HuffPost*, October 11, 2013. https://www.huffpost.com/entry/comedian-sam-hyde-pranks-ted-talks_n_4086129.

Lutz, Eric. "The Latest Batch of Jan 6-Related Text Messages Are Even Dumber (And More Sinister) Than You Could Imagine." *Vanity Fair*, April 26, 2022. https://www.vanityfair.com/news/2022/04/mark-meadows-january-6-texts-marjorie-taylor-greene-marshall-law.

MacGillis, Alec. "Inside the Capitol Riot: What the Parler Videos Reveal." ProPublica, January 17, 2021. https://www.propublica.org/article/inside-the-capitol-riot-what-the-parler-videos-reveal.

Mack, David. "Todd Phillips Blamed 'Woke Culture' for Killing Comedy and Leading Him to Make 'Joker.'" *BuzzFeed News*, October 1, 2019. https://www.buzzfeednews.com/article/davidmack/todd-phillips-joker-woke-culture-comedy.

Mahadevan, Tara. "Comedian Josh Denny Gets Roasted for Comparing 'N-Word' to 'Straight White Male.'" *Complex*, May 19, 2018. https://www.complex.com/pop-culture/2018/05/comedian-josh-denny-gets-roasted-for-comparing-n-word-to-straight-white-male#:~:text=On%20Friday%2C%20comedian%20Josh%20Denny%20was%20dragged%20by,diminish%20the%20recipient%20based%20on%20assumption%20and%20obias.

mark normand. "Joe Rogan Explains the Cult Origins of the Mothership | Protect Our Parks." YouTube, June 9, 2023. https://www.youtube.com/watch?v=SzDqbxV2nHc.

Marx, Nick, and Matt Sienkiewicz. "A Fox News Host's Strange Backstory Shows How Liberals Lost Comedy." *Slate*, June 13, 2022. https://slate.com/culture/2022/06/greg-gutfeld-fox-news-show-conservative-comedy.html.

Matthews, Dylan. "The Joe Rogan Controversy Revealed Something Important about the American Left." *Vox*, January 27, 2020. https://www.vox.com/future-perfect/2020/1/27/21081876/joe-rogan-bernie-sanders-henry-kissinger.

Matzo, Paul. *The Radio Right: How a Band of Broadcasters Took on the Federal Government and Built the Modern Conservative Movement*. New York: Oxford University Press, 2020.

Mayr, Chrissie. "Comedy Does NOT Have an Alt-Right Comedy Problem ft. Gavin McInnes." YouTube, April 27, 2021. https://www.youtube.com/watch?app=desktop&v=Ww1QtqmZD_s.

BIBLIOGRAPHY

McClear, Sheila. "David Chapelle Attacker Says Comedian's Jokes 'Triggered' Him." *Los Angeles Magazine*, May 23, 2022. https://lamag.com/news-and-politics/david-chapelle-attacker-says-comedians-jokes-triggered-him.

McDermott, John. "How the Alt-Right Made 'Cuck' the Word of the Year." *Medium*, November 28, 2016. https://medium.com/mel-magazine/how-the-alt-right-made-cuck-the-word-of-the-year-2164dac01e66.

McDonough, Katie. "Die Laughing at the Capitol." *New Republic*, January 11, 2021. https://newrepublic.com/article/160846/die-laughing-capitol.

McLeod, Kembrew. *Pranksters: Making Mischief in the Modern World.* New York: New York University Press, 2014.

McManus, Doyle. "Another Day, Another Vulgar Trump Tweet. The President Clearly Isn't Learning on the Job." *Los Angeles Times*, June 29, 2017. https://www.latimes.com/opinion/op-ed/la-oe-mcmanus-trump-tweet-mike-20170629-story.html.

Meaney, Thomas. "Trumpism after Trump." *Harper's Magazine*, February 2020. https://harpers.org/archive/2020/02/trumpism-after-trump/.

Media Matters for America. "Limbaugh on 'Second American Revolution.'" August 2, 2010. https://www.mediamatters.org/rush-limbaugh/limbaugh-second-american-revolution-i-would-not-call-it-revolution-id-call-it.

Mele, Christopher. "Creepy Clown Hoaxes Lead to 12 Arrests in Multiple States." *New York Times*, September 29, 2016. https://www.nytimes.com/2016/09/30/us/creepy-clown-hoaxes-arrests.html.

Mencken, H. L. "The Clowns in the Ring." In *H. L. Mencken on Politics: A Carnival of Buncombe*, edited by Malcolm Moos, 13–16. Baltimore: Johns Hopkins University Press, 1996.

Mencken, H. L. "The Struggle Ahead." In *H. L. Mencken on Politics: A Carnival of Buncombe*, edited by Malcolm Moos, 149–52. Baltimore: Johns Hopkins University Press, 1996.

Meredith, George. *Beauchamp's Career.* New York: Charles Scribner's Sons, 1922.

Meredith, George. *The Egoist: A Comedy in Narrative.* London: C. Kegan Paul, 1879.

Meredith, George. *An Essay on Comedy and the Uses of the Comic Spirit.* Edited by Lane Cooper. New York: Charles Scribner's Sons, 1918.

Meredith, George. *The Tragic Comedians: A Study in a Well-Known Story.* New York: Ward, Lock, Bowden, 1892.

Miller, Cassie. "Why Are The Proud Boys So Violent? Ask Gavin McInnes." Southern Poverty Law Center, October 18, 2018. https://www.splcenter.org/hatewatch/2018/10/18/why-are-proud-boys-so-violent-ask-gavin-mcinnes.

Miller, Matt. "Joe Rogan, Whose Podcast Reaches Millions, Is Afraid Woke Culture Will Silence Straight White Men." *Esquire*, May 18, 2021. https://www.esquire.com/entertainment/a36463910/joe-rogan-woke-culture-silencing-straight-white-men/.

MillionDollarExtreme2. "John Oliver Shoutout! Joke Video Political Commentary." YouTube, November 26, 2016. https://www.youtube.com/watch?v=nCN-JE8of5Q.

Milner, Ryan M. *The World Made Meme: Public Conversations and Participatory Media*. Cambridge, MA: MIT Press, 2016.

MILO. "'Cuckservative' Is a Gloriously Effective Insult That Should Not Be Slurred, Demonised, or Ridiculed." *Breitbart*, July 28, 2015. https://www.breitbart.com/politics/2015/07/28/cuckservative-is-a-gloriously-effective-insult-that-should-not-be-slurred-demonised-or-ridiculed/.

Minkin, Tracey. "The Building of Joe Rogan's Austin Empire." *Austin Monthly*, June 2022. https://www.austinmonthly.com/the-building-of-joe-rogans-austin-empire/.

Mishan, Ligaya. "The Long and Tortured History of Cancel Culture." *New York Times*, December 3, 2020. https://www.nytimes.com/2020/12/03/t-magazine/cancel-culture-history.html.

Mitchell, W. J. T. *Picture Theory*. Chicago: University of Chicago Press, 1994.

Mogelson, Luke. "Among the Insurrectionists at the Capitol." *New Yorker*, January 15, 2021. https://www.newyorker.com/magazine/2021/01/25/among-the-insurrectionists.

Molloy, Parker. "How Fox News Helped Turn Proud Boys Founder Gavin McInnes into a Right-Wing Media Star." Media Matters for America, October 2, 2020. https://www.mediamatters.org/gavin-mcinnes/how-fox-news-helped-turn-proud-boys-founder-gavin-mcinnes-right-wing-media-star.

Moore, John Hammond. *Carnival of Blood: Dueling, Lynching, and Murder in South Carolina, 1880–1920*. Columbia: University of South Carolina Press, 2006.

Moore, Tina, and Emily Saul. "Disgraced Shock Jock's Girlfriend Live-Streams Alleged Abuse." *New York Post*, December 20, 2015. https://nypost.com/2015/12/20/disgraced-shock-jock-arrested-for-beating-his-girlfriend/.

Morgan, Danielle Fuentes. "Dave Chappelle the Comedy Relic." *Vulture*, October 21, 2021. https://www.vulture.com/article/dave-chappelle-the-comedy-relic.html.

Morris, David B. *The Culture of Pain*. Berkeley: University of California Press, 1991.

Moser, Bob. "Rush Limbaugh Did His Best to Ruin America." *Rolling Stone*, February 17, 2021. https://www.rollingstone.com/politics/politics-features/rush-limbaugh-dead-trump-ruined-america-1129222/.

MSNBC. "'Sociopath': Trump on Track to Win 2024 & Be a 'Dictator' Warns His Coauthor from 'Art of the Deal.'" YouTube, December 8, 2023. https://www.youtube.com/watch?v=lDhSgYVGqPk.

Nagle, Angela. *Kill All Normies: Online Culture Wars From 4Chan and Tumblr to Trump and the Alt-Right*. Alresford, UK: Zero Books, 2017.

National Association for the Advancement of Colored People. "History of Lynching in America." Accessed April 12, 2021. https://naacp.org/find-resources/history -explained/history-lynching-america.

Neiwert, David. "What the Kek: Explaining the Alt-Right 'Deity' Behind Their 'Meme Magic.'" *Southern Poverty Law Center*, May 9, 2017. https://www .splcenter.org/hatewatch/2017/05/08/what-kek-explaining-alt-right-deity -behind-their-meme-magic.

Nelson, Amy. "'Gutfeld!' Roasts Stanford's List of Harmful Words like 'American': 'The Idiots Are Running the Show.'" *Fox News*, December 22, 2022. https:// www.foxnews.com/media/gutfeld-roasts-stanford-list-harmful-words-american -idiots-running-show.

Nietzsche, Friedrich. *The Gay Science*. Translated by Walter Kaufmann. New York: Vintage Books, 1974.

Nilsen, Alleen Pace, and Don L. F. Nilsen. *The Language of Humor: An Introduction*. New York: Cambridge University Press, 2019.

Nobles, Wilborn P., III. "Trump Calls Baltimore 'Disgusting . . . Rodent Infested Mess,' Rips Rep. Elijah Cummings over Border Criticism." *Baltimore Sun*, July 27, 2019. https://www.baltimoresun.com/politics/bs-md-pol-cummings -trump-20190727-chty2yovtvfzfcjkeaui7wm5zi-story.html.

"Notes and Gatherings." *Bulletin of the Society for the Preservation of New England Antiquities* 13 (July 1922–April 1923). https://babel.hathitrust.org/cgi/pt?id =uc1.$b728204&seq=9.

NPR. "'Joker' Opens to Controversy over Film's Depiction of Violence." *All Things Considered*, October 4, 2019. https://www.npr.org/2019/10/04/767339474/joker -opens-to-controversy-over-film-s-depiction-of-violence.

Nussbaum, Emily. "How Jokes Won the Election." *New Yorker*, January 15, 2017. https://www.newyorker.com/magazine/2017/01/23/how-jokes-won-the-election.

Nwanevu, Osita. "The 'Cancel Culture' Con." The Soapbox, *New Republic*, September 23, 2019. https://newrepublic.com/article/155141/cancel-culture-con-dave -chappelle-shane-gillis.

Oller, Jacob. "*A Glitch in the Matrix* Documentary Is More 'Oh' Than 'Whoa.'" *Paste*, February 3, 2021. https://www.pastemagazine.com/movies/sundance-2021 /a-glitch-in-the-matrix-review/.

Olson, Alison. "Political Humor, Deference, and the American Revolution." *Early American Studies* 3 (2005): 363–82.

Ott, Brian L., and Greg Dickinson. *The Twitter Presidency: Donald J. Trump and the Politics of White Rage*. New York: Routledge, 2019.

Otto, Beatrice K. *Fools Are Everywhere: The Court Jester around the World*. Chicago: University of Chicago Press, 2001.

Panreck, Hanna. "Joe Rogan Fights 'F—ing Cult' at New Comedy Club, Welcomes Canceled Comedians." *New York Post*, May 9, 2023. https://nypost.com/2023

/05/09/joe-rogan-fights-fing-cult-at-new-comedy-club-welcomes-canceled
-comedians/.

Parry, Robert. "The Rise of the Right-Wing Media Machine." Fairness & Accuracy
in Reporting, March 1, 1995. https://fair.org/home/the-rise-of-the-right-wing
-media-machine/.

Parsons, Elaine Frantz. "Klan Skepticism and Denial in Reconstruction-Era Public
Discourse." *Journal of Southern History* 77 (2011): 53–90.

Peacock, Louise. "Battles, Blows and Blood: Pleasure and Terror in the
Performance of Clown Violence." *Comedy Studies* 11 (2020): 74–84.

Pearce, Matt. "This Is Another Article about Stuff Joe Rogan Has Said about the
Coronavirus. With Bonus Timeline!" *Los Angeles Times*, September 3, 2021.
https://www.latimes.com/entertainment-arts/story/2021-09-03/joe-rogan
-podcast-coronavirus-vaccine-hestitancy-ivermectin.

Pérez, Raúl. *The Souls of White Jokes: How Racist Humor Fuels White Supremacy.*
Stanford, CA: Stanford University Press, 2022.

Peters, Justin. "Rush Limbaugh Wasn't Funny." *Slate*, February 18, 2021. https://
slate.com/news-and-politics/2021/02/rush-limbaugh-wasnt-funny.html.

Petri, Alexandra. "The Most Glorious Ted Talk Takedown You Will Witness
before 2070." *Washington Post*, October 14, 2013. https://www.washingtonpost
.com/blogs/compost/wp/2013/10/14/the-most-glorious-ted-talk-takedown-you
-will-witness-before-2070/.

Phillips, Whitney. *This Is Why We Can't Have Nice Things: Mapping the Relationship
Between Online Trolling and Mainstream Culture.* Cambridge, MA: MIT Press,
2015.

Pierce, Marge. "The Low Road." *The Sun*, October 2017. https://www.thesun
magazine.org/issues/502/the-low-road.

Poetry Foundation. "Ambrose Bierce." Accessed June 29, 2022. https://www
.poetryfoundation.org/poets/ambrose-bierce.

Polhemus, Robert M. *Comic Faith: The Great Tradition from Austen to Joyce.*
Chicago: Chicago University Press, 1980.

Politico. "Giuliani: 'Let's Have Trial by Combat.'" February 8, 2021. https://www
.politico.com/video/2021/02/08/giuliani-lets-have-trial-by-combat-122543.

Pollowitz, Greg. "Rush Limbaugh vs. Bill Clinton." *National Review*, April 19, 2010.
https://www.nationalreview.com/media-blog/rush-limbaugh-vs-bill-clinton
-greg-pollowitz/.

Porsalin. "Blacklisted | A Million Dollar Extreme Documentary." YouTube,
October 29, 2018. https://www.youtube.com/watch?v=8cugXJ84CMw.

Porsalin. "Sam Hyde Interview | Blacklisted." YouTube, October 31, 2018. https://
www.youtube.com/watch?v=EwvgDXfBxic.

PowerfulJRE. "Breakthrough Cases and Vaccine Passports." YouTube, August 6,
2021. https://www.youtube.com/watch?v=tiwsv51Il4k.

BIBLIOGRAPHY

PowerfulJRE. "Dave Smith Passionately Opposes Vaccine Passports." YouTube video, 8:13, April 23, 2021. https://www.youtube.com/watch?v=x9c3w_QFfbE.

PowerfulJRE. "Joe on the Outrage around Dave Chappelle's New Special." YouTube, October 19, 2021 https://www.youtube.com/watch?v=cqcslpX1hGo.

PowerfulJRE. "Joe Rogan Clarifies His Vaccine Comments." YouTube video, 5:51, April 29, 2021. https://www.youtube.com/watch?v=PloZ-GB9tzA.

Prieb, Natalie. "Rogan Mocks Controversies in Return to Stand-Up Comedy: 'I Talk S—for a Living.'" *The Hill*, February 9, 2022. https://thehill.com/blogs/in-the-know/in-the-know/593521-rogan-mocks-controversies-in-return-to-stand-up-comedy-i-talk-s.

Radford, Benjamin. *Bad Clowns*. Albuquerque: University of New Mexico Press, 2016.

Ravitch, David. "Al Franken on Rush Limbaugh's Squalid Legacy." *Diane Ravitch's Blog*, February 23, 2021. https://dianeravitch.net/2021/02/23/al-franken-on-rush-limbaughs-squalid-legacy/.

Real Time with Bill Maher. "Explaining Jokes to Idiots: Oscars Edition | Real Time with Bill Maher (HBO)." YouTube, April 8, 2022. https://www.youtube.com/watch?v=p-c2eUltH58.

Real Time with Bill Maher Blog. "New Rule: Just Don't Go There." November 17, 2018. https://www.real-time-with-bill-maher-blog.com/index/2018/11/17/new-rule-just-dont-go-there.

Reddit. "Who's Samuel Hyde and Why Are There Memes around Him and Shootings/Terrorist Attacks?" r/NoStupidQuestions. https://www.reddit.com/r/NoStupidQuestions/comments/xzkr5f/whos_samuel_hyde_and_why_are_there_memes_around/.

Reilly, Dan. "What *Joker* Gets Right about Stand-Up Comedy." *Vulture*, October 15, 2019. https://www.vulture.com/2019/10/joker-gary-gulman-sam-morril-stand-up-comedy.html.

Reilly, Nick. "Kevin Smith Says Batman Was Killed Off in Alternative 'Joker' Ending." *NME*, December 31, 2019. https://www.nme.com/news/film/kevin-smith-says-joker-had-a-seriously-dark-alternative-ending-2591803.

Remnick, David. "The Inciter-in-Chief." *New Yorker*, January 9, 2021. https://www.newyorker.com/magazine/2021/01/18/the-inciter-in-chief.

Remski, Matthew. "Bro Science Manifesto." *Medium*, July 7, 2021. https://matthewremski.medium.com/bro-science-manifesto-b6f6ec7d5481.

Remski, Matthew. "Bro Science (w/ Dr. Dan Wilson)." *Conspirituality*, December 11, 2020. https://www.podchaser.com/podcasts/conspirituality-1233098/episodes/29-bro-science-wdr-dan-wilson-80775856.

Rich, Frank. "Can Conservatives Be Funny?" *New York Magazine*, May 15, 2014. https://nymag.com/news/frank-rich/conservative-comedians-2014-5/.

BIBLIOGRAPHY

Robertson, Adi. "Alt-Right: Age of Rage Is a Snapshot of One of 2017's Darkest Moments." *Verge*, March 14, 2018. https://www.theverge.com/2018/3/14/17113514 /alt-right-age-of-rage-antifa-film-review-sxsw-2018.

Rock, Chris. *Selective Outrage*. Directed by Rikki Hughes. Netflix Special, 2023. https://www.netflix.com/title/81625055.

Rodrigues, Ashwin. "The Far-Right Has Deep Roots in New York Comedy." *Vice*, February 12, 2021. https://www.vice.com/en/article/dy8j4k/alt-right-new -york-comedy-new-republic.

Rogan, Joe (@joerogan). "I GOT COVID." Instagram video, 1:39, September 1, 2021. https://www.instagram.com/tv/CTSsA8wAR2-/.

Romano, Aja. "Joaquin Phoenix's Oscars Speech Was a Sprawling Sociopolitical Epic." *Vox*, February 10, 2020. https://www.vox.com/culture/2020/2/10/2113 0778/joaquin-phoenix-oscars-speech-awards-season.

Romano, Aja. "What Dave Chappelle Gets Wrong about Trans People and Comedy." *Vox*, October 23, 2021. https://www.vox.com/culture/22738500/dave -chappelle-the-closer-daphne-dorman-trans-controversy-comedy.

Rosenberg, Howard. "Truthman Slips Up in His Rush to Judgment." *Los Angeles Times*, June 29, 1994. https://www.latimes.com/archives/la-xpm-1994-06-29-ca -9739-story.html.

Rosenberg, Matthew. "He Looted Speaker Pelosi's Office, and Then Bragged about It." *New York Times*, January 6, 2021. https://www.nytimes.com/2021/01/06/us /politics/richard-barnett-pelosi.html.

Rosenwald, Brian. *Talk Radio's America: How an Industry Took over a Political Party That Took over the United States*. Cambridge, MA: Harvard University Press, 2019.

Rosenwald, Brian. "They Just Wanted to Entertain." *Atlantic*, August 21, 2019. https://www.theatlantic.com/ideas/archive/2019/08/talk-radio-made-todays -republican-party/596380/.

Ross, Rollo. "Cancel Culture Takes the Fun Out of Life, Says Comedian John Cleese." Reuters, July 21, 2020. https://www.reuters.com/article/us-people-john -cleese/cancel-culture-takes-the-fun-out-of-life-says-comedian-john-cleese -idUSKCN24M2QV.

Roy, Jessica. "Analysis: 'Cuck,' 'Snowflake,' 'Masculinist': A Guide to the Language of the 'Alt-Right.'" *Los Angeles Times*, November 15, 2016. https://www.latimes .com/nation/la-na-pol-alt-right-terminology-20161115-story.html.

The Rush Limbaugh Show. "Barack the Magic Negro, Explained." March 23, 2007. https://www.rushlimbaugh.com/daily/2007/03/23/barack_the_magic_negro _explained2/.

The Rush Limbaugh Show. "El Rushbo, the Prankster, April 1, 2021." April 1, 2021. https://www.rushlimbaugh.com/daily/2021/04/01/april-fools-el-rushbo-the -prankster/.

BIBLIOGRAPHY

The Rush Limbaugh Show. "The Global Warming Stack." April 8, 2008. https://
www.rushlimbaugh.com/daily/2008/04/08/the_global_warming_stack/.
The Rush Limbaugh Show. "Rush's Second 35 Undeniable Truths of Life." https://
www.rushlimbaugh.com/second35undeniabletruthsoflife/.
Ryan, Erin Gloria. "Rush Limbaugh Spent His Lifetime Speaking Ill of the
Dead." *Daily Beast*, February 17, 2021. https://www.thedailybeast.com/rush
-limbaugh-spent-his-lifetime-speaking-ill-of-the-dead.
Sam & Nick's Perfect Clips. "KSTV2 EP. 2—Fuck-Drumpf-App [Sam Hyde]."
YouTube, June 19, 2019. https://www.youtube.com/watch?v=w8XuNsSnXUE.
Sam & Nick's Perfect Clips. "Sam Hyde—Action 6 News [HWD_e04]." YouTube,
May 16, 2019. https://www.youtube.com/watch?v=Zom56GOLlV0.
Sam & Nick's Perfect Clips. "Sam Hyde—Beating Women [KSTV2 EP.4]."
YouTube, December 20, 2019. https://www.youtube.com/watch?v=cOG5y
poX_Dw.
Sam & Nick's Perfect Clips. "Sam Hyde—Deal with the Devil [TOA Cut]."
YouTube, July 16, 2019. https://www.youtube.com/watch?v=wB5KKdkRyfg.
Sam & Nick's Perfect Clips. "Sam Hyde—FBI & Shooter Meme [HydeWars_040]."
YouTube, August 4, 2019. https://www.youtube.com/watch?v=ILTR3DKFfws.
Sam & Nick's Perfect Clips. "Sam Hyde—Women Stories [HW_047]." YouTube,
August 5, 2020. https://www.youtube.com/watch?v=Q9yyeNG68g4.
Sam & Nick's Perfect Clips. "Shane Gillis & Sam Hyde Talk MillionDollarExtreme
& World Peace." YouTube, November 30, 2023. https://www.youtube.com/watch
?app=desktop&v=7DTVGnkSxjA.
Sam & Nick's Perfect Clips. "WORLD PEACE 2: Sam Hyde & Nick Rochefort
REVEAL Sketch List." YouTube, January 5, 2023. https://www.youtube.com
/watch?v=uSdVDNFb1X8.
Schaeffer, Carol. "Inside the Proud Boys Event That Sparked Violence
Outside of Uptown GOP Club." *Bedford + Bowery*, October 13, 2018. https://
bedfordandbowery.com/2018/10/inside-the-proud-boy-event-that-sparked
-violence-outside-of-uptown-gop-club/.
Schreckinger, Ben. "The Alt-Right Manifesto That Has Trumpworld Talking."
Politico, August 23, 2019. https://www.politico.eu/article/right-wing-manifesto
-that-has-trumpworld-talking-military-rule-bap-bapism-cult-book-bronze-age
-mindset/.
Schwartz, Ian. "Joe Rogan: We Will Get to the Point Where 'Straight White Men
Aren't Allowed to Talk' Due To Privilege." RealClearPolitics, May 18, 2021.
https://www.realclearpolitics.com/video/2021/05/18/joe_rogan_we_will_get
_to_the_point_where_straight_white_men_arent_allowed_to_talk_due_to
_privilege.html.
Schwartz, Rod. "Remembering Rush Limbaugh." Pullman Radio, February 23,
2021. https://pullmanradio.com/remembering-rush/.

Scott, Terry Anne. *Lynching and Leisure: Race and the Transformation of Mob Violence in Texas*. Fayetteville: University of Arkansas Press, 2022.

Sedensky, Matt. "Rush Limbaugh, 'Voice of American Conservatism,' Has Died." *Salt Lake Tribune*, February 17, 2021. https://www.sltrib.com/news/2021/02/17/rush-limbaugh-voice/.

Semley, John. "Corrupted Headspace: *Joker* and the Vacuity of Influence." *Baffler*, October 7, 2019. https://thebaffler.com/latest/corrupted-headspace-semley.

Serwer, Adam. "The Cruelty Is the Point." *Atlantic*, October 3, 2018. https://www.theatlantic.com/ideas/archive/2018/10/the-cruelty-is-the-point/572104/.

Serwer, Adam. *The Cruelty Is the Point: The Past, Present, and Future of Trump's America*. New York: One World, 2021.

Serwer, Adam. "Latching onto L.A. Times Op-Ed, Limbaugh Sings 'Barack, The Magic Negro.'" Media Matters for America, March 20, 2007. https://www.mediamatters.org/rush-limbaugh/latching-la-times-op-ed-limbaugh-sings-barack-magic-negro.

Seymour, Richard. *The Twittering Machine*. London: Verso, 2020.

Shapiro, Ben. "The House That Rush Built." *New York Times*, February 20, 2021. https://www.nytimes.com/2021/02/20/opinion/politics/rush-limbaugh-conservative-media.html.

Sharf, Zack. "Quentin Tarantino Analyzes 'Joker' Climax: It Forces Viewers 'to Think Like a F*cking Lunatic.'" *IndieWire*, February 4, 2021. https://www.indiewire.com/features/general/quentin-tarantino-analyzes-joker-climax-subverison-1234614892/.

Sharlet, Jeff. "'Executing Politicians? Lulz.' For Trump's Zombies, 'Funny' Cosplay Is the Language of Deadly Fascism." *Vanity Fair*, January 8, 2021. https://www.vanityfair.com/news/2021/01/for-trumps-zombies-funny-cosplay-is-the-language-of-deadly-fascism.

Sheppard, Elena. "Pro-Trump Capitol Rioters Like the 'QAnon Shaman' Looked Ridiculous—By Design." *Think*, January 13, 2021. https://www.nbcnews.com/think/opinion/pro-trump-capitol-rioters-qanon-shaman-looked-ridiculous-design-ncna1254010.

Shine, Jacqui. "Not with a Bang, but a Retweet: The Rise of the Alt-Right." *Los Angeles Review of Books*, July 30, 2017. https://lareviewofbooks.org/article/not-with-a-bang-but-a-retweet-the-rise-of-the-alt-right/.

Sienkiewicz, Matt, and Nick Marx. *That's Not Funny: How the Right Makes Comedy Work for Them*. Oakland: University of California Press, 2022.

Simons, Seth. "The Comedy Industry Has a Big Alt-Right Problem." *New Republic*, February 9, 2021. https://newrepublic.com/article/161200/alt-right-comedy-gavin-mcinnes-problem.

Simons, Seth. "Right-Wing Comedians Are Right-Wing Media." *Paste*, March 22, 2021. https://www.pastemagazine.com/comedy/right-wing-media/ring-wing-comedians-are-right-wing-media.

BIBLIOGRAPHY

Sims, David. "The Battle over Adult Swim's Alt-Right TV Show." *Atlantic*, November 17, 2016. https://www.theatlantic.com/entertainment/archive/2016/11/the-raging-battle-over-adult-swims-alt-right-tv-show/508016/.

Sims, David. "The Comic That Explains Where *Joker* Went Wrong." *Atlantic*, October 7, 2019. https://www.theatlantic.com/entertainment/archive/2019/10/killing-joke-and-joker/599512/.

Sims, David. "Untangling the Controversy over the New *Joker* Movie." *Atlantic*, October 3, 2019. https://www.theatlantic.com/entertainment/archive/2019/10/joker-movie-controversy/599326/.

Sizemore, Jay. "The Day Rush Limbaugh Died." *Medium*, February 17, 2021. https://medium.com/parlor-tricks/the-day-rush-limbaugh-died-83cf04472a1f.

Skolnki, Jon. "'AmericaFest': Right-Wing Youth Just Held a Wild Carnival of Fun-Filled Fascism." *Salon*, December 21, 2021. https://www.salon.com/2021/12/21/americafest-right-wing-youth-just-held-a-wild-carnival-of-fun-filled-fascism/.

Sloan, Will. "The Limits of Liberal Comedy." *Current Affairs*, December 10, 2020. https://www.currentaffairs.org/2020/12/the-limits-of-liberal-comedy.

Smith, Blake. "Bronze Age Pervert's Dissertation on Leo Strauss." *Tablet Magazine*, February 14, 2023. https://www.tabletmag.com/sections/arts-letters/articles/bronze-age-pervert-dissertation-leo-strauss.

Smith, Justin E. H. "The End of Satire." *New York Times*, April 8, 2019. https://www.nytimes.com/2019/04/08/opinion/the-end-of-satire.html.

Snyder, Timothy. "The American Abyss." *New York Times*, December 28, 2021. https://www.nytimes.com/2021/01/09/magazine/trump-coup.html.

Sohn, Gigi B., and Andrew Schwartzman. "FAIRNESS—NOT SILENCE." *Washington Post*, January 31, 1994. https://www.washingtonpost.com/archive/opinions/1994/01/31/fairness-not-silence/cbe8b618-de11-4da3-8b63-83e04b4dec1c/.

Sonnad, Nikhil, and Tim Squirrell. "The Alt-Right Is Creating Its Own Dialect. Here's the Dictionary." *Quartz*, October 30, 2017. https://qz.com/1092037/the-alt-right-is-creating-its-own-dialect-heres-a-complete-guide.

Southern Poverty Law Center. "Alt-Right." Accessed March 17, 2022. https://www.splcenter.org/fighting-hate/extremist-files/ideology/alt-right.

Southern Poverty Law Center. "Proud Boys." Accessed March 17, 2022. https://www.splcenter.org/fighting-hate/extremist-files/group/proud-boys.

Southpaw (@nycsouthpaw). "Some of the Trump fanatics constructed a gallows near the Capitol reflecting pool and another group of them fashioned a crude noose from stolen AP camera cables and hung it from a tree." Twitter, January 8, 2021. https://twitter.com/nycsouthpaw/status/1347563271352676354?lang=en.

Spencer, Richard. "What It Means to Be Alt-Right." ALTRIGHT.com, August 11, 2017.

Stableford, Dylan. "New Video Shows Alleged Jan 6. Capitol Rioters Threatening Pence." *Yahoo!News*, February 7, 2022. https://news.yahoo.com/new-video-jan-6-capitol-riot-pence-threat-drag-through-streets-195249884.html.

Staples, Brent. "So the South's White Terror Will Never Be Forgotten." *New York Times*, April 25, 2018. https://www.nytimes.com/2018/04/25/opinion/american-lynchings-memorial.html.

Starkey, Arun. "How Kurt Cobain Reacted to 'Weird Al' Yankovic's Nirvana Parody." *Far Out*, August 17, 2022. https://faroutmagazine.co.uk/kurt-cobain-reacted-weird-al-yankovic-nirvana-parody/.

Stephens, Alexander H. "Cornerstone Speech." Savannah, Georgia, March 21, 1861. https://teachingamericanhistory.org/document/the-corner-stone-speech/.

Stocker, Paul. "Joker, the Far Right and Popular Culture." *Open Democracy*, November 1, 2019. https://www.opendemocracy.net/en/countering-radical-right/joker-far-right-and-popular-culture/.

Suebsaeng, Asawin, and Will Sommer. "Trump's Favorite Part of Jan. 6 Is Laughing at the Trauma." *Daily Beast*, January 6, 2022. https://www.thedailybeast.com/trumps-favorite-part-of-january-6-is-laughing-at-the-trauma.

Sutton, Kelsey. "Alec Baldwin on Trump: 'He's the Head Writer of His Own Comedy Routine.'" Politico, November 8, 2016. https://www.politico.com/blogs/on-media/2016/11/alec-baldwin-on-trump-hes-the-head-writer-of-his-own-comedy-routine-230939.

Taibbi, Matt. *Insane Clown President: Dispatches from the 2016 Circus.* New York: Random House, 2017.

Taussig, Michael. *Defacement: Public Secrecy and the Labor of the Negative.* Stanford, CA: Stanford University Press, 1999.

Taylor, David. "Willem Dafoe Has Fantasised about Playing a 'Joker Imposter' Opposite Joaquin Phoenix's *Joker*." *GQ*, June 8, 2022. https://www.gq-magazine.co.uk/culture/article/willem-dafoe-joker-sequel.

This American Life. "White Haze." September 22, 2017. https://www.thisamericanlife.org/626/transcript.

Tim Heidecker. "Jeremy Levick, Rajat Suresh on Office Hours Live." Office Hours Live. Episode 184. YouTube, November 25, 2021. https://www.youtube.com/watch?v=P6Iyg9fznvM.

Toto, Christian. "Mocking Woke May Be the New Norm in Comedy, Thanks to Sebastian Maniscalco." Fox News, December 13, 2022. https://www.foxnews.com/media/mocking-woke-new-norm-comedy-thanks-sebastian-maniscalco.

Towsen, John H. *Clowns.* New York: Hawthorn Books, 1976.

Trahair, Lisa. *The Comedy of Philosophy: Sense and Nonsense in Early Cinematic Slapstick.* Albany: State University of New York Press, 2007.

Trump, Mary L. *Too Much and Never Enough: How My Family Created the World's Most Dangerous Man.* New York: Simon and Schuster, 2020.

Tucker Carlson Originals. "The Death of Comedy." July 2023. https://nation.foxnews.com/tucker-carlson-originals-death-of-comedy-nation/.

BIBLIOGRAPHY

Ugwu, Reggie. "Tim Heidecker, Bard of the Anti-Trump Movement." *Buzzfeed News*, April 4, 2017. https://www.buzzfeednews.com/article/reggieugwu/tim-heidecker-trump-songs.

United States of America v. Jacob Anthony Chansley. Government's Memorandum in Aid of Sentencing, United States District Court for the District of Columbia, CR. NO. 21-CR-003 (RCL).

Urban Dictionary. "Clown World." June 10, 2020. https://www.urbandictionary.com/define.php?term=Clown%20World.

VanArendonk, Kathryn. "Joe Rogan Plays an Unconvincing Fool." *Vulture*, August 5, 2024. https://www.vulture.com/article/joe-rogan-burn-the-boats-netflix-comedy-special-review.html.

Wagner, John. "Trump Says It Was 'Common Sense' for Jan. 6 Rioters to Chant 'Hang Mike Pence!'" *Washington Post*, November 12, 2021. https://www.washingtonpost.com/politics/trump-hang-mike-pence/2021/11/12/64a17142-43b0-11ec-a88e-2aa4632af69b_story.html.

Walker, Hunter. "The 'JusticeForJ6' Rally Wasn't a Joke—It Was A Warning." *Rolling Stone*, September 18, 2021. https://www.rollingstone.com/politics/politics-features/justiceforj6-rally-insurrection-capitol-trump-1228690/.

Wallace, David Foster. "Host." *Atlantic*, April 2005. https://www.theatlantic.com/magazine/archive/2005/04/host/303812/.

Washington Post. "Identifying Far-Right Symbols That Appeared at the U.S. Capitol Riot." January 15, 2021. https://www.washingtonpost.com/nation/interactive/2021/far-right-symbols-capitol-riot/.

Webber, Julie A. *The Joke Is on Us: Political Comedy in (Late) Neoliberal Times*. Lanham, MD: Lexington Books, 2019.

Weiner, Robert G., and Robert Moses Peaslee. Introduction to *The Joker: A Serious Study of the Clown Prince of Crime*, xiv–xxxi. Jackson: University Press of Mississippi, 2015.

Weiss, Bari. "Meet the Renegades of the Intellectual Dark Web." *New York Times*, May 8, 2018. https://www.nytimes.com/2018/05/08/opinion/intellectual-dark-web.html.

West, Cornel. "Nietzsche's Prefiguration of Postmodern American Philosophy." In *The Cornel West Reader*, 188–212. New York: Basic Civitas Books, 1999.

Westwood, Robert. "Theory as Joke: A Hysterical Perturbation." In *Humour, Work and Organization*, edited by Robert Westwood and Carl Rhodes, 45–74. New York: Routledge, 2007.

Wieck, David Thoreau. "Funny Things." *Journal of Aesthetics and Art Criticism* 25, no. 4 (1967): 437–47.

Wilkinson, Alissa. "Joker Has Toxic Fans. Does That Mean It Shouldn't Exist?" *Vox*, October 3, 2019. https://www.vox.com/culture/2019/10/3/20884104/joker-threats-cancel-phillips-art.

Williams, Christian. "Take in the Work of the Comedy Provocateurs in Million Dollar Extreme." *AV Club*, April 23, 2013. https://www.avclub.com/take-in-the-work-of-the-comedy-provocateurs-in-million-1798237780.

Williams, Raymond. *Keywords: A Vocabulary of Culture and Society*. New York: Oxford University Press, 1976.

Williams, Raymond. *The Long Revolution*. Ontario: Broadview Press, 2001. Originally published 1961.

Willett, Cynthia. *Irony in the Age of Empire: Comic Perspectives on Democracy & Freedom*. Bloomington: Indiana University Press, 2008.

Winki, Luke. "What Those Animal Pelts Tell Us about the Future of the Far Right." *Atlantic*, January 12, 2021. https://www.theatlantic.com/culture/archive/2021/01/why-capitol-rioters-wore-animal-pelts/617639/.

Wolcott, James. "How Donald Trump Became America's Insult Comic in Chief." *Vanity Fair*, November 6, 2015. https://www.vanityfair.com/culture/2015/11/wolcott-trump-insult-comic.

Wood, Amy Louise. *Lynching and Spectacle: Witnessing Racial Violence in America, 1890–1940*. Chapel Hill: University of North Carolina Press, 2009.

Wood, Graeme. "How Bronze Age Pervert Charmed the Far Right." *Atlantic*, August 3, 2023. https://www.theatlantic.com/magazine/archive/2023/09/bronze-age-pervert-costin-alamariu/674762/.

Woodward, Bob. *Rage*. New York: Simon and Schuster, 2020.

Wordsworth, William. "Character of the Happy Warrior." Poetry Foundation. Accessed November 11, 2019. https://www.poetryfoundation.org/poems/45512/character-of-the-happy-warrior.

Wright, Megh. "Adult Swim Orders 'World Peace' Series from Million Dollar Extreme." *Vulture*, March 3, 2016. https://www.vulture.com/2016/03/adult-swim-orders-world-peace-series-from-million-dollar-extreme.html.

Wright, Megh. "Sam Hyde Lashed Out at Tim Heidecker over 'Million Dollar Extreme's Cancellation." *Vulture*, December 8, 2016. https://www.vulture.com/2016/12/sam-hyde-lashed-out-at-tim-heidecker-over-million-dollar-extremes-cancellation.html.

Yang, Jeff. "'Joker'—A Political Parable for Our Times." CNN, October 6, 2019. https://www.cnn.com/2019/10/06/opinions/joker-political-parable-donald-trump-presidency-yang/index.html.

Young, Alfred F. *Liberty Tree: Ordinary People and the American Revolution*. New York: New York University Press, 2006.

Young, Damon. "The Racist Roots of 'Cuck' (the White Supremacist's Favorite Insult), Explained." *Root*, August 15, 2017. https://www.theroot.com/the-racist-roots-of-cuck-the-white-supremacists-favo-1797868917.

Young, Dannagal Goldthwaite. *Irony and Outrage: The Polarized Landscape of Rage, Fear, and Laughter in the United States*. New York: Oxford University Press, 2020.

Young, Steve. "Rush Limbaugh, Comic Genius." *Philadelphia Inquirer,* March 7, 2012. https://www.inquirer.com/philly/opinion/inquirer/20120307_Rush _Limbaugh__comic_genius.html.

Zaretsky, Robert. "With Huckster Trump in Charge, the Carnival Goes On—And On and On." *Forward,* December 23, 2020. https://forward.com/culture/460850 /with-huckster-trump-in-charge-the-carnival-goes-on-and-on-and-on/.

Zaretsky, Robert D. "Return of the Grotesque." *Aeon,* July 3, 2017. https://aeon.co /essays/the-grotesque-is-back-but-this-time-no-one-is-laughing.

Zinoman, Jason. "In His Stand-Up Special, Joe Rogan Plays Dumb." *New York Times,* August 4, 2024. https://www.nytimes.com/2024/08/04/arts/television /joe-rogan-standup-netflix.html.

Zupančič, Alenka. *Odd One In: On Comedy.* Cambridge: Massachusetts Institute of Technology, 2008.

Zuppello, Suzanne. "'Killer Clowns': Inside the Terrifying Hoax Sweeping America." *Rolling Stone,* September 29, 2016. https://www.rollingstone.com /culture/culture-news/killer-clowns-inside-the-terrifying-hoax-sweeping -america-129505/.

INDEX

Academy Awards, 167

Accuracy in Media, 38

Adult Swim, 50, 142–43

Aesop's fables, 48, 70

Ailes, Roger, 32

Alamriu, Costin, 147

Allen, Tim, 136

All in the Family, 143

alter egos, comical, 8–9, 54. *See also* comic characters

alternate endings, for *Joker,* 99–100

alt.fan.rush-limbaugh, 40

alt-right comedy, 17, 64, 69, 135–56; language of, 135–56. *See also* Hyde, Sam

AMC Networks, 141

AmericaFest (Phoenix, AZ), 119–20

American Revolution, 120–21. *See also* Capitol Insurrection

"Angry Black Man," 167

animated cartoons, 180

anticomedy, 12; MDE and, 48–73. *See also* trolls/trolling

Anti-Defamation League, 64, 142

Antifa, 112

antisemitism, 57, 142

Anton, Michael, 146–47

Apatow, Judd, 141

Aristotle, 124

Asanuma, Inejiro, 154–55

Atlantic, 57

Attridge, Derek, 156

authoritarian impulse, in comedy, 171–72

authoritarian populism, in American tradition, 106

Babylon Bee, 173

Bakhtin, Mikhail, 6–7, 13–15, 18, 28, 90, 93, 97, 106, 108–9, 112, 114, 121, 123, 126, 175

Baldwin, Alec, 38

"bang" gun, 66–67, 99

BAP (Bronze Age Pervert), 149; *Bronze Age Mindset,* 146–48, 151. *See also* Alamriu, Costin

Barnett, Richard "Bigo," 113

Batman, 67, 81–82, 89, 99–100

Batman (Tim Burton, 1989), 90

Batman: The Killing Joke (Alan Moore, 1996), 67, 80

Beavis and Butt-Head (Mike Judge), 29

Benjamin, Owen, 136

Benny, Jack, 33

Bergson, Henri, 4, 34, 42, 59, 66, 72, 145, 155–56, 165, 169, 175–76

Berlant, Lauren, 14, 124

221

INDEX

Bernstein, Joseph, 54

Bierce, Ambrose, *The Devil's Dictionary,* 135, 137, 139, 143–44, 154

bigotry, and comic language, 140–44

BLACKLISTED (Porsalin, 2018), 65–66, 68–70

Blanc, Mel, 34

blue-collar comedians, 136

Blum, Alexander, 64

boogaloo movement, 116

Borowitz, Andy, 117

Bradbury, Ray, 126; *Something Wicked This Way Comes,* 119

branding, Limbaugh and, 25, 27

Bronze Age Pervert. *See* BAP (Bronze Age Pervert)

Bruce, Lenny, 154

Buckley, William F., Jr., 37

Burgis, Ben, 3

Burke, Kenneth, 83, 96, 172

Bush, President George H. W., 38

Cabrera, Ana, 58

cancel culture, 3, 49, 69, 83–85, 91–93, 106, 114, 172

capitalist laughter, 96, 100

Capitol Insurrection (January 6, 2021), 5–7, 17, 25–26, 39, 104–27, 174–75

caricature, 39. *See also* cartoons

Carlin, George, 150

Carlisle, Henry, 120–21

Carlson, Tucker, 152, 173–74

carnival, and revolution, 120–21. *See also* dark carnival, Capitol Insurrection as

carnival attitude, 175

carnivalesque, the, 5–9, 25, 40–41; and Capitol Insurrection, 104–27

carnival grounds, US Capitol as, 106–9

carnivalish, the, 7–9, 11

Carol, Charls, 48–49. *See also* Million Dollar Extreme

Carolla, Adam, 173

Caron, James E., 123

Carter, President Jimmy, 38

cartoons: animated, 180; editorial, 29, 39; political, 137

Carvey, Dana, 38

censorship, 96, 155

Chansley, Jacob (QAnon Shaman), 110

Chappelle, Dave, 12–13, 15, 168–71, 173; *The Closer* (2021), 84, 166, 169; *What's in a Name?,* 166

character study, *Joker* as, 80. *See also* comic characters

"charged humor," 117–18

Christian nationalism, 105, 111

class issues, 54

Cleese, John, 84

Clinton, President Bill, 31–32, 37

Clinton administration, 35–40

Clinton-Lewinsky sex scandal, 32

clownery, in *Joker,* 89–93

clown figure, 66–67, 141; in *Joker,* 78–100

clown panic, 140

clown props/tricks, 66–67. *See also* "bang" gun

Clown World Order, 137, 141, 144, 147, 174

Cobain, Kurt, 24, 28

Cohen, Roger, 118

Colbert, Stephen, 6, 68, 136–37, 173; *The Colbert Report,* 6; *The Late Show with Stephen Colbert,* 122; Rally to Restore Sanity and/or Fear (2010, with Stewart), 11

Columbus Dispatch, 33

"comedian," label of, 43

comedic commentary, 10

comedic process, 40

comedy: death of, 80, 135–56, 173–74; and democracy, 121–27; etymology of, 153; as index of culture, 164–77; infernal, purgatorial, or paradisal, 175; as property of Left, 121–25

comedy club, 87. *See also* Comedy Mothership (Austin, TX)

comedy machine, alt-right and, 149–53

Comedy Mothership (Austin, TX), 3, 172

Comerford, Michael Sean, 104–5

comic artfulness, 108–9

comic characters, 54–55, 176

INDEX

comic culture, 5
comic debasement, 125
comic degradation, 5–6, 11, 41–42
comic delight, 4–5, 105, 108
comic detachment, 53
comic dispirit, 1–18, 53. *See also* comic spirits;
  Million Dollar Extreme
comic effect, 10–12, 72–73, 96, 115, 122, 124,
  146, 165, 175–76
comic failure, 8, 14
comic freedom, 16, 123, 151, 169–71, 174, 177
comic gesture, 106–9
comic hoaxes, Limbaugh and, 32. *See also*
  internet hoaxes
comic idea, 4, 27, 39–40, 59, 70
comic imposture, in *Joker,* 80
comic judgment, 8, 11, 17, 80, 82–83, 85–89,
  96, 145, 173
comic language, alt-right and, 135–56. *See also*
  cuck; obscenities; vulgarity
comic license, 8, 11, 13, 35, 50, 165, 171, 174
comic license to kill, in *Joker,* 78–100
comic mask, 53, 64, 80, 82–83, 100, 111, 155
comic masquerade, 153–55
comic perception, 42
comic persona, cults of, 11
comic retribution, in *Joker,* 87
comic scapegoat, 172
comic seduction, 145
comic spirits, 148, 164–65, 167–68, 172,
  174–75
comic victims, 122
comic virtue, 113
conservatism, 5, 9, 15, 24–43, 52, 120–21, 138,
  140, 142, 144, 146, 151–52, 174. *See also*
  alt-right comedy; Capitol Insurrection;
  Carlson, Tucker; Gutfeld, Greg;
  Limbaugh, Rush; McInnes, Gavin;
  Rogan, Joe; Shanklin, Paul
control, pattern of, 169
Conway, George, 116
cosplay, at Capitol Insurrection, 109–11
coupologists, 109, 117
COVID-19 pandemic, 1–2, 58, 61–62
cringeworthy humor, 145

Critchley, Simon, 8
Crowder, Steven, *Louder with Crowder,* 42
cruelty, 14, 24, 33, 50, 53, 63, 69, 84, 148, 164;
  alt-right and, 135, 143–44, 148, 154; in
  Capitol Insurrection, 105, 109, 123; and the
  carnivalesque, 114–17; Joker and, 89, 91;
  and Trumpism, 117–20, 125, 127
Cuck (film, 2019), 158n32
"cuck," 140–44
cuck fetishists, 141
"cuckservative," 140–44, 155
cultural politics, 5, 10, 17, 51; alt-right and,
  137, 140, 144, 150, 152, 175–76; *Joker* and,
  80–82, 84; Shanklin and, 27–29, 34, 41;
  Trumpism and, 105, 110, 114, 123, 125–26
cultural war/warfare/warriors, 24, 30, 39, 63,
  69–70, 119, 136, 148–49, 164, 173
Cumnia, Anthony, 155
cyberfascism, 53

Dafoe, Willem, 82
The Daily Show, 116
dance, in *Joker,* 88
dark carnival, Capitol Insurrection as,
  104–27
The Dark Knight (2008), 81–82, 89–90
Davis, D. Diane, 86
DC Comics, 67
death, 24, 40–41, 52, 126; and the
  carnivalesque, 106–9; of comedy, 80,
  135–56, 173–74; of democracy, 120–21; in
  Joker, 94. *See also* killing joke
DeGeneres, Ellen, 84
demasculinization, 152
democracy, and comedy, 121–27
De Niro, Robert, 78. See also *Joker* (Todd
  Phillips, 2019)
Denny, Josh, 155
deregulation, and repeal of fairness doctrine,
  30–31
devil, wearing comic mask, 82
Dewey, Caitlin, 51
diminishment, 11
dispiritedness. *See* comic dispirit
dittoheads, 42

Donovan, Johnny, 34
Douglas, Mary, 169
dreamworlds, 176–77
Drexel University, 55
Duke Ellington School of the Arts (Washington, DC), 166

Eagleton, Terry, 9
Eco, Umberto, 170
editorial cartoons, 29, 39
effigy hanging, 118
egoism/egoistic, 36, 41–42, 81, 120–21, 125, 154, 177; and Capitol Insurrection, 117, 125; and identity politics, 172–73; Joker and, 81, 83, 90–91, 98, 100
egoistic comedy, 8–11, 13–15, 17, 27, 29–30, 35, 42, 53, 169–70, 172
ego trip, 42
Ehrenstein, David, 32–33
EIB Network, 31
Einstein, Albert, 56
Ellis, Emma Grey, 51
Emancipation (2022), 170
empathy, need for, 81
environmentalism, 52
excretion, 6, 8, 109

FAIR (Fairness & Accuracy in Reporting), *Extra!*, 25
fairness doctrine, repeal of, 30–31
fake news, satirical, 10, 123, 173
farce, 35, 40
Fauci, Dr. Anthony, 118
"feminazi," 137
Ferrell, Will, 141
4chan, 52–53, 58, 166
Fox, Jesse David, 4
Fox News, 136, 152
Franken, Al, *Rush Limbaugh Is a Big Fat Idiot...*, 40
Franklin, Benjamin, 137, 154
Freud, Sigmund, 9
Frost, Amber A'Lee, 140
Frum, David, 167

"fuck you spirit," at Capitol Insurrection, 111–14
fun/funniness, defining, 153
funniness, defining, 4
"funny ha-ha" *vs.* "funny peculiar," 153
Funny or Die, 137–39; "The Kings of Alt Right Comedy," 137–39, 141
Furie, Matt, *Boy's Club*, 64

gallows, erected during Capitol Insurrection, 104, 106–9, 125, 127
Gamergate, 51, 141
Garner, Eric, 165–66
gender issues, 12–13, 54, 166, 168–69. *See also* homophobia; misogyny; transphobia
"Ghost of Kyiv," 58
G.I. Jane (film), 167
Gillis, Shane, 70, 136
Giroux, Henry, 124
Giuliani, Rudy, 110
global warming, 52
Glopdemon's Law, 143
Golden, James, 33
Gomez, Luis J., 173
Gonzalez, Vicente, 58
Gore, Al, 36–38, 52
Gorrell, Bob, 29
Griffin, Kathy, 84
Grossberg, Lawrence, 105, 124
groypers, 112
gun violence, 48–49. *See also* violence
Gutfeld!, 136, 150–52
Gutfeld, Greg, 136, 150–52, 174; *The Joy of Hate*, 152; *Red Eye*, 151–52
Guthrie, Woody, 49

hanging: in effigy, 118, 125; as means of capital punishment, 106. *See also* gallows, erected during Capitol Insurrection
Hannity, Sean, 152
Harris, Mary, 52
Hart, Kevin, 12–13
hate, and humor, 13
hate groups, 15
Hate Machine, 64, 136

INDEX

hate speech, 166
hate symbol, Pepe the Frog as, 64. *See also* internet memes
Heidecker, Tim, 16, 50, 141–42; "I Am a Cuck," 141; *Office Hours,* 143; and Sam Hyde, 143–44
Hemmer, Nicole, 30
Hicks, Bill, 154
hoaxes. *See* comic hoaxes; internet hoaxes
Hochschild, Arlie Russell, 118
Hollywood Reporter, 63
Holmes, James, 50
homophobia, 15, 84, 142, 145
Hoppean Snake, 152
horror, comedy and, 92
HuffPost, 57
humorlessness, 123, 170
Hutcheon, Linda, 28
Hyde, Sam, 17, 48–73, 141, 143, 166, 171, 174; and Perfect Guy Life, 144; TED Talk "2070 Paradigm Shift," 50, 55–57, 59, 147; and Tim Heidecker, 143–44. *See also* Million Dollar Extreme
Hyers, Conrad, 8, 62, 72
hypermasculinity, 138, 151

"Identitarian Revolution," 145
identity politics, and egoism, 172–73
imposter syndrome, 78
infotainment, 10
Instagram, 2–3, 166
insult comedy, 26–27
Insurrection Day, 104–27
internet hoaxes, 58, 166
internet memes, 50, 58–60, 64, 112, 148–49; "Pepe the Frog," 64, 112, 141, 147; "Sam is the Shooter," 50, 58–60, 166
irony, 122–23
Isenberg, Nancy, 105
Ivy, Marilyn, 108

Joker (Todd Phillips, 2019), 17, 78–100, 116, 169, 174
Joker, the (DC Comics), 67
Joker: Folie à Deux (2024), 82, 116–17, 176

JRE Toons, 180–90
JRE Toons, "A Comedy of Earthly Survival Moment," 180–90
Judge, Mike, *Beavis and Butt-Head,* 29
Justice for J6, 117
"just joking," trope of, 14, 84–85, 88, 169–70

Kaufman, Will, 154
"Kek," 119
Kellogg, Stephen, *Objects in the Mirror,* 168
Kendi, Ibram X., 49
"killing it," in *Joker,* 78–100
killing joke, 66–67, 70, 89, 96, 148, 164–68; in *Joker,* 87, 93–95
Klepper, Jordan, 117–18
Ku Klux Klan (KKK), 110–11, 121

Lady Gaga, 82
Larson, Mary Strom, 25
last laugh, in *Joker,* 99–100
laughter: capitalist, 96, 100; derisive, 42; in face of death, 104; in *Joker,* 78–100; in public, 175; strength and weakness in, 169; thoughtful, 42
Ledger, Heath, 81, 83, 89–90. See also *The Dark Knight* (2008)
Left, the, 121–25; and comic language of alt-right, 135–56
Legion of Skanks, 136, 173
Levick, Jeremy, 15–16
Lewis, Paul, 10
lex talionis (law of retaliation), 106, 127
libtard, 141–42
Limbaugh, Rush, 6, 9–10, 50–52, 136–37, 140, 164–65, 171; Adventures of Rush Revere series, 26; *Limbaugh Letter,* 25–26; Operation Chaos, 24; *The Rush Limbaugh Show,* 30–34; *See, I Told You So,* 151; and Shanklin, 24–43
LMFAO (Laughing My Fucking Ass Off), 142
LOL, 119
Los Angeles Times, 32
Louis C.K., 84
low-road comedy, 164–77

lulz, 52
lynchings, 107

Maddow, Rachel, 11
Maher, Bill, 27, 171, 173–74; *Club Random,*
   174; *Real Time with Bill Maher,* 169
manifestos, 144–48
Manion, Clarence E. "Pat," 30
The Man Show (Comedy Central), 173
Marx, Nick, 53, 150
masculinists, 49, 142
mass shootings, 50, 58–59. *See also* "Sam is
   the Shooter" memes
Mayr, Chrissie, 151
McInnes, Gavin, 136, 151–54; "The Cognitive
   Dissidents Tour", 155; *The Gavin McInnes
   Show,* 152; *Get Off My Lawn,* 136
McLeod, Kembrew, 57
MDE.TV, 71
Mencken, H. L., 125
mental illness, as portrayed in *Joker,* 80–81,
   85–89
Meredith, George, 8, 15, 36, 42, 177
Miller, Dennis, 136
Miller, Paul, 116
Million Dollar Extreme (MDE), 48–73,
   136, 164; *How to Bomb the U.S. Gov't,* 70;
   *Million Dollar Extreme Presents: World
   Peace,* 50, 63–71, 143. *See also* Hyde, Sam
Million MAGA March, 112
Milner, Ryan M., 53
misogyny, 13, 51, 54, 57, 69, 80, 105,
   124, 142
Mitchell, W. J. T., 137
mock executions, 106–7
mockumentaries, 61–62
Montana, 38–39
Moore, Alan, *Batman: The Killing Joke*
   (1996), 67, 80
Morgan, Danielle Fuentes, 92
Morris, David B., 91
Muñoz, Henry R., III, 141
musical comedy, 34–41
music videos, 28–29

Nast, Thomas, 137
National Public Radio, 11
Netflix, 166
New Right, 121
NewsRadio, 12
New World Order, 137
New York Times, 11
Ngai, Sianne, 14, 124
Nietzsche, Friedrich, 148
Nirvana, 27–28. *See also* Cobain, Kurt
Noah, Trevor, 116; *The Daily Show with
   Trevor Noah,* 122
NRA (National Rifle Association), 48
Nussbaum, Emily, 105

Oath Keepers, 113
oaths and oath-taking, 112–13
Obama, President Barack, 32–33
obscenities, and the carnivalesque, 111–14
Old Americanism, 111
Oliver, John, 136; *Last Week Tonight,* 48
The Onion, 6, 10
outcast status, in *Joker,* 78–100
outrage, 122–23

parody, 27–29, 34
peculiar/peculiarity, 136, 149–56
Pelosi, Nancy, 113
Pennsylvania State University, 155
Pepe the Frog, 64, 112, 141, 147
Perez, Lou, 173
Phillips, Todd, 84; *Joker* (2019), 17, 78–100
Phillips, Whitney, 52
Phoenix, Joaquin, 78, 83–84, 116. See also
   Joker (Todd Phillips, 2019)
pilgarlics, 140
Pinochet Ugarte, Augusto, 152
Poe, Nathan, 51
Poe's Law, 50–53, 70, 139
Policy Review, 37
political cartoons, 137
political identity, 41
political parable, *Joker* as, 80
Poole, Christopher "Moot," 53

INDEX

pop music, 27–29, 34

pranks/pranking, 48–49, 51–52, 143; MDE and, 55–58

presidential election of 2020, 104–27

principles, statements of, 144–48

Proud Boys, 136, 152, 162n100

pseudobulbar affect, 80, 98

QAnon Shaman (Jacob Chansley), 110

race/racism, 32–33, 54, 142, 165–66

radio personality, Limbaugh as, 31–34

rage: and the carnivalesque, 8; right-wing, 135–56; white rage, 111–14

"Rage on the Right," 149

Ramirez, Michael, 39

Rand, Ayn, 41

recognition, 82–83

Remski, Matthew, 1–2

retaliation, law of. *See* lex talionis (law of retaliation)

Rife, Matt, 145

rightist extremism, 53

right-wing media machine, 149

right-wing rage machine, 149–53

Rip Van Winkle figure, 121

Rochefort, Nick, 49, 71–72. *See also* Million Dollar Extreme

Rock, Chris, 167–71, 173; *Selective Outrage,* 171–72. *See also* Slapgate

Rogan, Joe, 1–3, 5–6, 12–13, 15, 49, 169, 171–72; *Burn the Boats,* 2; *Joe Rogan Experience (JRE),* 1–3, 177; *The Sacred Clown Tour,* 2

Ryan, Erin Gloria, 24

"Sam is the Shooter" memes, 50, 58–60, 166

Sam & Nick's Perfect Clips, 50, 60

satire, 39

Saturday Night Live, 38, 136

Schumer, Amy, 138

Schwartz, Tony, 116

"Second American Revolution," 26

selective outrage, 171–72

self-protection, 48–49

sending in the clowns, 89–93

sentimentality, 24, 50, 138–39, 145

Serwer, Adam, 119

Seymour, Richard, 52–53

Shaffir, Ari, 173

Shanklin, Paul, 17, 24–43, 52, 174; "Barack, the Magic Negro," 32–33; *Bill Clinton: The Comeback Kid Tour,* 38; *Bill Clinton: The Early Years,* 36; *The Usual Suspects,* 39

Shine, Jacqui, 138–39

The Shining (1980), 113

shitposters, 127, 139, 145, 156, 164, 167

Sienkiewicz, Matt, 53–54, 150

Sinatra, Frank, "That's Life," 98

Sizemore, Jay, 40–41

Slapgate, 167–70, 173

slavery, 121, 156

slave trade, 121

Smith, Dave, 1

Smith, Kevin, *Fatman Beyond,* 99

Smith, Will, 167–70, 173. *See also* Slapgate

sociopathy, 115–16

Something Awful, 140, 143

Sondheim, Stephen, "Send in the Clowns," 86–87, 89

Southern Poverty Law Center, 139, 142

Spencer, Richard, 145, 148; "What It Means to Be Alt-Right," 144–45

Stanford University, "Harmful Language," 150–51

Stewart, Jon, 11, 105; Rally to Restore Sanity and/or Fear (2010, with Colbert), 11

Stewart-Colbert Effect, 121

suicide, 99–100

Super Happy Fun America, 5

Suresh, Rajat, 16

survival, comedies of, 17

tabloid journalism, 60

Takimag, 152

talk radio, 9–10, 17, 24–25, 41, 50, 136, 143; Limbaugh and, 30–34. *See also* Limbaugh, Rush

Tarantino, Quentin, 95–96

TEDx, TED Talks, 55–57
"third rail" comedy, 3
thought leadership, Limbaugh and, 33
Tim and Eric's Billion Dollar Movie (2012), 142
TIME, 11, 25
Tim & Eric, 141–42
Trahair, Lisa, 69
transgender community, 84, 166, 171
transphobia, 15, 142
travesty: of the carnivalesque, 109–11; Limbaugh and, 35
tricks/tricksters, 52–53; Sam Hyde as, 53–58. *See also* pranks/pranking
trolls/trolling, 50–53, 57–59, 68–69, 143, 145, 149, 164
Trump, President Donald, 31, 33, 38–39, 105, 138, 145, 149, 162n100, 166. *See also* Capitol Insurrection (January 6, 2021)
Trumpism, 25–26, 39, 50, 135–56; and Capitol Insurrection, 104–27
Trumpsters, and Capitol Insurrection, 104–27
Trump World Order, 137
truthiness, 137
Truth Social, 114
Tsongas, Paul, 36
Twain, Mark, 154
Twitter Presidency, 111–12, 114. *See also* Trump, President Donald

Uncensored America, "Stand Back & Stand By," 155
Ungar-Sargon, Batya, 120
Unite the Right rally (Charlottesville, VA), 146
unmasking, 42
US Capitol, as carnival grounds, 106–9

videos, 59–63, 71; "Beating Women," 61; "Deal with the Devil," 62; "Fuck Drumpf-App," 61; "HydeWars," 60; "John Oliver

shoutout!," 48–49; Lil Shitposts, 60–61; "Psycho Serial Killer (Documentary)," 60; "Women Stories," 61–62
violence: in Capitol Insurrection, 114–17; promoting, 80
"Violent Trumpism," 111. *See also* Trumpism
Vonnegut, Kurt, 154
vulgarity, in Capitol Insurrection, 111–14

Wallace, David Foster, 9–10
Wareheim, Eric, 50
Washington Post, 30, 57
Watson, Paul Joseph, 116
Wayne, Thomas, 93
weaponizing, of language, 135–56
Westwood, Robert, 67
white male resentment, 69, 80, 155
white nationalism, 111–13, 119, 137, 141–42, 146, 151
white rage, politics of, 111–14
white supremacy, 49–51, 54, 111, 144–45
Whitmer, Gretchen, 118
Wieck, David Thoreau, 4
Willet, Cynthia, 123
Williams, Raymond, *Keywords*, 135, 137, 144, 153
WIRED, 51
wokeness/wokeism, 49, 69, 80, 167, 171
Wordsworth, William, 26
Wright, Edgar, 95–96

X/Twitter, 168

Yamaguchi, Otoya, 154–55
Yankee Doodle figure, 121
Yankovic, "Weird Al," "We're All Doomed," 27–29
Young, Dannagal Goldthwaite, 122–23
YouTube, 2–3, 48–50, 59–60, 71, 99, 138, 180

Ziegler, John, 9
Zoomers of Gen Z, 50

Christopher J. Gilbert is Associate Professor of English at Assumption University. He is author of *Caricature and National Character: The United States at War*. He is also author of numerous articles published in a wide variety of academic journals and several chapters in edited volumes and coeditor (with John Louis Lucaites) of *Pleasure and Pain in US Public Culture*. When he is not teaching and writing, Gilbert is a farmsteader and an avid cyclist.

For Indiana University Press

Sabrina Black, Editorial Assistant
Tony Brewer, Artist and Book Designer
Allison Chaplin, Acquisitions Editor
Anna Garnai, Editorial Assistant
Sophia Hebert, Assistant Acquisitions Editor
Samantha Heffner, Marketing and Publicity Manager
Katie Huggins, Production Manager
David Miller, Lead Project Manager/Editor
Dan Pyle, Online Publishing Manager
Jennifer Witzke, Senior Artist and Book Designer